Catholic Shrines

in the United States and Canada

Architects' sketch of the National Shrine of the Immaculate Conception, being built in Brookland – District of Columbia

CATHOLIC

SHRINES

IN THE

United States and Canada

FRANCIS BEAUCHESNE THORNTON

NEW YORK : : WILFRED FUNK, INC.

Nihil Obstat
Fr. William Busch
Censor Deputatus

Imprimatur
✠ John Gregory Murray
Archbishop of St. Paul, Minn.
Paulopoli da Octobris 26, 1953

CONTENTS

To Mary
Mother of Shrines and Mother of Men

Who is She, in candid vesture,
   Rushing up from out the brine?
Treading with resilient gesture
   Air, and with that Cup divine?
She in us and we in her are,
   Beating Godward: all that pine,
Lo, a wonder and a terror—
   The Sun hath blushed the Sea to Wine!

            Assumpta Maria
            Francis Thompson

PREFACE

THE WORD *SHRINE* COMES TO US FROM OLD ENGLISH. *Schrin,* as it was originally spelled, was applied to a box, cabinet, or chest. In both Old and Middle English it had particular reference to the Ark of the Covenant, which held the Tablets of the Law and in which the glory of God came to rest between the adoring angels.

A second early usage applied the word *shrine* to either a box, a casket, or a repository in which the relics of a saint are preserved or to any tomblike erection of rich workmanship enclosing the relic of a saint.

In time these meanings were extended to include any object of religious veneration and, occasionally, to a niche built to house a sacred image.

Through figurative usage and transference the word *shrine* widened to mean "that which encloses, enshrines or screens, or in which something dwells." Finally it was applied to any place where worship is offered or devotions are paid to a saint or deity.

In the wide sense of the term, then, any church is a shrine, but there remains something special about the precise application of the word. A specific place, a special devotion or emanation, is implied, and it is in this narrower sense that the word *shrine* is used in this book.

The United States and Canada both have many unusual and gorgeous churches—amazing tributes to God and to the faith of the men who built them. Along with these places of daily worship there have grown up a number of particular places and buildings that have a note of the extraordinary about them, in the sense that they touch the heart and move it to fervent devotion and confidence. The great cathedrals and parish churches of England were a magnificent expression of medieval faith, but in a popular sense they could not hold a candle to the drawing power of Mary's shrine at Walsingham or the Shrine of Saint Thomas of Canterbury. Religion, like life, needs its special occasions of warmth and inspiration. The shrines of the world are an answer to this need, and it is not astonishing that there should be so many of them in the United States and Canada.

The large number of well-known and well-loved shrines in this country and in Canada may prove something of a surprise to casual students of culture and religion. Only a few years ago a prominent English visitor to the United States made a statement that the only Catholic contribution to American culture was the sugar bride and groom atop the multiple layers of a wedding cake. How much of our history and background the distinguished visitor had missed is obvious when the pattern of shrines is traced out through the various states.

The French and Spanish influences on the Northeast, Southwest, and West, and the German, Irish, Polish, and Italian impact on the East and Midwest, can be seen in the variety of architectural styles employed in the building of shrines, into which went the most profound love and sacrifice of these pilgrims of freedom. They brought with them their strange languages, but in the vaults of the mind were all the treasures of world culture: the never-stale variety of Romanesque, Gothic, Baroque, and Classical architecture. Painting, sculpture, glassmaking, woodcarving, and mosaic blending—these and the lesser arts were immeasurably furthered through the shrines and churches that sprang up everywhere.

The delicate mission style went out from the sanctuary and the cloister to invade the humblest homes of workmen and the palaces of millionaires. In this one instance the influence is amazing, but it is equally massive for many other styles, especially the Gothic. So strong is the influence, in fact, that even among non-Catholics the meeting-house style of church building has been largely abandoned for richer modes of expression first brought by the immigrants and expressed in their shrines.

With the architectural heritage came a deep appreciation of music: old German and Polish hymns, the *cantiques* of France, the grave Latin hymns of the Spaniards. This folk music was backed with a casual but thorough appreciation of the Masters. The *Masses* of Bach, Handel, and Mozart were heard in the forests of Kentucky and Wisconsin long before they became the exclusive property of so-called scholars and musical highbrows. Pageantry, architecture, music, decoration—immigrants tuned their harps and sang the songs of Zion in the new Jerusalems they had created from next to nothing on the edge of vast plains and towering mountains.

Above all, the shrines brought a message of faith and love to the new land. Faith can never be the exclusive privilege of the mind or it will not long be the faith that moves mountains. The Scriptural account of Christ's coming and His life is intensely human and natural. His Mother, His friends, a series of appearances, of touching and miraculous incidents—it is a moving story of human love and the divine penetration of the flesh and blood of humankind. We are sons by adoption, sharers in the divine, but we remain human and sinful—we need the help of every resource of tenderness and creative genius

viii

to further the work of grace, to bolster our belief, and to warm our love. Religious shrines are a materialization of that need.

Along with the log houses of the frontier were built the log churches. Always there went into the house of God the most beautiful workmanship and ornaments available among talented and adventurous men. Sometimes a lovely grove reminded them of a shrine to Mary or some other saint of the homeland. So the grove was set aside, an oratory or a chapel inevitably came into being, and a devotion began. Signs and portents, favors granted in time of peril, or the sheer beauty and repose of hidden places soon marked the mountains, hills, and secluded valleys with little cross-topped spires.

Home is where the heart is. That was the lesson the Jews learned in Babylon, when the vision of Solomon's temple blinded them to the fabulous hanging gardens, the parks and terraced houses of the great king. Unlike the ancient Hebrews, the Catholic immigrants in America were at home with their God and the saints. They wanted God in their midst: he was a Father to Whom they could tell their troubles. And Mary was the Mother of mothers. As she had at Cana, she could intercede for men and help them in all their little problems and good designs. The saints too had been the favored friends of Christ and Mary. On earth they were kindly, charitable, and brave. They could be expected to lend a ready ear to the problems of their devoted followers. It was in this family spirit that the shrines of Canada and the United States came into being and grew into the beauty they are today.

This book is a tribute to the riches of faith and beauty that have touched our culture and our lives. Men will always long to go on pilgrimage to the shrines of patriotism and of beauty, and to the shrines where a whisper or a shout of divinity helps to enrich life and make it worth living. Many among us will never see Lourdes or Fatima, or watch the play of changing light on the dome and pinnacles of Saint Mark's, but here in our midst are many native shrines that call to the heart and speak the same message.

In setting down this record for the convenience of pilgrims I do not claim that it is in any sense complete. There are, for example, numberless Lourdes grottoes scattered up and down the land. They may be found in the grounds of parish churches, in colleges and schools, and to give a history of every one would require several volumes. It is for this reason that the Lourdes Grotto at the University of Notre Dame has not been included, though I know from personal experience how potent an influence it has been in the lives of generations of students. The shrines of Saint Joseph in the college chapel at Saint Norbert's at West de Pere, Wisconsin, and at Mount Angel, Oregon, were excluded for the same reason. Basically they are college shrines and as such do not come within the scope of my book.

What I have tried to do is to give the history of noted places of popular pilgrimage: places where the attraction of a saint, an atmosphere, or a devotion has drawn men and women with the compelling magnetism Chartres had for Henry Adams. Never before in our history have the men and women of this continent so sorely needed a living message of faith and hope. They will find it written large in the shrines of the United States and Canada.

FRANCIS BEAUCHESNE THORNTON

Orchard Beach, Long Island, N. Y.
August, 1953

x

ACKNOWLEDGMENTS

MANY PEOPLE HAVE HELPED ME WITH THIS BOOK. To the following I owe a sincere debt of gratitude: Monsignor Patrick J. O'Connor; Monsignor Nicholas H. Wegner; Monsignor William T. Greene; Monsignor C. Blanshard; Very Revd. J. W. De Pencier, O.S.M.; Revd. Ambrose Diamond; Revd. Anthony G. Schirmann, S.J.; Revd. Louis A. Devaney, S.J.; Revd. John J. Fitzpatrick; Revd. Joseph F. Trexler; Revd. Bonaventure Oblasser, O.F.M.; Dom David, O.S.B.; Revd. Rodolfo Ortega, O.F.M.; Revd. Joachim De Prada, C.M.F.; Revd. Father Dominique, O.F.M.; Revd. Father Hubert; Revd. Theodore Eichholtz, O.F.M. Conv.; Revd. Peter Minwegen, O.M.I.; Revd. John B. Tackaberry, C.M.; The Revd. Father Sebastian, O.C.D.; Revd. Father Richard, O.C.D.; Revd. L. A. Sullivan; Revd. John Gorman; Revd. John M. McPherson; Revd. P. M. Dobberstein; Revd. Charles E. Coughlin; Dom. Victor Ronellenfitsch, O.S.B.; Revd. Joseph E. Manton, C. SS.R.; Revd. Leonardo Pavone; Revd. Thomas Shanahan; Revd. Joseph G. McIntyre; Revd. Nicholas Perschl, O.F.M.; Revd. Cletus Kistner, O.F.M.; Revd. Father Winifrid.

To Revd. G. W. Caffery; Revd. W. J. Thibodeau, S.S.S.; Revd. Gerard Calkins, O.S.M.; Revd. F. B. Schultzen; Revd. Albert J. Nevins, M.M.; Revd. Father Armand, O.F.M. Cap.; Revd. Francis B. McHugh, O. Praem.; Revd. Louis S. Derruisseaux; Revd. T. J. Lally, S.J.; Revd. Lionel Dionne; Revd. Alexander C. Wangler; Revd. J. H. Johnson, S.J.; Revd. Father Patsuck, M.SS.T.; Revd. Joseph Skelly, C.M.; Revd. Gerard Decorme, S.J.; Revd. Joseph A. Finney, C.M.; Dom. Kenneth Ozmon, O.S.B.; Revd. Father Raymond, O.C.D.; Revd. Albin J. Scheidler, C.PP.S.; Dom. Lawrence Riebenthaler, O.S.B.; Revd. Alcuin F. Egan, S.A.; Revd. Patrick Moore, M.S.S.S.T.; Revd. M. R. Roth; Revd. F. G. de Quevedo, S.J.; Revd. Abdón Zuñiga, S.J.

To Revd. James H. Wilett; Revd. Charles J. Carroll; Revd. Daniel J. Fant; Revd. Terence McNally; Revd. Joseph M. McSherry; Revd. Joseph E. Martin, C.S.S.R.; Revd. Winfrid Herbst; Revd. Charles W. Lacy, S.P.M.; Revd. John J. McCormick; Revd. Paul Bussard; Revd. Thomas J. O'Brien; Revd. Eugène Lefebvre, C.SS.R.; Revd. Father Ostermann; Revd. Roland Bedard, M.S.; Revd. Honorat Gauthier, M.S.; Revd. Paul T. Hoban, O. Carm.; Revd. Joseph Fontaine, M.S.; Revd. Henry Bernard, C.S.C.; The Revd. Paul Henry Barabé, O.M.I.; Revd. Romeo Juneau, O.M.I.; Revd. William Terrasas, S.J.; Revd. Wilfred Laurier; Revd. L. Dion; Revd. Thomas J. O'Brien; Revd. Peter Caballer, C.M.F.; Revd. J. S. Feldmeir; Revd. George Julian, O.M.I.; Revd. L. H. Greung; Revd. John H. Archibald; Revd. C. Kelly; Revd. F. Lambert, O.F.M.

To The Benedictine Fathers of Saint Benoît-du-Lac; The Capuchin Fathers of Saint Ann De Micmacs; The Oblate Fathers of Colebrook, New Hampshire; The Franciscan Friars of Atonement of Graymoor, Garrison, New York; The Franciscan Fathers of Pointe-aux-Trembles; The Capuchin Fathers of Lac-Bouchette; The Carmelite Fathers of Holy Hill, Hubertus, Wisconsin; The Holy Cross Fathers of Saint Joseph's Oratory; The Oblate Fathers of Cap De La Madeleine; The Passionist Fathers of Saint Anne of Scranton; The Franciscan Fathers of Mount Saint Sepulchre; The Redemptorist Fathers' Pilgrimages of New York City; National Confraternity of Saint Roch; The Fathers of Mercy, New York City; Basilian Fathers of Detroit; The Franciscan Fathers of Detroit.

To Revd. Mother Mary Agnes, O.F.M.; Mother Curtin, R.S.C.J.; Mother M. Columba, O.S.U.; Revd. Mother O. Lapere, R.S.C.J.; Sister M. Friedburga; Sister M. Lucy, C.S.C.; Sister M. Dominica; Sister M. Norbert; Sister Marie Rosaria, O.P.; Sister M. Philomena; Missionary Sisters of the Sacred Heart; The Dominican Nuns; Monastery of Our Lady of the Rosary of Summit, New Jersey; The Franciscan Nuns of the Most Blessed Sacrament of Cleveland, Ohio; Brother B. Lewis; Brother Aloysius, S.J.; Brother Jean Paul, O.F.M.

To Edna Meller; Joe Montoya; Carlos E. Castañeda; E. T. Elkin; Mrs. Robert A. Sands; Mulford Winsor; Stanley J. Guerin; Frank D. Reeve; Dorothy Dowd; Col. H. M. Henderson; Russell C. Ewing; Earl Jackson; Agnes F. MacLaren; Hawley Richardson; Thomas J. Lambert; C. B. Mayshark; C. Edgar Goyette; Ethel Bixby Leech; Joseph Fitzgerald; Robert C. Broderick; Robert K. Doran; Francis Van Eich; Roger Baudier, Sr., K.S.G.; M. J. Robb; Margaret Judge; M. Wassonseig; Ethel W. Harris; F. Lahti; Nellie Sinkinson; E. H. Thornton, Jr.; and E. T. Elkin.

A very special word of thanks is due to Cleofas Calleros; John W. Esau; Burton Frasher, Jr., of Frashers Fotos, Inc.; Ralph Buffon and Mission Trails, Inc.; the Santa Fe Travel Offices of the Santa Fe Railroad; the Tucson Chamber of Commerce; the El Paso Chamber of Commerce; The Albuquerque Chamber of Commerce; The Santa Fe Chamber of Commerce; The Texas Highway Commission; The United States Department of Interior National Park Service of Globe, Arizona; National Park Service of Tumacacori; The Library and Archives of Phoenix; the New Mexico State Tourist Bureau; the New Mexico State Highway Department; *Arizona Highways;* The New York Public Library; and Fordham University Library.

Above all I am grateful to Ralph L. Woods and to Timothy Murphy Rowe, who played a large part in the making of this book.

Catholic Shrines

in the United States and Canada

SHRINES OF THE NORTHEAST

THE IMMORTAL DRAMA ENACTED AT THE INDIAN village of Ossernenon, near what is now Auriesville, N. Y., kindled the Catholic faith in the eastern part of our country. The deaths of Isaac Jogues and his companion martyrs set a pattern of heroism that endured through the intolerant period of colonial times. From the Mass-house at Conewago, in Pennsylvania, Jesuit missionaries ministered to small congregations of Catholics in Pennsylvania, New York, and New Jersey. Quiet men of learning, wearing no distinguishing dress or outward signs of the priesthood, made long journeys on horseback in order to keep the faith alive.

This faint, bloody dawn presaged a glorious future. The religious freedom that emerged after the Revolutionary War drew countless thousands to the new land of freedom. On the foundation built by Jesuit sacrifice, nuns and priests of almost every community and order in the church participated in erecting a magnificent superstructure to the glory of God.

The entire story cannot possibly be told in the somewhat telescoped histories of the eastern shrines. Its full magnificence shines out of the monasteries and cathedrals, the schools and colleges, and the many historic churches that date from the earliest period of our national life.

But the shrines of the East do give us a map of ever developing devotion and tenderness toward Christ, Our Lady, and the saints. There is richness here, and variety; there is a depth of fervor such as Jogues foresaw in a vision the year before he was martyred. Shrines are nothing, and they will not long remain shrines if they are mere patterns of brick and mortar. It is their spirit that counts: the impulse they give to devotion, and the deepening of those reasons of the heart that make faith more than an individual, selfish preoccupation.

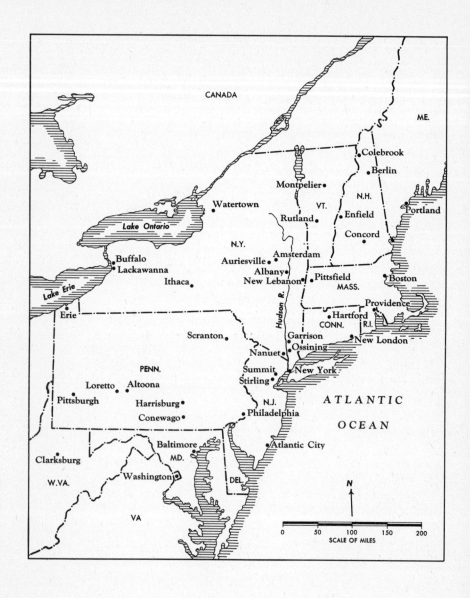

CANADA

ME.

Colebrook
Berlin

Montpelier

Watertown

VT.

N.H.

Rutland

Enfield

Portland

Lake Ontario

N.Y.

Concord

Amsterdam

Buffalo
Lackawanna

Auriesville

Albany

New Lebanon

Pittsfield

Boston

Lake Erie

Ithaca

MASS.

Providence

Erie

Hudson R.

Hartford

CONN.

R.I.

Scranton

Garrison

New London

Ossining

Nanuet

PENN.

Summit
Stirling

New York

Loretto

Altoona

Pittsburgh

Harrisburg

N.J.

Conewago

Philadelphia

ATLANTIC

OCEAN

Clarksburg

Baltimore

MD.

Atlantic City

Washington

W.VA.

DEL.

VA

N

0   50   100   150   200
SCALE OF MILES

THE SHRINES

Our Lady of Grace, Colebrook, New Hampshire
Shrine of La Salette of Enfield, Enfield, New Hampshire
Our Lady of Perpetual Help, Roxbury, Massachusetts
Shrine of the Little Flower, Nasonville, Rhode Island
Saint Peter's Church, New York, N. Y.
Saint Ann's Church, New York, N. Y.
Saint Patrick's Cathedral, New York, N. Y.
Saint Jean-Baptiste, New York, N. Y.
Church of Notre Dame, New York, N. Y.
Saint Anthony's Shrine, New York, N. Y.
Chapel Shrine of Mother Cabrini, New York, N. Y.
Shrine of Our Lady of Pellevoisin, New York, N. Y.
Grotto Shrine of Our Lady of Lourdes, Brooklyn, N. Y.
Saint Christopher's Shrine, Baldwin, New York
Saint Anthony's Shrine, Nanuet, New York
Maryknoll, near Ossining, New York
Graymoor, near Garrison, New York
Lourdes Grotto, New Lebanon, New York
Shrine of the North American Martyrs, Ossernenon, near Auriesville,
    New York
National Shrine of Our Lady of Victory, Lackawanna, New York
Our Lady of the Rosary, Summit, New Jersey
Saint Joseph's Shrine, Stirling, New Jersey
Saint Ann of Scranton, Scranton, Pennsylvania
Mary's Central Shrine, Germantown, Pennsylvania
Sacred Heart Chapel of Conewago, Conewago, Pennsylvania
Prince Gallitzin Chapel, Loretto, Pennsylvania
Saint Anthony's Chapel, Pittsburgh, Pennsylvania

OUR LADY OF GRACE

Colebrook, New Hampshire

Founded 1949

THE SHRINE OF OUR LADY OF GRACE, AT
Colebrook, N. H., began with a spontaneous act of
thanksgiving and has grown into a memorable experience through
the beauty of its natural surroundings and the attraction Mary has
for all men who love contemplation.

In 1922 the Oblates of Mary Immaculate were looking for a
suitable place to establish a junior seminary in which their young
men might be educated. After some searching they purchased a large
farm in the outskirts of Colebrook, which is on the Connecticut
River in northwestern New Hampshire, near the Canadian border.
Slowly the spacious old farmhouse was adapted to the needs of the
religious community, and for twenty-five years Fathers and students
pursued the religious life in an atmosphere of simplicity reminiscent
of their Master.

In 1947 the community wished to show its gratitude for twenty-five years of happy existence. After some discussion in the family
atmosphere of students and priests, it was decided to erect a statue to
Mary, Mother of All Graces, and a site was selected at the east side of
the farm, about a thousand yards from U.S. Route 3. A pedestal
of rich gray Vermont granite was erected, and when in 1949 the
white marble statue arrived from Italy it was publicly blessed by
Bishop Brady of Manchester and set up with appropriate ceremony.

The place that had been chosen was a lovely one on a low
knoll in a notch between two hills. The combination of intensely
blue sky, gleaming birches, and somber cedars and pines provides a
background of delicate beauty more opulent than any grille or mosaic.
The little knoll on which the pedestal stands has been made into a
rock garden glowing with flowers, as if nature had poured out an
abundance of fragrance and color to honor Mary.

6

The statue itself is graceful and impressive. The face is suffused with notable tenderness, the hands are outstretched in an openpalmed gesture that invites approach.

Seeing the statue from the road, travelers stopped to look; many lingered to offer a prayer. When they observed this public interest in the shrine the students and priests built a flagstone plaza before the statue, flanked with graceful steps and low balustrades of matching stone. Vigil lights began to appear; graveled paths were laid out, bordered with wide beds of flowers changing through the months of the years; and modest benches were acquired for the growing congregation of visitors. In Mary's months of May and October there were outdoor processions. Finally Mass and Benediction of the Blessed Sacrament became an established custom through all the warm months of the year.

In 1952 a permanent granite altar was erected. Marble Stations of the Cross, the work of a famous Italian sculptor, were installed the next autumn, replacing the temporary Stations, and in 1954 marble plaques exemplifying the fifteen mysteries of the rosary are to be erected. A five-year plan, drawn up by the Father Guardian of the shrine, calls for the creation of an artificial lake in the depression to the right of the central mall. This will be balanced by a gigantic rosary of flowers—the missionary rosary of Bishop Sheen with its decades of beads in white, red, blue, yellow, and green. The Fathers also plan to turn the old hayloft of the great barn into a rustic chapel, for it has all the qualities of design adaptable to such use. The Christian life began in a stable in Bethlehem, and there is a poetic beauty in simplicity that outmatches all show.

SHRINE OF LA SALETTE OF ENFIELD

Enfield, New Hampshire

Founded 1948

I N THE WEST CENTRAL PART OF NEW Hampshire, near the Vermont border and the Connecticut River, lies the little town of Enfield. The countryside is mountainous; the slopes of the hills are covered with great patches of dreaming woods; little lakes are set like silver mirrors in the lush green floors of the quiet valleys.

The spot was beloved by the Shakers, who in the middle of the nineteenth century came to Mascoma Lake, near Enfield, and acquired some twelve hundred acres of land. In the course of years a large group of buildings was erected along the shores of the lake; some were of stone, and all were beautifully simple, with hand-forged door hinges and other craftsmanlike adornment in which the Shakers excelled. Life there was plain and beautiful. Prayer, meditation, work—the tranquil days grew into years of accomplishment. But the Shaker community found few disciples and eventually was unable to look after the great reaches of farmland.

Many purchasers would gladly have acquired the property, for the gracious old buildings were adaptable to many purposes. But to the dwindling community of Shakers the spot was hallowed by their long love and worship of God. They were unwilling to see the place given over to profane uses, and when the La Salette Fathers offered to buy the property for the establishment of a junior house of study, the Shakers met poverty with a loving generosity. The entire property was sold to the Fathers for the amazingly small sum of $25,000.

The La Salette Fathers and students took possession in 1927, and the buildings were adapted to the uses of Catholic religious life.

The astonishing circumstance of the purchase price was the beginning of wonders. In 1928 Miss Mary Ann Keane, of Hartford,

8

Conn., visited the community. She was awed by the beauty of the spot and decided to settle there and to make it the goal of her charity. After she had built for herself on the ground a charming house with a little turret, her concern was the erection of a beautiful Renaissance chapel for the use of the Fathers and students.

The upper church is glorious, with colored marble and glittering artwork in honor of Our Lady of La Salette, who in 1846 appeared to two shepherd children near the little town of La Salette, in France, high in the bleak solitude of the French Alps.

Before the stained-glass windows could be installed, the financial crash of 1929 came and Miss Keane lost almost all her fortune. She continued to live at Enfield, where Fathers and students cooked for her and were butlers and chauffeurs as the occasion demanded. She died there in 1932, in the midst of her faithful friends, and was buried in the chapel she had built. The parishes of the Diocese of Manchester, N. H., provided the funds for completion of the excellent stained-glass windows. Of particular note are the windows of the crypt which tell in words and pictures the story and complete message of La Salette.

9

During the twenty years after its founding many curious pilgrims came to La Salette of Enfield. A thriving boys' camp was established on the shores of Lake Mascoma, and the life of work and worship continued in immortal rhythm. In 1948 the La Salette Fathers determined to establish a shrine that would help to make known the message of La Salette. On the side of Shaker Hills, in the midst of thick woods, Fathers, students, and the people of Enfield cooperated in building the first shrine.

The message of Mary at La Salette was a call to atonement for sin and renewal of Christian life. The Shrine of La Salette of Enfield dramatizes that story. Beginning at the right, the first statue portrays the Virgin as the children saw her, weeping bitterly for the sins and hardheartedness of men. In the next scene the two children draw near the figure while she makes known her message, and then follow her up the hillside until she vanishes. There at the top of the cleared space is a superb Calvary group in white marble. Before it are the Holy Stairs, a replica of the staircase in the palace of Pontius Pilate which Christ walked with bleeding feet long ago. Pilgrims ascend these steps on their knees and make atonement for the sins of their own lives and the sins of others.

Across the center of the hill stretch the life-size groups of the Stations of the Cross which invite meditation on the scenes of the Passion and death of Our Lord. A shelter has been built for the sick and the aged, and one of the old Shaker buildings has been made into a dining room with wide windows looking out on the natural beauty of the shrine and the countryside. It was in the alteration of this building that a lath was found in the wall with "1846" written on it in colored pencil—the same year in which Our Lady of La Salette gave her message to the world.

Townspeople and the La Salette religious community have cooperated in building at the edge of the meadow a delightful rustic chapel to the glory of Mary. The hand-cut quartz altar enshrines a memorable statue of the Virgin. Another devotional place is the "Serviceman's Shrine." For this the old brick sugaring house of the Shakers has been used. Tiny American flags, one for each pilgrim who had a son in the service, flank the altar from which the face of the Mother of Men looks down. Here Masses are offered for all the men in the service of their country and for the chaplains of the community of La Salette who serve them.

Every night the shrine is beautifully illuminated. Even in the depth of winter it offers a luminous call to pilgrims, inviting them to atonement for their sins and to the beauty of religious life which has long made La Salette a holy place.

10

OUR LADY OF PERPETUAL HELP

1545 Tremont Street

Roxbury, Massachusetts

Founded 1870

THE CHURCH OF SAINT ALPHONSUS LIGOURI is on the Via Merulana in Rome. It is a graceful Gothic structure, built in 1854 on the site formerly occupied by the ancient Augustinian church which the French destroyed in 1812. Saint Alphonsus' Church is famous the world over for its miraculous portrait of Our Lady, known as Our Lady of Perpetual Help. The picture is painted in the precious but flat style employed in the painting of ikons, and has a real primitive charm. Two archangels, identified by Greek abbreviations as Saint Michael and Saint Gabriel, bear in their veiled hands the symbols of Our Lord's Passion: the sponge, the spear, and the Cross itself. The head of the Mother is bent toward her sage-looking Child in pity for the suffering to be endured, but her eyes look out with a pitying glance on all who gaze on the portrait.

Some authorities suggest that the picture is the work of Saint Luke, but it was probably painted by a Greek artist of the thirteenth or fourteenth century. Its first recorded appearance was in the home of a wealthy merchant in Crete near the end of the fifteenth century. The picture was carried to Rome under extraordinary circumstances, and was eventually enthroned in the Church of Saint Matthew after being borne through the streets of Rome in triumph. A series of miraculous cures quickly established devotion to the picture, and for over three hundred years crowds of pilgrims made long journeys to visit the wonderworking portrait.

In 1812, with the razing of Saint Matthew's, the picture was

11

hidden away and did not emerge until January 19, 1866. By order of Pius IX the portrait was given to the Church of Saint Alphonsus Ligouri, since that church occupied the spot on which the Virgin herself had originally indicated that she wished her portrait exposed for veneration.

The full story of the picture has the naïve charm of *The Golden Legend*. This alone would have fixed the attention of the world on the finding of the portrait in 1866.

When, in 1870, the Redemptorist Fathers in the United States were asked to establish a mission church in Roxbury, near Boston, they dedicated their humble building to Our Lady of Perpetual Help. Meanwhile, at the mother shrine in Rome, copies of the portrait had been made, touched to the original, and forwarded to the Redemptorist houses of the United States. One came to the new establishment at Roxbury, where it was solemnly enthroned over the main altar of the church on May 28, 1871.

The effect was immediate, for the following day little Louise Kohler was healed of asthma and lameness in the course of a novena made by her mother. Other cures followed in rapid succession, beginning with two elderly women who were restored to health. In 1878 a new church was built with a special shrine, glowing with mosaic and gold, for Our Lady of Perpetual Help. There the copy of the ancient Madonna and Child gazes out at her thronging children.

The procession of cures continued, and in 1883 a very remarkable case engrossed the attention of most newspapers in the United States. Grace Hanley, of Roxbury, was the daughter of an army colonel. Injured in a fall at the age of four, she suffered incessantly. Added to the pain of her disability was the discomfort of a canvas and iron corset and the heavy crutches whereby the girl was able to achieve some freedom of movement. Noted specialists treated her without success. Then on the final day of a novena made by Grace and her family at Our Lady of Perpetual Help the girl felt a sudden thrill and was instantly cured.

Cures and favors have been multiplied since those first years. A full record of the exceptional cures up to the year 1921 is given in *The Glories of Mary in Boston,* a book published in Boston by the Mission Church Press.

Joseph R. Marcello

SHRINE OF THE LITTLE FLOWER

Nasonville, Rhode Island

Founded 1923

THÉRÈSE MARTIN, BETTER KNOWN AS THE Little Flower of Jesus, was beatified by Pius XI on April 23, 1923, and canonized two years later. She had entered the Carmelite convent at Lisieux, France, in 1888 as a girl of fifteen and died nine years later, surrounded by devoted members of the community. Her autobiography, published after her death, revealed a soul of rare spiritual perception and a life lived entirely in the presence of God. On the surface the way of perfection chosen by this girl seemed childlike and ingenuous, but beneath the surface was the iron heroism of the saints—merciless to self, loving and frank to others.

From the hour of her death great miracles were worked in the name of Therese. Her beauty and the inner romance of her life captured the modern imagination, and there was a great outpouring of devotion to the "Saint of the Little Way."

At Nasonville, a suburb of Providence, R. I., the first parish church in honor of the new *beata* was built scarcely four months after the ceremony of beatification in Rome. Immediately a series of extraordinary cures and favors focused attention on this humble shrine. Two of the cures were so extraordinary that a report of them was forwarded to the Sacred Congregation of Rites in Rome.

So great was the press of people at the Shrine of the Little Flower that it was necessary to organize special devotions at various hours of the day and evening, both in the church itself and in the modest shrine outdoors. The outdoor shrine, which draws the greater crowds, is a simple sanctuary of ornamental stone and brick. Behind the unadorned altar is a plaster statue of the saint flanked by vigil lights and palms. A smaller stone statue crowns the sanctuary arch.

Many privileges for pilgrims have been granted to the shrine at Nasonville. Letters and testimonials show that Saint Therese still scatters her showers of roses on those who come to her shrine.

15

SAINT PETER'S CHURCH

16 Barclay Street

New York, N. Y.

Founded 1786

CATHOLICS, QUAKERS, AND JEWS WERE PRO-
scribed in several of the American colonies, but the
attitude toward these minorities changed during the Revolution.
In New York City after the war some two hundred Catholics began
to think of establishing a parish. J. Hector St. John de Crévecœur, a
doubtful Catholic at best, made arrangements for transfering to the
group several lots of land that had been a part of the Trinity Church
farm. Father Charles Whelan, an Irish Capuchin, began to collect
funds for the building of Saint Peter's Church, in lower New York.
He was ably assisted by Don Diego de Gordoqui, the Spanish minister to the United States, who secured a gift of $1000 from King
Charles IV of Spain. Governor Clinton, Mayor Duane, and many
outstanding Protestants also contributed, and when the new church
was opened on November 4, 1786, a distinguished company of emi-
nent Americans witnessed the ceremony and, after the Mass was over,
were entertained by Gordoqui at a lavish banquet.

The early days of the church were plagued with quarrels.
Father Whelan, the first pastor, was assisted by a brother Capuchin,
Father Andrew Nugent, and both priests found partisans among the
lay trustees. Father Whelan, a rough-and-ready sort of man who spoke
better French than English, envied the preaching ability of his assistant. The Nugent faction won, but Father Nugent too was soon at
swords' points with the trustees and was eventually retired with a
pension. Only after his retirement did the church enter a period of
prosperity under the amiable guidance of Father William O'Brien, a
Dominican preacher of considerable eloquence.

16

From these tumultuous beginnings Saint Peter's Church became the cradle of the New York Archdiocese and developed a very distinguished history. Among significant events were the organizing of the first cathedral parish on Mott Street, the baptism of Elizabeth Seton, and the establishment of the first free elementary school in New York City.

A particularly important episode happened in 1813. A man named Philips and his wife were accused by a Catholic merchant named Keating of receiving stolen goods. Before their case could be tried, Father Kohlmann, the Jesuit pastor of Saint Peter's, restored the property to Keating. The police insistently demanded that Father Kohlmann reveal the names of the persons who had given him the stolen property. The pastor firmly refused, because the revelation had been made to him in the confessional and he was bound by Church law to reveal such things to no one. The case was taken to court and Father Kohlmann was upheld. In this fashion the inviolability of the seal of the confessional was established in American law.

Another seven-day wonder in the history of Saint Peter's was the life of Mother Adelaide of Saint Teresa O'Sullivan. Born of a distinguished Irish family living in New York, the girl, though baptized a Catholic, was brought up in the Episcopal Church. A chance

17

meeting with Bishop Fenwick returned the child to her own faith and began the journey that led her through unbelievable difficulties to the Visitation Convent, in Washington, and eventually to the realization of her call to contemplation among the Discalced Carmelites of Spain, where she had a profound influence.

Most appealing of all the events connected with Saint Peter's is the story of Pierre Touissant, a Negro slave brought to New York from Santo Domingo by a wealthy French family named Bérard. After the death of Touissant's master the family fortune disappeared and Madame Bérard, old and ill of a throat infection, was unable to look after herself. Touissant established himself as a hairdresser with a fashionable clientele of wealthy customers, and so supported his mistress until her death. Then, as a freeman, he married well and was for sixty-two years one of the most popular parishioners in Saint Peter's, revered and loved by Catholics and Protestants alike.

The trustees of Saint Peter's overextended themselves in building (1837-44) a new church in the Greek style. It was a source of much artistic controversy. Eventually, with a mounting debt of $135,000, the parish went into bankruptcy and Archbishop Hughes bought the property at a public auction for $46,000. The whole affair was taken to court but the Archbishop won the case. After several years the parishioners paid off the entire claims of the creditors.

Saint Peter's history is fascinating, so closely knit is it in the fortunes of New York. Saints and sinners have found in it a shrine of hope and a mecca of refreshment. Surrounded as it is by business, Saint Peter's today, through its services and through its superb library and lecture hall, offers to the slaves of paper and finance the same inspiration that it gave to the infant city of New York.

18

SAINT ANN'S CHURCH
National Shrine of the Motherhood of Saint Ann

110 East 12th Street

New York, N. Y.

Founded 1852

W HERE WANAMAKER'S DEPARTMENT STORE
stands today, between 8th and 9th streets facing on
Astor Place, was the first site of Saint Ann's Church. The original
building had an interesting and checkered history. It had been built
on Murray Street as a Presbyterian place of worship, but with the
northward trend of New York's population it had been moved piece-
meal to Astor Place and successively occupied by Presbyterians, Episcopalians, and Swedenborgians. Archbishop Hughes bought this
building in 1852. With some slight alterations, and perhaps an extra
dose of Holy Water, it was turned into the Church of Saint Anne.
(Anne was the spelling in vogue until 1862, when the shorter form
was adopted.)

The first years of the church were difficult ones, as misunderstandings, defections, and the turbulent history of midcentury affected
Saint Ann's and the life of her people. With the arrival of Father
Thomas Preston in 1862, however, Saint Ann's entered into a long
period of quiet influence in the city. Father Preston had great ad-
ministrative gifts and, in addition to his work as pastor, was Chancel-
lor of the Archdiocese of New York and later Vicar General. He was
an enthusiastic defender of parochial schools, and it was his desire
to build a school for his parish as well as the crowded condition of
the church on Astor Place that led to the purchase of property on
East 12th Street.

The principal building at the new site had been first a Baptist
temple and then a synagogue. Under the supervision of Napoleon

19

Le Brun, the architect, only the front wall of the synagogue was retained, and on this Le Brun grafted a tower. The interior of the church was in thirteenth-century French Gothic style, much as we see it today except that the gallery, which formerly ran along the sides to within thirty feet of the sanctuary, has fortunately been removed.

For years Saint Ann's Church was the most fashionable of New York's Catholic churches. Much of this popularity was due to the gifts and commanding position of Monsignor Preston. Although he was succeeded by many talented pastors, time and the continuing northward movement of the residential section eventually brought temporary difficulties to the church. Then Monsignor George Waring became pastor, and under his energetic leadership the church was renovated and embellished and entered into a new era of prosperity and influence.

Under Father Sinnot came the development of Saint Ann's as a shrine church. The novena preceding the Feast of Saint Ann was begun by his assistant, John J. Southwick, in 1915 and brought crowds of people to the church. A confraternity was formed; in time, by Papal rescript of August 26, 1929, Saint Ann's became the American National Shrine of the Motherhood of Saint Ann and the Primary Church of the Confraternity in the United States.

Today, in a dingy street, Saint Ann's stands like some dowager of Victorian times. The interior of the building is spacious and beautiful, with the kind of mellowness that comes to places long loved and long used by many people.

The shrine is a simple affair. A first look draws the eyes to the far reaches of the sky-blue ceiling with its delicate groining. An expressive Carrara marble statue of Saint Ann is set against a fluted drape of old rose at the immediate right of the sanctuary. The Saint looks down at her daughter, who is engrossed in the book she holds in her hands. For the veneration of the faithful, a relic of Saint Ann is exposed in a glass case slanted above the communion rail, and another relic reposes in a gilded bronze reliquary below the statue.

SAINT PATRICK'S CATHEDRAL

Fifth Avenue at 50th Street

New York, N. Y.

Founded 1858

IT WAS ONCE POPULAR IN MILLIONAIRE circles to refer to Saint Patrick's Cathedral as "the housemaids' cathedral," because so many cooks and maids went there and hoarded their wages and tips to adorn it. Today the term has been almost forgotten, and there is hardly a pilgrim to New York who does not pay a visit to the gracious old building whose lacy twin spires look up at the glass and steel of Radio City.

The property on which the Cathedral stands was purchased by Father Kohlmann, S. J., early in the nineteenth century. There he started a college called the Literary Institution. American Catholicism was not then ready for this flight of fancy, and it is not surprising that the undertaking failed, later to be revived as Fordham University.

The cornerstone of Saint Patrick's was laid on August 15, 1858. Seven bishops and one hundred and thirty priests participated in the ceremony while a hundred thousand people watched.

During the Civil War work on the cathedral was discontinued, but afterward Archbishop McCloskey, who succeeded Archbishop Hughes, resumed the undertaking. To raise money, a cathedral fair was held in the building between October 22 and November 1, 1878. Many New Yorkers attended the affair and swelled the building fund with $172,000.

Saint Patrick's was dedicated on May 25, 1879. Although the spires were still unfinished the whole city took pride in an achievement that at one time had seemed too grandiose ever to be realized.

23

A pulpit was given to Archbishop McCloskey in 1884 on the fiftieth anniversary of his ordination. The spires were finished in 1888, and the Lady Chapel was added between 1901 and 1906. By 1910 the church was completely free of debt and was solemnly consecrated by Archbishop Farley in October of that year. Since that time many alterations have added to the beauty and convenience of the cathedral. Of these, the new Lady Chapel and the high altar are the most memorable.

Pilgrims and tourists who visit the building today are charmed with its spaciousness and beauty. The high Gothic style is accurately carried out in all the decorations and furnishings. The splendid stained-glass windows warm the monotony of the stone groining and pillars. The high altar is dignified and pure in style, and the delicate tracery in the bronze baldachin adds a note of upward flight that lifts the eye toward the finely arched roof.

The Lady Chapel is a bright bower for the Virgin. The radiance of colored windows falls down upon the white marble figure enthroned on the marble altar and backed by hangings of gold and blue damask. The statue is a triumph of the sculptor's art. Fluted marble draperies frame the face and figure in musical lines. The head is slightly bent, the long-lashed eyes are lowered in contemplation of Her Son, and an enigmatic smile plays about the mobile lips. The two hands of the Virgin, graceful but strong, are raised in the ancient gesture of prayer first sketched on the walls of the Catacombs.

Saint Patrick's is woven into the joys and sorrows of American life, and it will always be a place of pilgrimage for men of faith and love. The houses of most millionaires who called Saint Patrick's "the housemaids' cathedral" are closed or sold. But the poor and forsaken find courage in the beautiful church built by housemaids for the Eternal God.

SAINT JEAN-BAPTISTE
Saint John the Baptist

Lexington Avenue at 76th Street

New York, N. Y.

Founded 1882

THE CHURCH OF SAINT JEAN-BAPTISTE WAS founded in New York City in 1882 as a national church for French and French Canadian people. It has always retained its French name. The parish was first opened modestly in a loft above a stable on East 77th Street, where the smell of horses and the rattling of harness disturbed the devotions so often that it became known popularly as the "Crib of Bethlehem."

Father Charles De La Croix, the pastor of the church, was a member of the French ducal family of Castries and was the brother-in-law of Marshal McMahon, president of France from 1873 to 1879. He had taken the name of De La Croix to conceal his identity and eminence. In 1882, after he had obtained funds, Father De La Croix had the architect Napoleon Le Brun draw up plans for a church building. The new church was a success, attracting many from the district who spoke no French but appreciated the convenience of a church in the neighborhood.

In 1892 the first extraordinary event in the history of Saint Jean-Baptiste occurred. A visiting Monsignor, en route to Canada, brought with him from Rome a relic of Saint Ann given him by Leo XIII. When the relic was exposed for the veneration of the people on the first Sunday of May, the response was electric. Throughout the early weeks of May crowds of pilgrims fairly mobbed the church in their desire to obtain favors, but amid the cries and tears of a huge crowd the relic was finally taken from the church to Canada on May 20. Not until ten years later did Cardinal Taschereau divide

25

the relic and send part of it back to Saint Jean-Baptiste. Saint Ann had found her shrine in the United States.

In 1900 the Canadian branch of the Fathers of the Blessed Sacrament took over control of Saint Jean-Baptiste. With their coming, daily exposition of the Blessed Sacrament led to a marked increase of devotion and fervor in the parish. Saint Ann still attracted her large crowds of devoted patrons, and old Saint Jean-Baptiste grew too small for the people it served. In 1912 the cornerstone of a splendid new basilica was laid at the corner of Lexington Avenue and 76th Street. There were many building difficulties, and the expenses could not have been met except for the princely munificence of Thomas Fortune Ryan, who contributed over $1,000,000. Cardinal Farley dedicated Saint Jean-Baptiste in 1914, while a distinguished group of prelates and laymen filled the spacious reaches of the church.

The Church of Saint Jean-Baptiste is a combination of classical and Renaissance styles, with the interior expressing the splendor of art which should surround the daily exposition of the Blessed Sacrament. The long lines of penitents waiting at the confessional are a sign of the vivid faith that pulses here.

Altars of various saints, including Saint John and Saint Ann, were moved from the old building to new and splendid shrines in the crypt of the new church. The shrine of Saint Ann in the crypt is especially splendid. Here the lame, the blind, and the sick light their candles and bend in prayer before the beautiful statue of Mary and her mother. Among the many noted visitors to the shrine was Herman ("Babe") Ruth, who came to ask help for an incurable throat cancer. The famous, the unknown, the destitute and the rich —all have cooperated in building and keeping a shrine whose spiritual influence is incalculable.

Through the efforts of the late Cardinal Hayes, Saint Jean-Baptiste in New York City was granted affiliation with Saint John Lateran in Rome. Saint John's is the Mother Church of Christendom, and the privilege of affiliation brings with it the many rich indulgences granted to Saint John's, a golden opportunity for New York pilgrims and those who visit the metropolis.

27

CHURCH OF NOTRE DAME

114th Street and Morningside Drive

New York, N. Y.

Founded 1911

L IKE THE PROW OF A SHIP, MORNINGSIDE Heights juts out above the cluttered tenements of Harlem. The apse of the Cathedral of Saint John the Divine is like a gigantic carved design on the prowlike mass of the hill. Several blocks north of Saint John's, at the corner of 114th Street and Morningside Heights, may be seen the classical-pillared front of the Church of Notre Dame. It is designed on the pattern of the Invalides in Paris, which enshrines the body of Napoleon I in a superb and dramatic setting. The Church of Notre Dame houses a still greater drama, but its exterior is not yet finished, and the noble dome that will crown it some day is a dream of the future.

The interior of Notre Dame is classical in expression. Ornate cornices and friezes brighten the gentle warmth of Caen stone and Hauteville marble. Beyond and to the right of the lovely high altar shines the statue of Our Lady of Lourdes. Her grotto, to which thousands of people come every year; is behind the high altar, a second church as it were, beautifully made out of the natural escarpment of rock that is Morningside Heights. The grotto, a faithful reproduction of the Lourdes shrine, was designed with remarkable artistry. Devotion to Our Lady is a commonplace here, and the sick and diseased of mind come to receive a blessing and to ask their favors of Mary's maternal heart.

Originally the church was begun as a national French church in 1911. Many wealthy French families contributed to the early building, but pilgrims and devoted souls have given this shrine of Our Lady a national importance.

29

F. S. Lincoln

SAINT ANTHONY'S SHRINE

Church of Saint Francis of Assisi

135 West 31st Street

New York, N. Y.

Founded 1930

S AINT ANTHONY WAS A TRUE SON OF SAINT Francis of Assisi. Anthony found the key of life when he discovered the meaning of love. An absolute simplicity distinguished his every act. He was wholly devoted to the poor and the sick; he saw Christ shining out from the faces of children and in the beauty of creation. The saint had a passionate devotion to the Infant Saviour, a devotion fostered by Saint Francis. One day a brother, unannounced, opened the door of Saint Anthony's cell. The little room blazed with light, and Anthony, oblivious to everything else, was holding the Divine Child in his arms. Dazzling rays came from the face of the Infant. One baby finger was curled about the workworn hand of the ecstatic saint.

Even in his lifetime Anthony was known as a wonderworker. He healed the sick and brought radiance and help to the lonely and poor. It is scant wonder that many people venerate him for his tenderness of heart and ask his help in their worries and troubles.

The National Shrine of Saint Anthony was established in the Church of Saint Francis, on West 31st Street, in 1930. The entire crypt of the church was placed in the hands of competent decorators: walls were paneled in fumed oak; gorgeous mosaics were put together piece by piece; bronze and wrought iron added subtle touches of beauty. The whole effect achieved was one of warmth and simplicity that paralleled the life and character of Padua's saint. From the delicate plaque of Saint Anthony over the main altar to the many

31

shrines at the back and sides of the crypt, a welcome is breathed out to the weary and harassed.

At every hour of the day both the upper and lower church echo with the footfalls of pilgrims. Long lines of people wait outside the confessionals, and the shrines glow with innumerable vigil lights. With the simplicity of children coming into their Father's house, all pilgrims seem at home here. Gray-haired old ladies, discarded by the present, relight their old loves and memories. Young men and old, battered by life, find courage to face the "abashless inquisition" of the day. Fashionably dressed secretaries and successful business-men are there too, and young couples in the first radiance of their honeymoon. Twenty-six Sunday Masses are said for overflowing crowds in the upper and lower churches.

It is an astonishing manifestation, because the Church of Saint Francis is in a business section of New York City and should be living mainly on its memories. Yet it has that indefinable patina of constant use, a warm aura which comes from the fact that Saint Anthony's Shrine has given rise to a spirit of practical love that touches all kinds and conditions of people.

From the time of the Depression to the present moment thousands of men and women have been fed and helped temporarily until they could begin life anew. Here the spirit of Saint Francis and Saint Anthony is kept alive by the sons of Saint Francis, who seem to savor with a special fervor the knowledge that holy places can be measured in terms of unquestioning love and service.

F. S. Lincoln

CHAPEL SHRINE OF MOTHER CABRINI

Mother Cabrini High School

701 Fort Washington Avenue

New York, N. Y.

Founded 1933

MOTHER CABRINI HIGH SCHOOL IS A BUSY place. Its wide halls ring with laughter and the clatter of young feet. A rhythmic succession of classes and school activities, performed with verve and dash, make this an intensely American atmosphere. You will see its counterpart all over the United States in the many schools where youngsters endure the pains and joys of learning. What makes Mother Cabrini High School exceptional is its chapel. The long, low room has warmth and friendliness about it. The sanctuary glitters with marble and bronze. And underneath the main altar there is a crystal casket wherein reposes a figure clad in the graceful habit of the Missionary Sisters of the Sacred Heart—it is the body of Mother Cabrini, the first American saint. Her story should be known to every American, for it suits our genius and destiny.

Marie Frances Cabrini was born of peasant parents in the little town of Saint Angelo of Lodi, in Italy. The province of Lombardy is famed for its smiling vinyards and strong people. Simplicity speaks out from the tranquil fields and mountains.

Marie Frances was the thirteenth child, but she found an abundance of love poured out on her in a house where the pieties of land and altar were the boundaries of self-discipline. She was a delicate child, with a wide forehead, heart-shaped face, generous mouth, and wide nose. The best of her was concentrated in her intense blue eyes; under the delicate wings of her brows they looked out with

33

exceptional vividness, as if to speak of the unique intelligence that made them sparkle.

Like the great Teresa of Avila, Marie Frances lived in two worlds. The one universe was composed of simple duties about the house and school, the clatter of clogs in the garden, songs, gentle words of praise or rebuke, studies by the light of the flickering fire. The second world was contrary to all of this. It pulsed with romantic feeling centered about God and the saints. All the make-believe of childhood, and all its poetry, was centered here. In that world the doors of the heart could open on all the glory of God and the great and thrilling tasks to be done for Him. The pagodas of the Orient, the wide plains of the United States, the pampas of South America, towering mountains, and endless rivers—the little girl yearned over them like Christ yearns over the world.

Maturity comes with the fusing of the two worlds. How deeply that happened to Marie Frances we can see in the events of her life. By the twelfth of November, in 1880, when she founded her community and took possession of her first orphanage, she had proved herself an exceptional student and teacher, a competent executive, and a woman of large dreams. Outracing them all was a love of God so intense that it burned up all the thought of self.

The founding of the new community gave wings to accomplishment. Wide success in Italy was like a great stone pillar from which she could look out on faraway worlds still to be won for Christ. The Orient, particularly, was beckoning, but an audience with Leo XIII changed all that. "Go with God, my daughter. But not to the East. Whole sections of our Italian people have gone to the United States. They suffer there and they need your help. It is a great generous land, and you will love it and help your people find themselves."

To Mother Cabrini no dream of her own could live in the light of this command. With six sisters she arrived in New York on March 31, 1889. The voyage had been rough and her reception was depressing. No one wanted to receive the little band. Italian peasants! What were they but "wops" who couldn't even speak English? Mother Cabrini said, "The Pope sent me here and here I shall stay."

The future saint occupied the dirty basement on the edge of the Italian section of the Lower East Side, given her by the church authorities for teaching catechism to immigrant children. She and her nuns lived in two squalid rooms. "We will beg!" They went from door to door. "For the orphans, for God." The little nuns were smiling. Within a month they were in their own respectable orphanage looking after the thronging children. Prudence said, "Consoli-

date." Imagination and the dream said, "Fly." Within a year she had purchased a vast estate on the Hudson, at West Park, near Hyde Park, N. Y. How? It was dream and imagination that gave her an intuitive grasp of paper credit. When she spoke of her dream, people could see it standing there more solid than stone. From this great foundation the dream kept growing and growing like Jack's beanstalk.

35

Those who knew her best knew that she was nothing of herself. God was all. The world was His, and she must take possession in His name. There was a shyness about her, but she made decisions with the quick surety of Napoleon. The core of her was of the iron that saints alone can mine. One who did not know her might never grasp how securely she pulled down the curtain on her personal feelings and heroic life. Yet those who knew her knew at once that she saw in them the good God meant them to show.

Many of her sisters knew the full story. They whispered among themselves, "Mother is a saint." One of them, troubled with varicose veins for years, took off the rubber stockings prescribed by the physician and put on a pair of Mother Cabrini's cotton stockings. She was instantly cured. Mother Cabrini, noting her brisk step, asked about the ailment. "It's gone! Your stockings cured me."

A twinkling laugh came from the Superior's throat. "My stockings? Don't be foolish. I wear them all the time and they don't do me any good. It was your faith that cured you. But don't talk about it."

In 1917, at the time of her death in the great hospital she had founded in Chicago, Mother Cabrini's foundations spanned three continents. She was alone when she died, but not lonely. The one direct Love of her life that she carried closer than her own heart lifted up the curtain that had partly veiled His face from her.

Frances Cabrini, United States citizen, was beatified in 1938 and sainted in November 1946, only twenty-nine years after her death. The whole process was swift because miracles were there in abundance. Delays had never stopped her flight, nor did they now. It is fitting that her heart should rest in one of the schools she founded, in the land she loved, while about her the brisk tempo of high-school life pulses with hope and laughter.

SHRINE OF OUR LADY OF PELLEVOISIN

Saint Paul's Church

113 East 117th Street

New York, N. Y.

Founded 1935

T HE SHRINE OF OUR LADY OF PELLEVOISIN is in the parish church of Saint Paul, on 117th Street between Park and Lexington avenues. In 1837, in the more gracious days of Manhattan's history, Saint Paul's was established in a green suburb on the edge of Harlem. Today the gray stone wall that supports the tracks of the New York Central Railroad closes in the littered street on the west; the once-fashionable brownstone houses teem with Puerto Rican and Negro children; but church and shrine are a constant refuge in a crowded neighborhood.

Saint Paul's Church is a spacious building. The interior is pleasantly light because of the huge windows of painted stained glass that are naturalistically beautiful in their portrayal of scenes from the New Testament. The Shrine of Our Lady of Pellevoisin is on the left side of the church. It was built on simple lines, in keeping with the severe style of the church.

The statue of Our Lady stands above a plain marble altar in a wide, shallow niche. The niche is square and its walls are of stone; it is framed like a huge picture in a massive stone molding. The statue is a charming one: a matronly figure clad in flowing robes. A gold-bordered veil frames the compassionate face of the Virgin and falls in graceful folds over her shoulders. From her outstretched hands, strands of crystal beads ray out to catch the colored light from the great windows in the walls above. The head of the statue is crowned with a heavy halo, and the whole figure is circled with a stylized garland of roses of wrought iron and enamel.

The Shrine of Our Lady of Pellevoisin was erected in 1935 by Father Thomas F. Kane, pastor of Saint Paul's, upon his return from a pilgrimage to the principal Marian shrines of France.

The Pellevoisin story is an interesting one. Estelle Faguette was a lady's maid in the employ of Countess Arthur de la Rochefoucauld. Toward the end of May 1875, Estelle fell dangerously ill. For some time she had suffered from an enlarging tumor, and to this was added a terrible pain in her lungs, which doctors said was from tuberculosis.

The Countess sympathized with the girl, and to help her gave her the use of a fine house in the village of Pellevoisin, a beautiful spot in the Diocese of Bourges. Estelle's father and mother came to Pellevoisin to nurse their daughter, assisted by three nursing sisters, but Estelle grew progressively worse. Several doctors said she could not possibly live, and her physical state seemed to bear out their opinion. Yet in her lucid moments Estelle announced that she would be cured on Saturday, February 19, 1876. On that morning, after receiving Holy Communion, she was miraculously and suddenly cured. Her tumor disappeared, and she was able to rise from bed and resume her duties. Estelle lived on in perfect health for fifty-three years and died only in 1929.

What had caused her sudden cure? According to Estelle, the Virgin had appeared to her for five successive nights and had told her she would be cured on that specific Saturday.

After Estelle's cure the Virgin appeared ten times more to the girl and in these later visions urged Estelle to propagate the wearing of a special scapular of the Sacred Heart of Mary. Estelle made her first scapular in the pattern of the one she had seen the Virgin wearing. With the permission of Cardinal Boyer, Archbishop of Bourges, an archconfraternity was formed to propagate devotion to the scapular and to the Blessed Virgin under the title of Mother All Merciful. The devotion was blessed by Pope Leo XIII, who granted many indulgences to members of the Confraternity.

It seems fitting that the statue of Our Lady of Pellevoisin, the Virgin All Merciful, should be enthroned in a church that by chance has become the inheritance of Mary's darker-skinned children. They have had scant social justice in their forcefully adopted land; they have been ground down by our money civilization. Above all they need the tender care of the Virgin and her smile that speaks of a new day slowly beginning to dawn.

39

John G. Schaefer

GROTTO SHRINE OF
OUR LADY OF LOURDES

Our Lady of Lourdes Church

Aberdeen Street and Broadway

Brooklyn, N. Y.

Founded 1871

THE FATHERS OF MERCY, A FRENCH COM-
munity dedicated to Mary Immaculate, came to
Brooklyn in 1871. The Bushwick section of Brooklyn to which they
were assigned still smelled of "Flora and the country green," and it
seemed at the time that the missionaries could hardly hope for more
than a modest destiny.

By the turn of the century their parish, Saint Francis de Sales,
had dropped its country ways and was as fashionable as its haughty
neighbors along New York's Fifth Avenue. Then, under the rector-
ship of Father Porcile, the Fathers of Mercy suddenly became prominent and the Church of Saint Francis changed into something rare
and beautiful.

The news from Lourdes had electrified an unbelieving world.
Father Porcile had been deeply touched by the revelation, and
wanted to create realistically for the people of Brooklyn what he had
seen with his own eyes. With this thought in mind he collected
funds for building a new church, imported French materials, and
in 1905, within the walls of a classical shrine, built an exact replica
of Bernadette's Grotto. Devotions at the new shrine were conducted
in the pattern of Lourdes—formal pilgrimages, processions of the
Blessed Sacrament, and blessing of the sick.

The sudden flare of devotion moved Bishop McDonnell to
change the name of the church from Saint Francis de Sales to Our

Lady of Lourdes. The Fathers of Mercy were jubilant. Dedicated as they were to Mary Immaculate, they were more than happy to be in charge of their Lady's shrine. Great days dawned for the renamed parish. Pilgrims came in streams, and their volume kept growing with the years. The maimed, the sick, and formal pilgrims from parishes all over the East came to ask Mary to intercede for them.

Half the attraction for the pilgrimages is the church itself. The exterior of the building is austerely Romanesque, which scarcely prepares the mind for the drama presented within. There the walls between the fine windows are heavy with marble pilasters and pillars. Beyond the low communion rail of precious marble stretches the fine sanctuary with its simplified altar. Behind this, within the gorgeous marble frame of the triumphal arch, is Lourdes. First the cave, a perfect replica in every detail as Bernadette saw it in her ecstasy. Behind it, filling the whole arch with something of the explosive beauty seen in El Greco's picture of Toledo, is a painting of Lourdes as it is today, with its aspiring basilica, forests, and great mountains backed with an infinity of light and sky.

Pilgrims love the shrine. They return to it again and again to experience the tranquil atmosphere of devotion that echoes like a thunderclap in the quietness of Lourdes. Many cures are reported of both major and minor ailments, some of them said to be as serious as cancer.

SAINT CHRISTOPHER'S SHRINE

Merrick Road

Baldwin, Long Island, N. Y.

Founded 1925

SAINT CHRISTOPHER, PATRON OF TRAVEL-ers, is well known to all who journey about the world. According to tradition, Christopher, a pagan and a tremendous giant of a man, earned his living by carrying travelers across a river ford. One evening a beautiful child came to the ford and Christopher made ready to carry him over.

"Are you sure you can bear my weight?"

Christopher gave a bellow of a laugh. "I've carried strong men and heavy women over. Your weight will be like a feather."

"Very well then, but I warn you I am heavier than I look." Christopher bent down and the child climbed up pick-a-back on the brawny shoulders. Christopher's massive sandals found the first stone of the ford. The water swirled about his knees. Truly this child is heavy, thought the giant. Each step of the way the weight grew and grew. Finally, with superhuman exertion, Christopher crawled up on the bank. The child got down.

"Who are you? How could you be so heavy?"

"I am Jesus of Nazareth, and I carry the world on my shoulders!"

It was in this fashion that Christopher was converted to the faith, eventually to become a martyr-saint and the patron of travelers.

With the advent of high-powered automobiles it is not surprising that Saint Christopher has attained wide popularity. Many Christians and those of no faith carry a medal of the Saint in their

43

cars. That Saint Christopher is not the saint of fools is summed up in the quip, "You know Saint Christopher gets out after 45."

Saint Christopher has a religious following who appreciate his virtues and staunchly believe in his power to protect them. One of the many interesting shrines raised to his memory is the Church of Saint Christopher, on Merrick Road, at Baldwin, Long Island. The simple brick front of the church, broken only by a huge rose window in the shape of a wheel, looks down on a modest white statue of the Saint, backed by masses of cedars and shrubs.

Each year on July 25, thousands of cars are brought to Saint Christopher's. When the solemn Mass is over the officiating priest blesses the cars and distributes medals of the Saint. It is the custom of the Church to bless everything, and the inclusion of cars expresses the positive attitude of the Church toward all things made to serve man and his destiny.

Many travelers stop at this shrine, and the Sunday Masses in summer fill the church to the doors and overflow into the school. The Holy See has granted Saint Christopher's Shrine many indulgences, and an active confraternity of the Saint of Travelers has its headquarters here.

44

SAINT ANTHONY'S SHRINE

Nanuet, New York, on Route 59

between Nyack and Suffern

Founded 1898

A CROSS THE HUDSON RIVER, AND NOT FAR above New York City, is the town of Bardonia, N.Y. Here, in 1898, Monsignor John A. Nageleisen founded Saint Anthony's Church, a fine frame building that served the neighboring German colony until August 21, 1912. On that night the church went up in flames. Firemen from all the neighboring towns worked fiercely to save the edifice, but their labors were in vain.

Father Strube, the pastor, started the work of rebuilding, but on the advice of Cardinal Farley moved the church to a new location in near-by Nanuet. The community served by Saint Anthony's was not wealthy, and at first only a basement church of fieldstone was completed.

In 1916, Father Nicholas W. Hans succeeded to the pastorate of the church. Father Hans was a man of vision and imagination. Under his direction the upper church was built in 1920. Relics of Saint Anthony were brought from Rome in 1923 and were enshrined in a beautiful new chapel built on at the right of the church. The League of Saint Anthony soon enrolled members from all over the United States. Pilgrimages came regularly in the summer to Saint Anthony's Shrine. For twenty-three years Father Hans labored on the shrine. In the beautiful cemetery grove at the back of the church a fine Calvary group and Stations of the Cross were erected. Picnic tables were set out under the trees for the convenience of the pilgrims.

45

Father Hans retired in 1940 and was succeeded by the Reverend Francis A. Ostermann, who is carrying on the apostolate of Saint Anthony with new vigor and vision.

The commodious church and shrine are of fieldstone. The exterior style is a kind of modified country Gothic with a notable beamed ceiling. The actual shrine is small but beautiful. A simple marble altar frames a statue of the Saint in the tranquility of death. Behind the altar a brilliant stained-glass window memorializes Padua's wonderworker. Outside, in the quiet of the little cemetery, crowds of pilgrims visit the several shrines and pray before the green-bowered statue of the saint.

N. R. Baker

MARYKNOLL

Near Ossining, New York

Founded 1911

THE CATHOLIC FOREIGN MISSION SOCIETY was founded in 1911 and its headquarters were established near the town of Ossining, on the Hudson River, some thirty-five miles north of New York City. The gentle slope of the land suggested a title, "Maryknoll." People began to apply this name to the priests of the society, and soon they were known everywhere as the Maryknoll Fathers or, more affectionately, as Maryknollers.

With a God-helps-those-who-help-themselves spirit the first priests and students began to build. They gathered fieldstone with their own hands and shaped it into buildings. Since their missionary activities were largely in the Orient, the builders capped their roofs with green tile in the Chinese style and touched up the heavy beams with Nile green and Mandarin red. The central tower has something of the strong beauty of the best Chinese architecture. The copper cross atop the tower may be seen for miles.

Maryknoll and its vision prospered. Today missionaries trained there are spread over the Orient, Africa, and much of South America. Always since its beginning the society has fostered a spirit of simplicity among its men. This atmosphere alone has attracted many to the spot where great things were begun.

Each June, after the ordination of the new class of priests, an ancient Japanese bell rings through the great quadrangle. The priests, their families, and friends gather around the lovely statue of Our Lady of Maryknoll. The assignments are solemnly read: Formosa, the Philippines, Korea, Africa, the far islands of the vast Pacific. The prayer for travelers is said with the heartwarming devotion. There are tears and laughter in the ceremony, and a spirit of martyrlike courage amply borne out by recent history.

One of the loved spots at Maryknoll is the Martyrs' Chapel, with its relics of the True Cross, of the Crown of Thorns, and of many martyrs of the early Church, such as Saint Stephen and Saint Paul. The growing list of Maryknoll martyrs will one day shine down from these walls like an illumination of blood: Bishop Ford and Bishop Byrne, who endured the slow martyrdom of the Chinese Reds; Father Otto A. Rauschenbach, killed by Red bandits; Fathers Cairns and Cummings, victims of Japanese brutality in World War II; Father Jerry Donovan, the Saint Stephen of the group, killed by bandits in 1938—they are the seeds of Maryknoll's faith and continuing glory.

At Maryknoll there are two interesting museums. The one assembled by the Fathers is rich in hand-carved ivory from China, tapestries from Japan, Buddhist beads from Manchuria, and various other exhibits from Maryknoll mission countries of the world. The beauty and meaning of this collection is amplified in the extensive museum of the Maryknoll Sisters, where can be seen miniature models of homes in the Philippine Islands and other countries of the Far East, an immense hand-carved crucifix from Manchuria, teakwood chairs from India, and other examples of native culture from many mission lands.

48

GRAYMOOR

Near Garrison, New York

Founded October 3, 1899

T HE NAME GRAYMOOR EVOKES THE BAR-
ren, furze-studded reaches of English wasteland beloved of dramatic writers. In fact, Graymoor on the Hudson, near
Garrison, N.Y., is a collection of beautiful monastic buildings set
in a smiling, sun-drenched countryside only fifty miles from New
York on Route 9. Graymoor is both a place and a force.

How Graymoor came to be is the story of Lewis Thomas
Wattson, who was born in Millington, Maryland, on January 16,
1863. His father was an Episcopal clergyman, a model of gentleness
and probity, who led Lewis into the ranks of the Episcopal min-
istry. On the Eve of Saint Francis, October 3, 1898, Father Wattson
met Sister Laurana White, an Episcopalian nun. Their extended
conversations and the retreat that followed led them to the formation
of the Society of the Atonement. This society, built on the rule
and spirit of the Franciscan Order, was to include priests, brothers,
and nuns.

Property was acquired at Garrison, and on October 3, 1899,
Father Wattson took up residence in an old paint shed at Graymoor.
Sister Laurana, who had preceded him there by several months, was
already busy founding her sisterhood. Life at Graymoor was lived
in austerity and abject poverty.

The community prospered under the direction of Father
Wattson. He took the name of Paul, and his foundation became
widely known as a favored retreat for deeply religious groups of
high-church Episcopalians.

Looking about him on a largely irreligious world, Father
Paul grieved most because Christians seemed divided in warring

sects and camps. He began to preach corporate union of the Episcopal Church with the Roman Church. This brought down on him the wrath of his bishop and many of his confreres, and gave rise to furious controversy. Father Paul was barred from many pulpits. Undismayed, he took his message to the streets and parks of New York, where in his brown robe and sandals he caused something of a sensation.

A magazine, *The Lamp,* was established in 1903 for the purpose of furthering reunion. In 1908, Father Paul inaugurated the Chair of Unity Octave, an eight-day period of prayers, beginning on the Feast of Saint Peter's Chair, January 18, and ending on the Feast of Saint Paul's Conversion, January 25. The intention of the novena was the return of all Christians to unity under the Pope. Father Paul had obviously reached the border of the Catholic Church. It astonished no one when he took his own advice and brought his community with him into the Catholic Church on October 30, 1909. Shortly afterward he was ordained a Roman Catholic priest.

From that time until his death in 1940, Father Paul's zeal found a wide range. The Graymoor Friars of the Atonement still followed the rule of Saint Francis. Their work and the Chair of Unity Octave was approved by Pius X and has received the warm encouragement of his successors.

The community has grown at an amazing rate. Missionaries of the Society labor among the Mexicans of the Southwest, the Negroes of the South, and the Japanese in Canada and in the Diocese of Yokohama in Japan. *The Lamp* reaches an ever-widening circle of readers. The Graymoor Mission Band conducts retreats, novenas, and missions in Canada and the United States. On the radio, the Ave Maria Hour, the oldest dramatic religious program in radio, offers artfully dramatized half-hours devoted to stories of Christian saints and heroes of the Church.

Graymoor has grown in beauty and size. A shrine to Saint Anthony attracts numerous pilgrims to the lovely center in the Hudson Highlands. Many visitors are particularly drawn to Saint Christopher's Inn, at Graymoor, which offers hospitality to homeless, friendless, and discouraged members of our society. No one is asked his creed, and no line is drawn because of color or disability; the hungry are fed, the homeless are sheltered, and the unhappy and defeated are encouraged to rebuild their lives. The ardent spirit of Father Paul still dominates Graymoor and reaches out to the ends of the earth.

Graymoor News Service Photo

LOURDES GROTTO

New Lebanon, New York

Founded about 1927

NEW LEBANON, N.Y., IN THE EASTERN SEC-
tion of the state, lies not far from Pittsfield, Mass.,
and the Berkshire Hills. The hill country around New Lebanon is
beautiful and serene. It was perhaps the latter quality that drew
the Shakers to the district and long before the Revolution led to
the establishment of a series of grist mills there. One of the attractions of the town today, in addition to its historical past and the
waters of near-by Lebanon Spa, is the shrine of Our Lady of Lourdes,
built about 1927 by the French Canadian Father Lefèvre.

The grotto is framed in lovely old trees and is a fine example of the stonemason's art. The materials employed in it are
fieldstone, brick, and dressed stone. From the beautiful statue of
the Virgin, set well back in the center of the grotto in a niche of
rough stone, five arches progressively increase in size with long
fieldstones disposed like rays of light forming the roof of the shrine.
The texture and design of the interior contrasts with a front arch
of brick into which white stone has been set at three points. The
brick arch is topped with a stone cross above a final raylike ledge
disposed between massive piers of fieldstone. A small stone altar
is cleverly blended into the left wall of the interior.

The statue of Our Lady of Lourdes is illuminated by concealed floodlights. The whole effect is dramatically beautiful and
worth going many a mile to see. Stones from Lourdes itself are incorporated in the grotto. One of them, which is heart-shaped, is
often called the "Heart of Bernadette."

The beauty of this shrine first attracted pilgrims from surrounding towns and villages tucked away in the hills. As the years
passed its fame grew, and today pilgrims have made the grotto
known throughout Canada and the United States. It is not astonishing, for here even the stones seem to sing a "song of Bernadette."

SHRINE OF THE
NORTH AMERICAN MARTYRS

Ossernenon, New York, near

Auriesville, 6 miles south of

Amsterdam on Route 5-S

Founded 1884

FATHER ISAAC JOGUES OF THE SOCIETY OF Jesus came to New France in 1636 and immediately went out to his mission among the Huron Indians. In 1642, a year of famine among the Hurons, Jogues and René Goupil, a Jesuit lay brother, courageously attempted to run the Iroquois blockade to get aid from Quebec but were captured. On the journey down into the heart of the Mohawk country (to the west of what is now Albany, N. Y.) the two men were beaten incessantly. At Ossernenon the tortures reached a peak of savagery; women chewed the ends of the men's fingers and children dropped hot coals down their necks. Jogues and Goupil were then given as slaves to the women of two different tribes. Some time later, Goupil was seen making the sign of the cross over an Indian child, and his skull was immediately split by a tomahawk. Jogues tried to protect the body of his companion in the ravine where it had been thrown, but his efforts to cover it with stones were in vain; the mangled corpse was removed by the Indians and was never found.

Jogues himself remained a slave for thirteen months. When he finally escaped to the Dutch at Albany, his condition appalled them and, though not of his faith, they nobly assisted the emaciated priest to return to France.

54

In 1646, in company with John La Lande, a nineteen-year-old layman, Jogues was back in Mohawk country. He came as ambassador of the French in the hope of discussing a peace treaty and of founding a mission. When Jogues arrived at Ossernenon on October 17, the Mohawks blamed him for the failure of their maize crop and received him and La Lande with ferocious beatings. La Lande was killed with a blow of a tomahawk. After a night of threats and torture Jogues received his crown of martyrdom in the same way.

55

The site of the martyrdom was set down in documents and the name of the village of Ossernenon was known and well described, but its exact location was long a matter of debate and sentimental preference. It was perfectly natural that the American provinces of the Society of Jesus should be interested in finding the exact place: it was linked in blood with their first beginnings in our nation, and it has always been the Catholic way to keep sacred the places where martyrs have died.

56

After considerable search and much debate John Gilmary Shea, the American historian, and General John S. Clark, a famous New York archaeologist, found in 1884 the only place that corresponded with the careful series of descriptions Jogues himself had written. It was a high bluff on the west bank of the Mohawk River, near Auriesville, N. Y. Extensive excavations on top of the bluff disclosed the remains of Ossernenon. The Jesuits immediately bought the property, six hundred acres of rolling land in and around the village of martyrdom.

The first pilgrimage was made in 1885. A small oratory was erected then, but with the passage of the years and an increase in the number of pilgrims a larger chapel was needed. A rustic church which seats five hundred people and is open on three sides was built in 1894. Its simplicity and devout atmosphere are admirably suited to the spirit of the men who died here. Unfortunately it too proved insufficient for the growing number of pilgrims, and in 1931 a vast amphitheater of buff-colored brick was built to seat sixteen thousand people. In the center of the huge interior is a square log palisade. Four altars face the cardinal points of the compass. Here on the feast days of summer and fall great crowds come to venerate the relics of the martyrs, to hear Mass, and to assist at Benediction of the Blessed Sacrament.

On the beautiful grounds there are a thousand reminders of the martyrs. Deeply affecting are the trees marked with a red cross and the exclamation "Jesus" such as Jogues carved with his mangled hands on the trees of the village long ago when he was a slave of the Mohawks. Deprived of every human consolation, he let the trees of the forest declare his undying love.

The west end of the village, where Jogues and Goupil ran the gantlet and were tortured incessantly; the deep ravine where the body of the noble-souled Goupil was thrown among the refuse of the camp—these holy places stir the compassion and faith of the most callous pilgrim. In the ravine, especially, the pathetic drama of the past becomes terribly real. It is a wild spot through which a tiny brook meanders, all that remains of the creek in which Jogues painfully gathered stones to cover the martyred remains of Goupil. Under a little canopy is a statue of Christ in the tomb, and from a niche in the bank the pitying face of Our Lady of Lourdes looks down on the crowds who go with the Blessed Sacrament along this modern Way of the Cross.

A museum houses many interesting relics of the missionaries and Indians, and there are many points on the bluff from which superb reaches of the Mohawk Valley may be seen.

NATIONAL SHRINE OF
OUR LADY OF VICTORY

Lackawanna, New York

Founded 1926

L ACKAWANNA IS A POLYGLOT SUBURB OF A
polyglot city, Buffalo, N. Y. Negroes, Poles, Serbs,
Croats, Italians, Hungarians, and many other nationalities live there
in harmony and justify the American dream.

To Lackawanna in 1876 came a young priest whose history
is a Horatio Alger story in reverse. At twenty-six Nelson H. Baker
was a partner in a successful feed and grain store. He sold his interest
to his partner, entered the seminary, and during his seminary days
went to Rome for the jubilee of Pius IX. Returning through Paris,
Nelson stopped at the great Church of Our Lady of Victory and
dedicated his life to her.

Father Baker was sent to Lackawanna to assist the priest in
charge of two orphanages, one for boys and one for girls. He found
the buildings bady in need of repairs and the orphans often on half
rations. Although he spent the money he had saved in the feed business, it proved a mere sop, so Father Baker took his problem to Our
Lady of Victory and found his solution. He formed the Association
of Our Lady of Victory and sent out letters far and wide. The mem-
bership fee was 25 cents a year, and all members were to share in
the spiritual benefits obtained through masses and the prayers of the
orphans. For a time the idea seemed to be a failure, but then a
deluge of letters poured in. Perhaps people recalled that the prayers
of orphan children were powerful with God. In any event, the Association provided the necessary funds to help the orphans and to give
them the comforts of homes they had never known. To aid the work
Father Baker established *The Victorian Magazine*.

58

There was one dream in the heart of the priest that clamored for realization: he was grateful for Our Lady's help, and he longed to show his gratitude by building a great shrine in her honor. Through the Association and its magazine, he worked toward the building of the shrine. Father Baker became Vicar General of the Diocese of Buffalo and, in 1905, a Prothonotary Apostolic. Through the years, the money came in little by little, and in 1926 the shrine was finished. Cardinal Hayes, in all the splendor of the Roman purple, presided at the dedication on May 25, while the sermon was preached by Bishop Turner. There was a mist in Father Baker's eyes on that morning when he paid his debt to Our Lady.

The shrine is built in flamboyant Renaissance style. Its dome and the great flanking towers are lovely against the northern sky. The interior of the great church is a forest of carved and twisted marbles from all over the world. Gold leaf, statues, and paintings reinforce the prodigal atmosphere. The main altar is dominated by a traditional statue of Our Lady of Victory, nine feet high, which was carved from a single block of Carrara marble.

When Monsignor Baker died in 1936, five hundred thousand people came to pay him honor. Today his shrine and his orphans are still calling men to God—an astonishing success story.

59

OUR LADY OF THE ROSARY

Summit, New Jersey, on Route 24

Founded 1920

P UBLIC DEVOTION TO THE SHRINE OF OUR
Lady of the Rosary began in 1920. In that year a
small group of nineteen pilgrims from Paterson, N. J., came to the
newly founded Monastery of Our Lady of the Rosary, at Summit,
asking to make a procession through the grounds. Permission was
readily granted, and the little group proceeded along the paths,
singing hymns and chanting the rosary.

From this small, spontaneous beginning many large pilgrimages have resulted, and sometimes as many as five thousand pilgrims
in the months of May and October have sung the praises of Mary
before her grotto or the more recent Fatima Shrine. On Sundays
and holy days and all through Mary's months the pilgrims come
from all over the East. Girls in white veils, the aged, the successful,
and the poor go in procession with colored banners and lights. The
climax of these pilgrimages is a visit to the superb Gothic chapel of
the monastery, consecrated by Archbishop Walsh on September 15,
1929. Here is the heart of the foundation.

The privilege of perpetual exposition of the Blessed Sacrament was granted to the monastery in 1926. Since that time, hour
by hour, cloistered Dominican Sisters have succeeded each other in
reciting the Eucharistic Rosary, making loving reparation to God
for the sins of men and the crimes of society.

The altar of repose is of fine Italian marble. Above it arches
an exquisite Gothic baldachin supported on four columns of Siena
marble with beautifully turned Corinthian capitals. A motif of adoring angels in low relief ornaments each side of the canopy. At the
four corners are four Gothic niches within which, standing on a

60

globe representing the world, are the statues of praying archangels. The throne of exposition is set in the center of the grilled wall behind the main altar. The monstrance is in plain sight of the nuns and the congregation in the chapel and a fine canopy of woodcarving shines above its rays.

The Fatima Shrine in the grounds is particularly delightful. Against a fine background of cedars a little mound has been built of earth and rocks. Flowers and grass and creeping vines mantle it. Standing at the apex of this mound is a replica of the Virgin of Fatima looking down at the kneeling figures of Francisco, Lucy, and Jacinta. Two sheep are seen in an attitude of extreme attention and a little lamb in the same expectant pose emerges at the corner of the mound.

The monastery is also noted for its replica of the Winding Sheet of Turin, which is said to be the cloth in which Our Lord was wrapped for burial. This cloth has engrossed the attention of scientists and savants for centuries. The replica itself, which was given to the monastery by the Dominican Nuns of Saint Dominic and Saint Sixtus in Rome, has an interesting history. It was made at the com-

61

mand of Austrian royalty in 1624 and after being completed was touched to the Winding Sheet venerated at Turin. In this process a stain as of blood was transferred to the replica. For this reason it has been long revered. Many indulgences have been attached to the veneration of this relic on special feast days, and a plenary indulgence was granted by Benedict XV to all pilgrims who visit the Monastery of Our Lady of the Rosary.

SAINT JOSEPH'S SHRINE

Stirling, New Jersey,

southwest of Summit on Route 512

Founded 1924

S AINT JOSEPH, THE FOSTER FATHER OF
Our Lord, was a carpenter. The little information
we have concerning his life would lead us to believe he had the
strength and silence of any craftsman who respects himself and his
craft. Today many people despise both work and workmen, and
the holiness of labor is almost forgotten except among cloistered
religious communities.

The theology involved in the saying of Saint Benedict, "To
labor is to pray," was well known to the Missionary Servants of the
Trinity, much of whose work was with the youth of our country.
To teach young people respect for themselves and their jobs was
the strong foundation on which the supernatural could be securely
built.

In 1924, the Missionary Servants acquired a small farm in
the Watchung Mountains, above Stirling, N. J. Immediately they
began a series of week-end retreats for young men, who were given
many conferences on the life and virtues of Saint Joseph and came
to have a particular veneration for him. Within a year a group of
young men asked and received permission to erect an outdoor statue
of Saint Joseph and immediately started to raise funds for the project.
They were so successful that a fine Carrara statue was ordered from
Italy. A pedestal of stone was set up, and on April 25, 1926, the statue
was unveiled and blessed. Four hundred boys and their friends and
parents greeted the occasion and joyed in their honor to the Saint
of Workmen.

63

It soon became the custom to end each retreat with prayers before the statue and, when time and train schedules permitted, Benediction of the Blessed Sacrament. By word of mouth the shrine was praised as only boys can praise things, so that people were soon coming to it in all sorts of weather. The little farmhouse became much too small to hold the visitors who crowded into it on bad days.

The dismantling of a neighboring barn led to the hauling of great beams and the building of a rustic chapel, which was blessed in 1928. A life-size statue of Saint Joseph was enthroned over the altar, and pilgrims left gifts for beautifying and enlarging the shrine. Flowers and shrubs were planted; a Fatima group and Stations of the Cross came into being. Today crowds of pilgrims learn to love Saint Joseph, who set an example for workmen and fathers and gave a glory to work.

SAINT ANN OF SCRANTON

St. Ann's Monastery

St. Ann Street, Round Hill

Scranton, Pennsylvania

Founded 1905

S CRANTON IS IN THE MIDST OF THE RICH anthracite-coal region of northeastern Pennsylvania, not far from the New York and New Jersey borders. Its citizens are a mixture of hardy peasant stocks that have bred generations of husky miners and football stars. The people of the region have their feet firmly on and *in* the ground, but they are equally notable for the simplicity of their religious life and the tenacious manner in which they keep their eyes on the stars. The poetry and meaning of life have not passed them by.

It was to this interesting combination of people and circumstances that the Passionist Fathers came in 1900, at the invitation of Bishop Hoban. They selected a site, which they called Roundwoods, and erected a monastery, a retreat house, and a chapel. The buildings were dedicated in 1905 to Mary's mother.

Hardly had the buildings been occupied when cracks began to appear in the brick walls and the foundations began to slant alarmingly. In Scranton this was an old story. Everyone knew what had happened: one or several of the mine shafts that riddle all the earth around the city had caved in. It seemed merely a question of time until the building collapsed, and experts warned the Passionists to vacate the property. They prepared to do so, but they kept on praying to Saint Ann. Suddenly the sinking movement of the ground subsided, and it was found that a huge drift of coal had backed up into the shaft, stabilizing the earth above. The Fathers were jubilant.

Saint Ann had lived up to her fabulous reputation. So that she might not again be dared to work a miracle, the amount of coal was estimated and paid for by the Fathers and their friends.

Coal miners who always live near to death from explosion and burial alive are religious people. In strikes and disputes, in disaster too, they came to Saint Ann. Expectant mothers came, and children with their petitions for a fair day for a picnic or success in studies or games. Everyone felt sure that Mary's mother would help. On her feast days crowds trooped to the monastery to honor their patron. Over the years the numbers grew and soon the chapel was too small, so the Passionist Fathers built a new one which was dedicated on April 2, 1929.

66

The church is in the Lombardy Renaissance style and has all the charm that comes from a combination of rough brick and artfully smoothed stone. The statue of Saint Ann on the main altar is patterned after the one at Sainte Anne-de-Beaupré in France. In the shrine, in jeweled glass and telling symbolism, the glories of the Saint and salvation shine about the touching figures of Saint Ann and her glorious child enshrined on the altar.

Under the old trees outside sanded paths carry the feet of pilgrims to a simpler shrine of Saint Ann and to Stations of the Cross. On Saint Ann's Day as many as sixty-five thousand pilgrims come to show their devotion and gratitude. Conspicuous are those in wheelchairs, while out in the enormous parking lot are those too ill to alight from their cars. To these the kindly Fathers go, bringing hope and a blessing for health.

The people of Scranton feel that Saint Ann has brought them many blessings, particularly the blessing of peace among many different nationalities and beliefs. Now pilgrims from afar come to share in that blessing.

MARY'S CENTRAL SHRINE
National Shrine of the Miraculous Medal

449 East Locust Avenue

Germantown, Pennsylvania

Founded 1915

T HE MIRACULOUS MEDAL IS WELL KNOWN and venerated over the entire world. It came into being through the express command of the Virgin herself in a series of visions granted to Catherine Labouré. The story is a charming saga of faith and real humility.

Catherine Labouré was born of peasant stock in Burgundy, a French province whose very name evokes plain speech and the joy of life. Catherine's days as a child were filled with household tasks: sewing, cooking, cleaning. Family discipline was strict but affectionate. When Catherine was nine, her mother died and the child, wise beyond her years, embraced the statue of the Virgin enthroned above the kitchen fireplace. "Now, dear Blessed Mother, you will be my mother!"

There was nothing weak or clinging in this resolution. Rather it strengthened the child to supervise her father's house. In addition to this demanding task Catherine had a passion for prayer—she spent hours in the church—and a love of the sick that took her into every afflicted home in Fain les Moutiers.

In the mind of this girl, at the edge of her teens, was a growing conviction that she wanted to join a religious community. One night in a dream Catherine found herself at Mass in the village church. The celebrant of the Mass was a venerable priest. At the end of the Mass he beckoned to Catherine, who became frightened and took refuge in the home of a sick friend. There again she found the same kindly looking priest, and when she started at the sight of

69

him, he said, "It is a good thing that you visit the sick, child. You turn away from me now, but one day you will be glad to see me!"

Catherine pondered the dream and at twenty-two decided the time had come to realize her vocation. Her sister Tonine was twenty, and Catherine had trained her well in looking after their father.

Strangely enough, her father refused to allow Catherine to enter a convent. He sent her to Paris to work in his brother's restaurant, where she was very unhappy. From Paris, Catherine went to live with her sister-in-law at Chatillon, to assist in the work of running a boarding school. Catherine herself, who had never had one day's schooling, joined the first grade. How the young girls laughed to see her struggling over the lessons in the primer!

At Chatillon, Catherine visited the convent of the Sisters of Charity. Her eyes almost popped out when she saw the picture of her dream priest hanging on the wall. It was Saint Vincent de Paul, founder of the Daughters of Charity. Catherine told the story of her dream to the group of nuns. They were deeply impressed, but were not half so moved as Catherine's sister-in-law, who wrote a vigorous letter to the girl's father. Almost magically the way was cleared for Catherine's entry into the Sisters of Charity.

The young girl fitted well into the community, which was recruited mostly from the strong ranks of peasants. She went her way unnoticed, but the finger of God touched her in an extraordinary fashion. In a series of dazzling night visions Catherine saw the Mother of God. These visions culminated in the precise revelation of a medal to be struck, the very scene and symbols displayed on the Miraculous Medal we see today. The Virgin also requested that a statue of herself be made. Great favors were promised to those who wore the medal. Catherine revealed the whole affair to her confessor, Father Aladel, and to no one else. Father Aladel kept her identity a secret but took the story to the Archbishop of Paris. The Archbishop was impressed and ordered a thousand medals struck, then thousands—then hundreds of thousands. Catherine was overjoyed, but she went about her duties with the sick and aged with the unassuming manner of any other nun.

At the age of seventy, in 1876, Catherine felt impelled to do something about making the statue the Virgin had desired. First she asked to have Father Aladel moved back as her confessor. When the Superior General refused the request, Catherine in desperation confided the story to her own Mother Superior. The good woman was amazed. All these years when everyone had speculated on the identity of the nun to whom the great revelation was made, she had been at the Motherhouse in the Rue du Boc, known only for her

unflagging love of the Virgin, her precise devotion to the rule, and the heroic character of her service to the poor and the old. The statue was made under Catherine's direction, and she died on December 31, 1876.

The fame of the medal went flying over the world. In 1895, Cardinal Masella instructed the Sisters of Charity to introduce the cause of Catherine Labouré. She was beatified in 1933 and in 1947 was declared a saint.

Devotion to the Miraculous Medal is widespread in the United States. The National Shrine of the Miraculous Medal is under the direction of the Vincentian Fathers at their house of

71

studies in Germantown, Pa. Attached to the chapel is a splendid shrine whose lofty tower is crowned with a heroic statue of Mary. The interior is decorated with precious marble and golden mosaic in the Venetian style. The gorgeous altar is a jeweled setting for a life-size Carrara statue of Mary. She seems poised in greeting and her slightly bent head is like some exquisite flower.

The shrine is a fountain of religious fervor:

A baker or a milkman leaps from his truck and hurries in for a word with Mary. An insurance collector pauses here on his daily rounds. Three high school girls; an old man who is hard put to hobble up the high steps; a young soldier; a middle-aged man and his wife who have driven from Chicago; mechanics and college boys; two girls scarcely seven; a nondescript man; a procession of stenographers and other office workers in the late afternoon; a woman down at the heels; a city official who is followed in by his chauffeur; mill workers and housewives . . . so they troop in through the livelong day like pilgrims of old.

To these individual visits from the district and city must be added cars and buses from every part of the United States carrying their thousands. There is a reason for this popularity, for since the foundation of the Central Association of the Miraculous Medal in 1915, more than 350,000 favors have been obtained. The letters are filed in the archives. The favors are varied: "work secured," "health restored," "financial assistance obtained," "ills of the mind and soul cured."

So the work of Saint Catherine Labouré grows and prospers. Every Monday in the year a continuous novena keeps the shrine vocal, and in a single year over a million people attend the novena prayers. For the past eight years the money taken up in collections at novena services has been given to the poor and unfortunate.

SACRED HEART CHAPEL OF CONEWAGO

Conewago Township, Hanover,

Pennsylvania, 35 miles south of

Harrisburg on Route 234

Founded 1721

C ONEWAGO VALLEY WAS ONCE A PART OF Maryland. It was settled by Welsh and English Catholics and became a link in the mission chain established by the Jesuits, who came to minister to the Catholics of Maryland. When a famous royal order, tentatively establishing the boundary between the colonies of Maryland and Pennsylvania, placed Conewago under the authority of the Penns, Robert Owings, son of the original owner, obtained confirmation of his grant in 1733.

The original log Mass-house, built at Conewago in 1721, had three living rooms and a chapel and was owned by Robert Owings. (The property is still in the possession of this old Catholic family.) Soon large numbers of German settlers of Catholic origin from Alsace and Lorraine came to Pennsylvania and settled in the countryside near the original Mass-house. In 1740, Father William Wappeler, S.J., arrived in Conewago and the next year became the first resident pastor of Sacred Heart Chapel. At that time Catholics in many of the colonies were still harassed by proscriptive laws and the Test Oath, and Father Wappeler, for reasons of concealment, took the name of Mister Manners and dressed in the drab style affected by the Quakers. After the beginning of the Revolution, religious minorities were freed from the legal constrictions.

The old log Mass-house was pulled down and in its place a fine stone church in colonial style was completed in 1787, the year

73

of the signing of the Constitution of the United States. The brownstone used was quarried in East Berlin and carted twelve miles to
the chapel site.

A succession of famous priests served the enormous parish,
which comprised large parts of Maryland and Pennsylvania. Some
time after 1847, Father Joseph Enders, S.J. added the thin spire to
the church tower and enlarged the church to its present size. He
imported a Tyrolean artist, Franz Stecher, who covered the walls
and ceiling with delightful frescoes in keeping with the title of the
church.

Father Enders had a poetic-minded assistant, Francis de
Necker, S.J. Father de Necker is remembered particularly for his
organization of picturesque Corpus Christi processions which attracted thousands of visitors from the neighboring towns and as far
south as Baltimore.

In 1901 the Chapel of the Sacred Heart passed into the control of the Bishop of Harrisburg and became a parish of the diocese.

74

PRINCE GALLITZIN CHAPEL

Loretto, Pennsylvania, on Route 53,

south of Altoona by Route 36

Founded 1832

A BOUT THE MIDDLE OF THE EIGHTEENTH
century the works of Jean Jacques Rousseau played
a great part in creating an admiration for the "noble savage" and a
love of the simple life. Divine Providence took advantage of this
fad and in many cases turned it toward good ends. Not the least
extraordinary of the many cases that could be cited is that of Prince
Demetrius Gallitzin.

Born on December 2, 1770, at The Hague, where his father
was the admired ambassador of the Russian government, the young
prince was brought up in the luxurious circle of Russian and German court life. Magnificence surrounded him on every side, such
magnificence that we hardly find it credible today, yet the young
man was early attracted to the priesthood.

At the age of twenty-one, Prince Gallitzin was so enchanted
by a visit to the United States that he became filled with a desire to
settle here permanently and give his life to the men and women of
the frontier. Everything was done to dissuade him from carrying
out his plan—parental and imperial disapproval, punishment, dis-
inheritance, threats—but nothing availed. He sacrificed most of his
inheritance, came to the United States, and entered the primitive
but influential Saint Mary's Seminary, staffed by the Sulpician
Fathers, at Baltimore. On March 18, 1795, Gallitzin was ordained by
Bishop Carroll, the first American Bishop.

Under the assumed name of Father Smith, the young priest
spent some time at the Jesuit mission at Conewago, Pa. (p. 73). Then

75

with the remnants of his princely fortune Father Gallitzin established a center at Loretto, Pa., and for over forty years endured unbelievable hardships in serving his people. Worn with austere living, the "Apostle of the Alleghenies" died at Loretto on May 4, 1840. In 1899 his body was transferred to a beautiful bronze and granite monument erected by the grateful people of Loretto.

His house in Loretto and the chapel he built in 1832 are kept much as they were when the prince-priest died. The wooden altar he used has been encased in stone. His chalice and Mass-book, his relic of the True Cross, and many other souvenirs are preserved as he left them. Outside the humble chapel is a cemetery where many famous Revolutionary and Civil War heroes are buried.

SAINT ANTHONY'S CHAPEL

1700 Harpster Street, Troy Hill

Pittsburgh, Pennsylvania

Founded 1880

S AINT ANTHONY'S CHAPEL, IN BUSY PITTS-
burgh, is not so widely known as it deserves to be.
Judged as architecture, it has no particular distinction that would
make it memorable, for its high, pointed towers and bronze statue
of Saint Anthony are like those of any number of the many small
churches that may be seen in the spire-dotted landscape of French
Canada. Munich and Luxemburg glass, and unusual Stations of the
Cross done in the realistic, life-size style popular among pious Germans toward the end of the nineteenth century, help to make it
notable. But it is the large number of relics in the chapel that give
the shrine its special importance.

The group of relics is the work of one priest, Father Anthony
Mollinger, who for forty years spent many of his waking hours in
assembling the collection. During Prince von Bismarck's mistaken
kulturkampf, German monasteries and convents were often robbed
of their treasured mementos of saints and the plundering of the
Papal States in Italy in 1872 (see p. 280) brought other thousands
of reliquaries into the windows of pawnshops. Father Mollinger was
a wealthy man in his own right, and he was able to rescue many relics.

When these were assembled he built a chapel in Pittsburgh,
intending to house them in the splendor that ought to distinguish
the resting place of the saints. In their lives they had been in a special
way beautiful temples of the Holy Spirit, and whether they were
martyrs or confessors, the Church from the very days of the Catacombs had honored their relics and had placed them in the stones of

her altars. Father Mollinger's chapel was built in 1880, but it proved insufficient to house the relic collection, and the priest enlarged the shrine in 1892. The formal opening of the more commodious building took place only three days before Father Mollinger's death.

The altars and shrines in the transept and sanctuary are made of beautifully polished walnut in the Gothic style. The entire body of Saint Demetrius lies in state beneath the main altar. In the center, behind the tabernacle, is a gold case with relics of the saints whose names are mentioned in the Canon of the Mass, the most sacred group of prayers in the treasury of the Church. Embedded in the altar itself is a splinter said to be taken from the table of The Last Supper. All the saints of the year are represented in this remarkable collection of more than five thousand relics, which also has stones and mementos from various shrines and revered places in Italy and the Holy Land.

The Shrine of Saint Anthony, which is really a shrine of all saints, is open every Sunday and Tuesday of the year. By special favor of the Holy See, pilgrims who visit Saint Anthony's may gain the same indulgences granted to the Chapel of Portinuncula, the Assisi shrine so beloved of Saint Francis. When Saint Francis found Portinuncula it was abandoned and in ruins, but it suited his love of poverty and once he and his little band had cleansed and restored the simple place it became the center of his life. There is a kind of poetic similarity between Father Mollinger's work and the labor of rescue and love spent by Saint Francis on Portinuncula.

SHRINES OF THE WEST COAST

THE HISTORY OF THE CALIFORNIA MISSIONS BEGINS in 1769 with the arrival of Father Junípero Serra. Until 1821 the missions were under the rule of Spain, and most of the priests who staffed the churches were Spanish born. That was the magnificent period, during which the mission civilization grew and prospered.

Mexican independence came in 1821, and from that time forward the missions were largely neglected or harassed. Their glory was extinguished with the decrees which secularized the mission lands during 1831-36. Arbitrary governors and their relatives robbed the Indians and padres of their lands and their living. Churches were sold or turned to vulgar uses, and most of the mission buildings fell into total or partial ruin.

The decay continued rapidly for some years after the United States acquired California, but gradually our government returned parts of the mission property to the Catholic Church. It was Charles F. Lummis, the historian, who wrote vividly of the missions and, aided by many men of many faiths, played a primary part in the movement to restore them. For years now California has loved its missions and has taken pride in the spiritual and cultural beauty of its early history.

Many men have played a part in the rise, the fall, and the resurrection of the missions, but towering above them is the strong figure of Father Serra. "In those days there were giants in the earth," but Serra overtopped them all in the height of his moral stature and the breadth of his vision. The whole California mission story is really the story of Junípero Serra.

Apart from California and the mission civilization, the West Coast has many small shrines like that of Saint Joseph at Mount Angel, Oregon. Mount Angel is well worth seeing because of its beautiful situation. For sheer splendor and poetry, however, the Shrine of Our Sorrowful Mother, in Portland, Oregon, outranks all the shrines in this section.

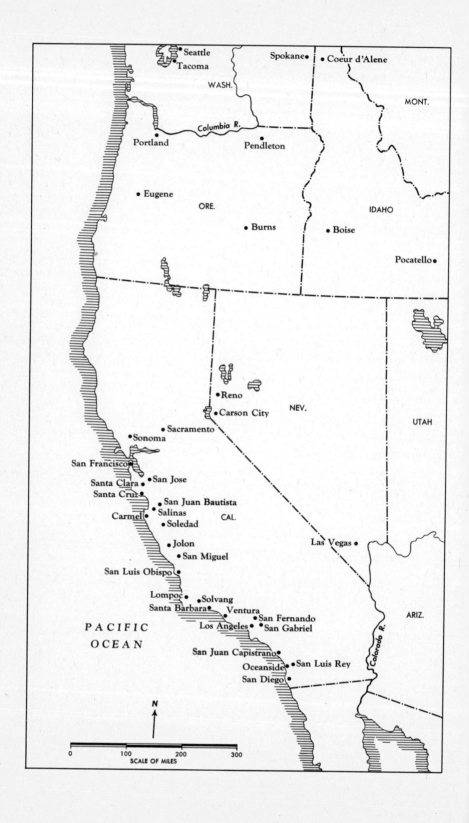

Seattle
Tacoma
Spokane • Coeur d'Alene

WASH.

MONT.

Columbia R.

Portland
Pendleton

Eugene
ORE.
IDAHO

Burns
Boise

Pocatello

Reno
Carson City
NEV.
UTAH

Sacramento
Sonoma
San Francisco
San Jose
Santa Clara
Santa Cruz
San Juan Bautista
Carmel Salinas
Soledad
CAL.
Jolon
San Miguel
Las Vegas
San Luis Obispo
Lompoc Solvang
Santa Barbara Ventura
San Fernando
Los Angeles San Gabriel
ARIZ.
San Juan Capistrano
Oceanside San Luis Rey
San Diego

PACIFIC
OCEAN

Colorado R.

N

0   100   200   300
SCALE OF MILES

THE SHRINES

San Diego de Alcalá, San Diego, California
San Juan Capistrano, San Juan Capistrano, California
San Luis Rey de Francia, San Luis Rey, California
San Gabriel Arcángel, San Gabriel, California
San Fernando Rey de España, San Fernando, California
San Buenaventura, Ventura, California
Santa Barbara, Santa Barbara, California
Santa Inés, near Solvang, California
La Purísima Concepción, Lompoc, California
San Luis Obispo de Tolosa, San Luis Obispo, California
San Miguel Arcángel, San Miguel, California
San Antonio de Padua, near Jolon, California
Nuestra Señora de la Soledad, Soledad, California
San Carlos Borromeo, Carmel, California
San Juan Bautista, San Juan Bautista, California
Santa Cruz, Santa Cruz, California
Santa Clara de Asís, Santa Clara, California
San José de la Guadalupe, south of San Francisco, California
San Francisco de Asís, San Francisco, California
San Francisco de Solano, Sonoma, California
Sanctuary of Our Sorrowful Mother, Portland, Oregon

SAN DIEGO DE ALCALÁ
Saint Didacus of Alcalá

Old Town, San Diego, California

Founded July 16, 1769

S AN DIEGO DE ALCALÁ WAS THE FIRST MIS-
sion established by Father Junípero Serra in Upper
California. The Jesuits had labored to civilize the long finger of land
known as Lower California, but, with their suppression in the middle of the eighteenth century, the missions of Spanish Mexico were
handed over to the Franciscan Order. Father Serra had done missionary work in Mexico since 1749. He had been Father-President of
the northern missions for nine years, and for eight he had taught
in the Franciscan college in Mexico City. In his heart there flourished
an ardent hope that he might be able to evangelize Upper California
and duplicate or outshine the record of the Jesuits in the peninsula.

The political and religious situation in Spain and her colonies
brought Father Serra's hope to the threshold of realization, and he
drew up an ambitious plan with the aid of his friends, Fathers Palou
and Crespi. The three Franciscans were immensely helped with
advice and influence by José de Galvez, the military aide of the
viceroy of Mexico.

Today in California we see a land radiant with fruit and
flowers. In 1769, when Serra first went there, many parts of it were
almost a desert. The coastal Indians scattered over the sandy plain
were easygoing, eking out an existence. The Spaniards thought them
ugly, squat, and "evil smelling." Much of this was changed by Father
Serra and his band of devoted missionaries. The gardens of Spain
and Mexico were rifled for slips of olive, fig, pear, and apple trees.
Vegetables, roses, flowering vines; all the delights of Spanish rural
life were poured into the new territory. The revolution accomplished

83

can hardly be appreciated today without some knowledge of the California missions and the men who founded them.

With almost incredible hardship the Mission of San Diego de Alcalá was founded by Serra on July 16, 1769. At first it barely survived. Supplies dwindled; the Indians were hostile; and the soldiers sent with the expedition were lazy and made trouble with Indian women. Too often this situation was the source of difficulty for the California missions: the Spanish forts and homes for the Spanish soldiers were too near to the buildings of the padres. After a considerable period of uncertainty, supplies became adequate, olive groves and gardens were planted, and this first mission became one of the most active and productive of Father Serra's chain.

The first small church and monastery were built too near San Diego Fort, or Presidio, and in 1774 the two Franciscan fathers in charge of San Diego Mission, Luis Jáyme and Vincent Fuster, moved their base of operations six miles up the valley from the Presidio. Indians soon came to the mission for instruction, and the little establishment seemed assured of uninterrupted growth. However, on November 4, 1775, two renegade converts engineered an attack in which Father Jáyme was beaten to death and the mission was destroyed. A new church was dedicated in October of the same year, and within two years Father Fuster had added a number of other needed buildings. In 1780 the church was enlarged, and finally, in 1808, a still larger church was erected. It was five years in building and occupied the same ground plan as that of the restored church we see today.

After the independence of Mexico in 1821 the Mission of San Diego suffered neglect and pillage. Eventually it was sold to Governor Argüello's family and soon afterward was taken over by American soldiers. During the first years of American occupation the old church was used as a barracks. In 1862 the mission was given back to the Church, but it was neglected for three decades. In 1891, Father Antonio Ubach, pastor of Saint Joseph's Church, in the section of San Diego known as Old Town, began the work of restoration. His small beginning became an important movement when in 1915 Mayor Mayrhofer of San Diego became interested in collecting funds for the mission and $100,000 was raised by popular subscription. The rededication ceremonies took place on September 13, 1931.

The restoration so far is accurate. A wide sweep of brick steps narrows in from the sidewalk between high brick walls. The walls spread wide like a pair of welcoming arms. The front of the church is broken only by the arched doorway and a narrow arched window. A bell tower, in three steps like a dovecote, rises at the side of the church and gives a sense of rhythm to the whole front. The bells, mellow in tone, are the original ones, although some of them have been recast. The story of how they were traced down and recovered is an interesting tale in itself. The oblong of the interior church is gracious and beautiful, with soft lights and shadows pointing up the tones of an old Spanish painting of the school of Murillo. Five padres are buried in the sanctuary. Among them is Father Jáyme, who gave his life to the Indians and the mission.

The church museum contains records of the mission in the precise hand of Father Serra and some of the ancient vestments once worn by the Franciscan Fathers in the days when the Mission of San Diego was the solid, prosperous anchor of the Camino Real, the Royal or King's Highway, which ran north through a series of sparkling missions nestled in trees and gardens of flowers.

Photos by "Frashers"—Pomona, Calif.

SAN JUAN CAPISTRANO
Saint John Capistran

San Juan Capistrano, California

Founded November 1, 1776

E VERYONE KNOWS ABOUT THE SWALLOWS of San Juan Capistrano. Each year, late in the fall, they take wing into the trackless blue and each spring, on or near Saint Joseph's Day, March 19, they return to build their nests in the friendly eaves of the mission. Where they go and whence they come is a mystery, but you will hear their twitterings in the eaves if you visit the mission in summer. Or, if you are fortunate enough to be there around Saint Joseph's Day, you can watch them arriving in air-borne clouds, happy to be home again.

In its day San Juan Capistrano was one of the most beautiful of the missions. An adobe church was built by Father Junípero Serra in 1776, soon after the beginning of the American Revolution. By 1806 it had been replaced with a stone building worthy of being called a cathedral, whose gilded cock atop its soaring sandstone tower could be seen nine miles away in Los Angeles. Its great cloister, which enclosed an acre of ground, was a place of peace and beauty redolent with the scent of innumerable flowers from the gardens of Mexico and Europe. Workshops hummed, the shuttles of the Indian weavers clacked steadily, and their work carried the name of the mission all over the world.

On December 8, 1812, the Feast of the Immaculate Conception, a terrible earthquake demolished the church and buildings. The destruction took place during the hour of one of the early Masses and forty Indians died amid the tumbling stones.

The mission was only partially restored and did not survive the period of lay domination decreed by the government of Mexico in the years following Mexican independence from Spain. It was

86

Photos by "Frashers"—Pomona, Calif.

returned to Catholic ownership by President Abraham Lincoln after California had been taken over by American troops. Several attempts were made to restore the glory that had been, one under Charles Lummis, the noted historian, but all were partial and unsuccessful. In 1910, Father John O'Sullivan, a diocesan priest thought to be dying of tuberculosis, came to Capistrano from Louisville, Ky., and, settling at the mission, began the real work of restoration and his own climb back to health.

No attempt was made to restore the great church, and today it stands in its massive ruins, literally bathed in flowers. Doves strut about the delightful fountain in the outer quadrangle and crowds of tourists wander through the magnificent gardens. In the soaring, unroofed walls of the church they can see the symphony of arches in pairs which made the original church an architectural wonder.

Only Father Junípero's adobe chapel has been perfectly restored. It houses a splendid gilt altar brought from Portugal by Archbishop Cantwell of Los Angeles. You may wander about for a whole day looking at the inspired beauty of this house of God and examining the interesting souvenirs of the mission past in the museum. But best of all is a quiet hour or two at rest in the sun-washed gardens. There you will understand why the swallows love Capistrano and always return.

SAN LUIS REY DE FRANCIA
Saint Louis, King of France

San Luis Rey, California

Founded June 13, 1798

I N 1798 THERE WAS STILL A GAP IN THE MIS-
sion chain between San Diego and San Juan Capistrano. This gap was closed with the building of San Luis Rey de
Francia. The mission was built in the floodtide of mission success,
and a great deal of experience and know-how gleaned from much
building went into it. In our time we take into account all the
practical considerations of convenience before choosing a location
for a building. The mission Fathers were no less wise; they erected
their new mission in the very heart of the Indian country, one day's
journey north of San Diego.

The King's Highway was near at hand. Below the eminence
selected as the mission site stretched the broad and fertile valley
watered by the San Luis River. Behind and to the east were range on
range of superb blue hills. The spot was ideal and the mission, which
became known as the "King of the Missions," was the most prosperous and successful of all those in Spanish America. Much of the
success of the project was owing to Father Antonio Peyri, the man
put in charge by Father Lasuen, who had succeeded Serra as Father-
President of the northern missions. For twenty-three years he ran
the establishment with firm mildness. Loved by the Indians, he did
his best to cooperate with the Mexican government, but in the end
his amiability and success only invited encroachment and theft.

Great orchards were laid out; irrigation was inaugurated with
a series of fine aqueducts; extensive gardens spread on every side;
fields and hay meadows greened in the lancing sun; and vineyard
terraces climbed the softly rounded hills. By 1831, San Luis Rey
could boast a harvest of 2500 barrels of wine and 395,000 bushels of
grain. The totals of the stock farms of the mission lands were equally
amazing: 12,150 horses, 26,000 cattle, and 25,500 sheep.

Photos by "Frashers"—Pomona, Calif.

A great quadrangle, 500 feet square, was walled in with dormitories, shops, the monastery, and the fine church and chapel which made the mission noted as a place of pilgrimage.

The restoration of the church today makes it possible for us to visualize something of its former beauty. The arched entrance is framed in pilasters flanked with niches for statues. Above the cornice on the pilasters a deeply recessed round window leads the eye up to the ornamented gable in which a deeper niche holds a statue of Saint Louis. The bell tower has solid grandeur. The monastery section makes a great sweep to the left. The balcony rail above the cloisters contains panels of burnt brick artfully disposed in a diamond pattern between low square posts. Above this balustrade shine the windows of the padres' quarters topped with a red tile roof.

Inside the church a happy arrangement of arches and huge pilasters painted to resemble black marble offers the eye variety and balance. An excellent paneled pulpit breaks the wall on the left at the point where four arches reveal the full beauty of the sanctuary. Behind the old tomb-style altar a fine altar screen is centered in a giant crucifix.

The chapel to the right of the sanctuary is the famous mortuary chapel, one of the outstanding artistic achievements of mission genius. It is octagonal in shape, and brick pillars support the graceful arches of the domed ceiling. In a shallow recess on the east wall the chapel altar stands under the radiance shed from a magnificent lantern fixed in its own dome. Above the altar is a small balcony tribune from which mourners or distinguished guests could watch the final drama of the funeral Mass before the bearers lifted up the bier and departed through the side door which led to the garden cemetery.

Because Father Peyri really loved the Indians, he also established an *asistencia* or chapel of ease near the northeast corner of the far-flung mission lands. The chapel (now on the Warner Ranch) has an extremely interesting bellcote, some fine Indian murals, and lovingly carved statues. The Indians particularly loved this little church, and even in their poverty, after the Americans took their lands and impoverished them, still made the Pala chapel a place of pilgrimage. Today the Indians gather there on Sundays and feast days. The old bells still call out the hour of Mass, and the place is filled with memories of the great old days. Yet it is hard for us to imagine what San Luis Rey was in the years of its glory, when Father Peyri ruled there. Work then was a pleasure, because it was leavened with *fiestas,* dances, bullfighting, and the obvious enrichment of all who labored in this communal paradise.

Though Peyri from his abundance made extensive grants to the Mexican soldiery, loyally took his oath of allegiance, and did everything in his power to cooperate with the new regime, he was unable to cope with greed. The Indian lands were taken away bit by bit through false promises and outright theft. In the end, when Peyri, heartbroken, secretly left the mission and went to board the ship that carried him to Spain, some five hundred of his neophytes raced after him on horseback and stood on the shore begging him to return. As Peyri blessed them his eyes filled with tears, for he knew he could never return to the spot from which the beauty of simplicity and the glory of trust had departed.

Father Peyri was right. The Indians were dispossessed and herded into the reservation. The beautiful mission itself was allowed to fall into ruins. Abraham Lincoln restored the buildings to the Church in 1865, but the real work of restoration had to wait until 1892, when two Franciscan fathers, Joseph O'Keefe and Peter Wallischeck, began a loving restoration. Today, for the thoughtful pilgrim, San Luis Rey offers a wealth of beauty and the charm of solitude. Enough of the rich past is left to help us understand why San Luis was called "King of the Missions."

90

SAN GABRIEL ARCÁNGEL
Saint Gabriel Archangel

San Gabriel, California

Founded September 8, 1771

THOSE WHO ATTEND THE SUMPTUOUSLY staged pageant of the missions at San Gabriel, California, a suburb of Los Angeles, come away more impressed by the mission church than by the drama of the pageant. The church as it appears to the eyes of the pilgrim is largely the same as it was in 1791, twenty years after it was founded by Father Cambon and Father Somera, although half the beauty of the exterior is lost among the crowding buildings of the bustling city of Los Angeles. This is unfortunate, because San Gabriel's front is really one of the long sides of the church. Nine bold pilasters crowned with pyramidal caps break the plain surface of the wall and bring into high relief the gently arched windows with their deep recesses. An interesting variation of texture was achieved by building the church half in stone and half in brick.

The bell tower, at the left end of the front, is in the dovecote style. Though its individual bell arches are not harmonious, they are arranged in a manner that refreshes the eye and pleases the sense of balance. This bell tower was built in 1812 to replace a loftier one destroyed in the earthquake which so severely damaged many of the missions. Several romantic tales are told of the bells; how much is fact and how much is legend is difficult to determine. The four bells that remain today are remarkably sweet in tone. Three of them are of Mexican origin, and the fourth was cast in Boston in 1828.

The sanctuary of San Gabriel is especially worthy of note. Behind the altar are six painted Mexican statues. The central statue is of Saint Gabriel and is executed with the naive feeling and movement that go with fine Baroque sculpture. Other treasures of the

California Mission Trails Assn., Ltd.

92

old church are the paintings, some from Spain, some from Mexico. One is said to be a genuine Correggio. The church also displays a handsome copper baptismal font, carved candlesticks, and many delightful relics of the great days of mission civilization. The interior of the church was considerably deformed by restoration; plaster walls, enlarged windows, and a paneled oak ceiling abolished most of the old atmosphere.

The history of this mission is filled with violence, brawling, bravery, and sanctity. The first mission was founded five miles away from the present site. The Indians flocked to the place, which under Fathers José Sanchez and Antonio Cruzado became a beehive of activity. Some idea of its importance can be gathered from the fact that it once boasted 40,000 cattle and a wheat harvest of 37,000 bushels. Groves of citrus fruit dotted the rolling landscape and a grist mill and workshops hummed with trade.

Because the Fathers were kindly and hospitable, the mission had many early settlers and adventuresome riffraff hanging about. These drifters were not always of savory character, any more than were the soldiers and the women who lived in the near-by pueblos. Governor Fages wisely moved the pueblos nine miles away, to what is now the center of Los Angeles, and a church was dedicated there to Our Lady of the Angels. Begun in 1814, it was not finished until 1822. There it still stands, much the same as it first appeared, in the old plaza, across from the gigantic modern railway station. The station, with its fringe of royal palms, looks much like a glorified movie set, and seen against this pretension the little church of Nuestra Señora de los Angeles is like a joyous bar of music from a Mozart sonata. The simplicity of its arched entrance and gabled roof is balanced with a modest bell tower. Inside, the subtle old altar is worth seeing, as well as the mementos of the past, before the City of the Angels had become the haunt of gossip writers.

SAN FERNANDO REY DE ESPAÑA
Saint Ferdinand, King of Spain

San Fernando, California

Founded September 8, 1797

FATHER-PRESIDENT LASUEN FOUNDED SAN Fernando Rey de España with the usual ceremonies. He was assisted by Fathers Dumetz and Cortes. From its small beginning the place grew swiftly and prospered. Far-flung ranchos came into being; the orchards were heavy with fruit and the vineyards with grapes; gardens and fields had abundant harvests.

In the space of five years the Fathers at San Fernando paid off all their debts to the other missions and built up a reserve which enabled them to entertain magnificently the many travelers along the King's Highway. All visitors, regardless of creed, were welcomed with equal hospitality, and the Indians loved San Fernando.

The great quadrangle of buildings was completed near the end of 1804, and two years later a new church was built to replace the first small adobe building. It was a symphony of arches, each of sufficient difference to give the new church both balance and variety. The earthquake of 1812 damaged it and the roof and walls were strengthened with heavy beams and a strong brick buttress. It is this church, which remained in a half-ruined state until recent years, that is now in process of restoration through a large grant from the Hearst Foundation.

San Fernando did not long enjoy its great period of prosperity. When Mexican independence came, with its progressive alienation of the mission lands, Father Ibarra did his best to protect San Fernando against the looters, but in spite of his struggle he watched the ranchos being sold to members of the clique. The Indians deserted; used to the mild demands of the padres, they found their new masters arrogant and unjust.

94

Photos by "Frashers"—Pomona, Calif.

Governor Pio Pico leased the place to his brother Andreas, who had only a short time to enjoy the delights of the great cloister and guest house before the United States took over the government of California and San Fernando became the headquarters of General Frémont for a short period. Eventually the mission buildings were returned to the Church and the historian Charles Lummis did his best to restore them, but was never entirely successful. Lummis did, however, succeed in having a park made before the place and was instrumental in saving the great star fountain that had been one of the delights of the mission.

San Fernando was lavish with its hospitality and the monastery wing of the quadrangle had many guest rooms. The great parlor which echoed to the laughter of famous guests may still be seen today. One enters it through a magnificent doorway ornamented with a lovely wavy design, the "River of Life." Moorish windows let in the subdued light from the patio which is refracted from the warm floor tiles. Beyond this great room are other rooms scarcely less interesting, culminating in the Governors' Room, which almost all year

95

California Mission Trails Assn., Ltd.

long used to house some distinguished guest or other. In the beautiful old wall murals blue vases hold prim bouquets against a background of California poppies. An interesting corner cupboard is painted in the same design. The pilgrim may well wander about the monastery for hours. It is wealthy in relics of the past, such as the life-size statue of Saint Ferdinand. The whole hospitable group of buildings is worthy of investigation. It is interesting to see the great wine vat, with its ingenious system of pipes running to the large vats in the cellar, and the foot-washing basin for the convenience and cleanliness of the Indians who trod out the grapes. The romance of the past is here, and history itself, in the memories of writers, generals, and world travelers who left behind them vignettes of life in a place that was beautiful in its peace and willingness to serve.

SAN BUENAVENTURA
Saint Bonaventure

Ventura, California
Founded March 31, 1782

PLANS FOR SAN BUENAVENTURA WERE drawn up in Mexico long before Father Serra came to California, yet the actual founding of the mission had to wait for almost eleven years. It had been decided to space the missions along the coast a day's journey from one another, like gigantic Stations of the Cross. In each one, as it was founded, the mission cross was set up even before an altar was erected, screened in with woven reeds and tender branches of trees.

Fathers Serra and Cambon founded San Buenaventura on Easter Day in 1782. The first Mass was offered on the site selected, the seaward end of the Ojai Valley, where the thriving center of Ventura, California, has grown up.

The mission got off to a slow start. It was three years before the Indians relinquished their cautious attitude and joined the mission in ever-growing numbers and nearly thirty years before, in September 1809, a stone church was dedicated to replace the adobe building that had served the padres and Indians till then. Father Vicente Santa Maria, the architect of the growing mission, died before that church was completed. His body was transferred to the new church the day after its dedication, which was of unusual splendor. The celebrant of the Mass was Father José Señan, one of the rising young men among the Franciscans. Señan later became Father-President of the missions for two terms. He was one of the finest of the Fathers who labored in California. He loved Buenaventura above all the missions, and he was tireless in his efforts to ornament and perfect it.

97

The earthquake of 1812 was a great sorrow to Señan and all the Fathers. It twisted the lovely bell tower of the church, and the sea roared into the valley in such a menacing fashion that the Indians and the padres fled inland to safer ground and remained for three years. Later there were troubles with visiting bands of Indians, and the pirate Bouchard raided the mission, but for the most part the years were tranquil and fruitful. Orchards and fields throve, the Indians were polite and friendly, and the workshops and tannery did a tremendous business. Buenaventura suffered decay and pillage after Mexican independence in 1821.

The church today is in the center of Ventura. It has been restored, sometimes ineptly, but it suggests to the imagination more

98

than a hint of its former glory. Christmastime is especially memorable, for then its gardens blaze with poinsettias. Out of this sea of fire the massive tower rises in three steps, capped with a domed cupola and lantern. The door leading into the garden is a Moorish arch framed in massive pilasters, one of the most graceful touches in the whole building. The interior is spoiled by a wooden floor and a flat ceiling covering the old hand-hewn beams. The sanctuary, however, is much as it was in Father Señan's time. The flamboyant altar is original, as are many of the paintings and statues. The baptistery still uses the old hand-hammered copper baptismal font, and the original Indian decorations on the walls are soft and beautiful.

In the outer court a small modern building in mission style holds an interesting collection of relics. Among these are the wooden bells rung during the long silence from Holy Thursday Mass until the *Gloria* is sung at Mass on Easter Saturday. A marvelous example of Indian craftsmanship may be examined in the hand-carved confessional to which the Indians came for spiritual guidance and release from sin. Outside in the courtyard stands the old olive press, a reminder amid much beauty of the industry which once made this valley, in its frame of growing orchards, seem the gate of Paradise.

Opening pages of the first book of baptisms (March 31, 1782) and first book of deaths (April 1, 1782), written by Father Serra

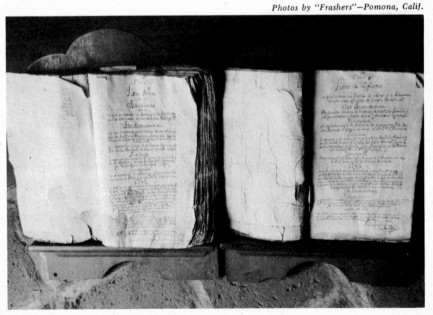

99

SANTA BARBARA
Saint Barbara

Santa Barbara, California

Founded December 4, 1786

I N THE WIDE ELBOW OF THE SANTA YNEZ
Mountains stands the Mission of Santa Barbara. In
the clear air its twin towers, crowned with graceful cupolas, have a
special lightness and grace and can be seen from anywhere in the
city. The front of the great stone church, between the towers, is
spaced off by soft pink pilasters that run up to the superb border
of the classical pediment. The interior of the church is a gracious
rectangle broken with two side altars and two chapels at the back.
With its fine inner and outer cloisters, fragrant with flowers, and its
tinkling fountain in the plaza, it is scant wonder Santa Barbara was
called "Queen of the Missions."

Santa Barbara as we know it today was not founded by Father
Junípero Serra. He came to establish a mission in 1782, but the military governor merely allowed him to found the chapel attached to
the military barracks. In 1786, Governor Fages finally permitted
Father Lasuen, Serra's successor, to select the site where the mission
stands today. There were quantities of fine sandstone near at hand,
and a copious mountain creek flowed through the land. The following spring the first side of the quadrangle was built—an adobe
building covered with gay tiles. By 1789 the two quadrangles had
been erected, and a spacious adobe church ministered to the Indians
and Spaniards.

In 1803 a large reservoir was finished some distance up the
mountain from the mission. At the same time a lovely octagonal
fountain was erected in the plaza. It adds a further delight for the
tourist when he discovers the graceful silhouette of the mission mir-
rored in the fountain basin.

The 1812 earthquake destroyed the adobe church and badly damaged the other buildings of the mission, but within eight years a newer and grander church arose. It was designed by a distinguished Franciscan architect, Father Antonio Ripoll, and the church and cloisters as they stand today are a monument to his genius.

The present church was badly damaged by an earthquake in 1925, and the $400,000 necessary for the work of restoration was raised largely by popular subscription. People of all faiths gave generously. Father Augustine Hobrecht, who was in charge of the project, saw to it that the restoration was faithfully and lovingly made, and the mission today remains the expression of all that was significant in Franciscan life.

Of all the splendid chain of mission buildings, Santa Barbara is the only one that has always been in Franciscan hands. In its exquisite gardens and extensive library and museum, in the very quiet air of its cloisters, you can find a breath of the ages of faith that built the missions and breathed out beauty on our land.

SANTA INÉS
Saint Agnes

Near Solvang, California

Founded September 17, 1804

FORTY-FIVE MILES NORTH OF SANTA BAR-
bara the Mission of Santa Inés was built in 1804, at
what is now Solvang, California. It was hoped that this mission
would provide a magnet for the pagan Indians who had so far remained unattracted to settled mission life.

The new superior of the missions, Father Estévan Tapis, who
had been elected after the death of Lasuen, expected great things
of the Santa Inés Mission. His expectations were never fully realized, because already the Spanish power was in its decline and the
new men of the rising colonial regime were out to make fame if they
could, but fortune in any event. Nevertheless, in spite of constant
friction between the Church and secular authorities, Santa Inés
prospered for a time.

By 1812 the buildings of the large quadrangle were nearly
finished. Then came the famous earthquake, and Santa Inés was
tumbled into ruins. Undismayed by the blow, the Fathers and their
neophytes had rebuilt the establishment by 1817. In the process of
building they instituted an extensive system of irrigation whose
worth was demonstrated in the growth of the mission's prosperity.
However, nothing could save Santa Inés from the greedy new
authority which now forced the missions to support both themselves
and the soldiers. Increased work hours and bad-mannered officers,
who demanded where the padres had only asked, made an era of bad
feeling. The resentment flared up in 1824, when the Indians re-
volted; they attacked the soldiers at Santa Inés. In the confusion
they burned many mission buildings, but when flames neared the
church the Indians gave over their anger and saved the edifice.

102

Most of the mission lands were taken over by the civil administration in 1836. The mission had a brief resurgence during the three-year regime of Governor Micheltoreña, who favored the padres and made a vain attempt to restore some of the mission lands for the foundation of a college at Santa Inés. Micheltoreña's gift prevented Pio Pico from seizing the property, but it did not prevent the progressive decay of the mission.

Restoration began under Father Alexander Buckler in 1904. At his death in 1930 the Capuchins were given charge of the mission. In 1949, through a gift from the Hearst Foundation, the tower of the church, which had been destroyed in an earthquake in 1911, was rebuilt in concrete.

Today the church and the remains of the monastery are lovely indeed. They rise like a white vision from the green fields of a drowsy pastoral landscape. Near by is the town of Solvang, with its quaint shops and Danish windmills. From the sturdy cote-style bell tower on the right, the front of Santa Inés Church juts slightly, with its simple pilasters running up just short of the eaves, and to the left stretch the ten cloister arches, about half the number in the original building.

The interior of the church has an unpretentious beauty. Parts of the walls are whitewashed, but many of the Indian decorations remain in bright shades of red, green, and yellow. The brilliant altar screen centers in the beautifully carved figure of Saint Agnes looking down on the altar from a shell-like niche. The beams of the ceiling are a particularly fine example of Indian painting. The bodies of Father de la Cuesta, the scholar, and Father Abella are buried in the sanctuary along with three other mission Fathers. Behind the altar is a short passage to the sacristy, which has wonderfully carved vesting cases and bright Indian decorations that make it well worth a visit.

Of special importance is the museum in one of the rooms of the monastery. Here may be seen the magnificent collection of vestments restored by the needlecraft of Father Alexander Buckler's sister. Registry books and many other volumes may also be examined. Remains of the grist mill and the water reservoirs are in the old quadrangle. It is to be hoped that the entire establishment will some day be restored.

Indians still come to Santa Inés for their great festivals. Then, especially on All Souls' Eve, the shadows cast by bobbing candles make the old mission come alive with a haunting beauty.

LA PURÍSIMA CONCEPCIÓN
The Immaculate Conception

Near Lompoc, California

Founded December 8, 1787

L A PURÍSIMA WAS FOUNDED ON THE FEAST
of the Immaculate Conception, December 8, 1787.
Rain and floods held up the work for almost a year after Father
Lasuen raised the mission cross. The original foundation was in the
lower Lompoc Valley, but floods and the earthquake of 1812 made
the site untenable and the following year a new beginning was made
higher up the valley, north of Santa Barbara and near Lompoc. Almost ten years later, in 1821, the church and its gardens and clustering shops, monastery, and Indian dwellings had been completed.
The presiding genius of the place, Father Mariano Payeras, had meanwhile become Father-President of the missions, but he carried on
his administration from La Purísima. He was succeeded at Purísima
by Father Antonio Rodriguez, and the new Father-President sent
Father Blas Odras to assist in the work of the mission.

In 1824, when trouble with the Indians began at Santa Inés
Mission, the Indians at La Purísima took up the quarrel of their
brothers. Four travelers were killed at La Purísima and the soldiers
came to put down the brief revolt. In the end Father Rodriguez succeeded in calming his excited flock and was instrumental in moderat-
ing the punishment meted out to the Indians responsible for the
outrages that had occurred.

From this point on, the course of La Purísima seemed entirely
downhill. The Mexican governor took it over in 1835, but he came to
a mission that had been practically abandoned. Little by little arches
fell, walls crumbled, and vines and weeds grew over the heaps of
rubble. The mission was gone, but it was to have a most amazing
resurrection almost a hundred years after its finest days.

105

California Mission Trails Assn., Ltd.

In 1903 the Union Oil Company bought the mission property. Its superintendent became absorbed with history as he poked about in the ruins, and through his influence the oil company offered the site to the state and then to the county, on condition that La Purísima be restored. Both refused the offer. In 1910 an enterprising priest, Father John Raley, came to Lompoc and was instrumental in erecting a mission cross on the site of Father Lasuen's first foundation. This started tongues wagging, and an active movement to restore La Purísima began in 1914. The Union Oil Company gave the land on which the ruins stood; state and county added more acreage; and the whole piece of property was made into a state park named Purísima Park. The final push to the work came from the interest of the National Park Service in forwarding the project.

A landscape engineer, Edwin Rowe, and an architect, Fred C. Hageman, were given charge of the restoration and after long and careful research the two men arrived at a fairly accurate idea of the arrangement and form of the old mission. The debris about the ruins was carefully cleaned away and sifted by boys from a neighboring CCC camp. They continued to work on the project as it progressed, and Indians of the district were also employed. Except for the concrete reinforcements so necessary in earthquake country, the methods of construction were those used by the padres when the mission had first been built.

Unlike most of the California missions, La Purísima was not built in a quadrangle. Beginning with the monastery, its buildings straggle up the valley like a crowd of happy children on a hike. The first building to be restored was the monastery. Adobe bricks were carefully made in the old way for the walls. The only column of the ancient cloister that still stood became the model for the cloister pillars, which are extremely beautiful and the only ones of their kind in all the missions. The monastery chapel, an integral part of the monastery, was restored next. Since there was no complete record of its decoration, the restoration was done in the spirit of the mission period by copying excellent detail from other missions. The vegetable dyes and distinctive patterns of the Indians were employed throughout. With the rebuilding of the church, the barracks, and the workshops, the main outlines of La Purísima were once more in existence.

The church is a fitting climax to the gracious group of buildings. A long gabled roof, with a strong, low tower in harmony with the horizontal lines of the building, holds the bells in three suave arches, one above, two below. Inside the church the restoration is excellent: altar, pulpit, and confessional achieve a delightful harmony.

At the dedication of the restored church, in 1937, famous people gathered from all over the world. The impulse of the whole work had come from an executive of a "soulless corporation" and community, state, and national government had cooperated in the rebuilding of something that spoke of faith and beauty. The youngest Americans from the CCC camp and the first Americans from the Santa Inés Reservation had labored side by side in perfect harmony. The lesson of this mission should be pondered by every pilgrim.

107

SAN LUIS OBISPO DE TOLOSA
Saint Louis, Bishop of Toulouse

San Luis Obispo, California

Founded September 1, 1772

NEAR THE CENTER OF SAN LUIS OBISPO, California, stands the mission of that name. It is a splendid example of unadorned Baroque, in which purity of line and balance of mass work their magic. The high gable of the church front, with its red-tiled roof, is broken by the unusually tall arches of three doors, and above these the bell arches suggest a delicate counterpoint. The church interior is equally severe. It is lightened with murals and an unevenly starred ceiling done by Indian artists; the same artists were probably responsible for the primitive Stations of the Cross hanging along the walls. The main entrance door is especially interesting for its fine panels and uneven motif of star-studded spikes.

The altar of the church has four wooden statues clustered about the central carved figure of Saint Louis, Bishop of Toulouse. The original copper baptismal font, with its hinged cover, is memorable because of its wooden pedestal covered with childlike Indian paintings in color.

The museum in the monastery boasts a considerable collection of brass candlesticks, rich vestments, wooden church benches, tiles, and all the registry books with their notations of deaths, burials, births, baptisms, and marriages. The church and remaining buildings are surrounded by superb gardens which alone make this mission worthy of a visit. Two of the bells are the same ones that called the Indians to Mass and Vespers long ago.

Father Junípero Serra himself founded this mission in the "Valley of the Bears." In its early days supplies were low and the Indians seemed reluctant, but after the first crop was harvested con-

Photos by "Frashers"—Pomona, Calif.

ditions improved. By 1776 the quadrangle of buildings was finished, and church and buildings continued to be enlarged and changed as the influence and prosperity of San Luis grew. Father Cavaller was the great builder and chief architect of most of the mission's growth. He was buried in the church with becoming pomp.

His successor was Father Luis Martinez. Martinez was a burly, two-fisted, virile man of great generosity and eccentric humor. For thirty-four years he ruled his mission justly and in a grand manner, which endeared him to the Indians. When the pirate Bouchard raided the California coast in 1818, Martinez was one of the few men unterrorized by the visit. He gathered a band of warriors about him and several times tried to come to grips with the raider. He was unsuccessful, but it would have been extremely interesting had the encounter taken place between a man who believed only in force and pillage and one who feared nothing but God.

After 1821 the church and mission buildings suffered the inevitable decay and pillage that went with Mexican independence and the misrule of bad governors. The last Franciscan, Father Ramón Abella, turned the mission into the hands of the secular authorities in 1833.

Governor Pio Pico auctioned off the mission to an American firm in 1845 and the United States Government later returned the central group of buildings to the Church. An unfortunate restoration in incredibly bad taste was made, but the Reverend John Hartnett began and carried out most of the improvements that make the mission the delightful group of buildings it is today.

109

SAN MIGUEL ARCÁNGEL
Saint Michael Archangel

San Miguel, California

Founded July 25, 1797

FATHER LASUEN FOUNDED SAN MIGUEL Arcángel, north of San Luis Obispo, in July 1797, a month and a day after founding San Juan Bautista (p. 121). Children were baptized after the mission cross was raised and Mass was celebrated. The Indians, who had requested a mission foundation in their midst, fell to work with the ardor of beavers, and within a short time dams for irrigation had been built and the first elementary buildings had been erected.

The new mission had many sorrows. The first was the summer heat which pressed upon the little valley pass and the lands about it like a red-hot iron glove. The rivers dried up, plants browned and died in the fields and gardens, the cattle bellowed mournfully, and even the thick adobe walls of the buildings were not able to withstand the heat. Perhaps this was part of the reason why Father Antonio Horra, one of the two resident Fathers, went insane. Another sad incident occurred in 1801, when three Fathers were supposedly poisoned at supper and one of them died. The kitchen help was suspected, and several Indians suffered the lash, although it was never proved that the tragedy was caused by anything more intentional than ptomaine.

The mission was almost wiped out in a terrible fire that destroyed granaries, workshops, storerooms, and one corner of the church, but the tragedy did not stop its steady growth. All the sister missions rushed to the aid of San Miguel and the new buildings erected to replace those destroyed were roofed with tile to make them as fireproof as possible. A new and grander church was begun in 1816. At that time there were over a thousand neophytes in residence

110

at the mission and mission farms, and they all took turns in building the new church. The foundations were of stone, the walls of adobe. Estaban Munras, a Spanish artist, was employed to superintend the decoration of the interior.

San Miguel suffered greatly under Mexican rule. Her lands were stolen and the monastic buildings and shops sold. Father Juan Cabot, who had labored for twenty-one years at the mission, finally gave up in despair and returned to Spain. The last Franciscan left San Miguel in 1841, and for almost twenty years the mission was without a priest. It was during this period that a famous multiple murder stained the history of the holy place. William Reed, who had married a daughter of the Vallejo clan, lived at the time in what remained of the monastic buildings. One day while giving his hospitality to five discharged American soldiers, Reed made the mistake of boasting about his wealth. The soldiers left but returned again in the night. Several days later neighboring families broke into the ranch house and they found ten bodies. The whole Reed family had been wiped out: men, women, and children. Along with them per-

111

ished the midwife who had come to attend Mrs. Reed, a Negro cook, and an Indian servant and his five-year-old nephew. The murderers were finally cornered at the Ortega Ranch. One of them was shot while resisting capture, one drowned in attempting to escape, and the other three were hanged at Santa Barbara.

The mission was a forsaken place until 1882, when Father Mut came to San Miguel from San Juan Capistrano. With his inspired labor and the intelligent work of Father O'Reilly, much of the mission was restored. San Miguel was returned to the Franciscan Fathers in 1928 and has since assumed something of its old splendid character. The pace of restoration has been stepped up with the establishment there of a school for Franciscan lay brothers.

Today San Miguel's plain front faces busy Route 101. A deeply recessed doorway and one window above are its only relief from severity. More than halfway back along the left wall of the church the monastery wing, bordered with flowers, juts out at right angles.

The interior of the church is notable because of its splendid Indian decorations, which give us some idea of the full beauty of the missions before time and greed brought about their decay. The six-foot statue of Saint Michael which looms behind the altar table is magnificently carved. Smaller statues of Saint Anthony and Saint Francis are of almost equal beauty. A complex design of twined leaves and odd patterns leads upward to the Gloria above the altar, which is exquisitely carved and painted in white and gold. Decorations on beams and walls, a lovely bell-canopied pulpit, superb carving on corbels and rafters, an interesting confessional built into the wall near the front entrance—these and the museum collection in the monastery wing urge you to linger at San Miguel.

Photos by "Frashers"—Pomona, Calif.

SAN ANTONIO DE PADUA
Saint Anthony of Padua

Near Jolon, California
Founded July 14, 1771

THE SITE OF THE PRESENT MISSION OF SAN Antonio de Padua is not the original one selected by Father Serra in 1771. That was in Los Robles Valley on the bank of San Miguel Creek, which runs into the San Antonio River. Church and river were both named by Serra.

The first small beginning was held down by famine and bad luck. In 1773 the mission was moved up the valley to its present location and from that time began to prosper. The establishment was enlarged in 1779 with the addition of a spacious church and buildings for Indian families in residence. Soon this mission became known for its cattle, flour, and fine horses. The padres in charge initiated a remarkable system of irrigation. They dammed the river three miles above the mission, and flumes and pipes carried the water to the buildings and the thirsty fields.

In 1810, under the direction of Father Pieras, a magnificent new church came into being. It was blessed in the summer of 1813.

Although it has been helped with gifts from various groups that love the missions, San Antonio has not yet been completely restored. From the work as it stands, however, it is possible to get a comprehensive idea of the beauty of the mission. It was built of tile and adobe brick. The once-proud dome of the church roof has been lowered and covered with tile, but the domed entrance, with its two exquisitely proportioned bell towers, remains as it was. The front of the church is broken with three arched doorways that give some clue to the strength of the building. High above the central door is a massive arch set in an oblong tiered frame. In this arch hangs the great bell of the mission, called the *Osquila*. The interior

113

Photos by "Frashers"—Pomona, Calif.

of the church shows few signs of its former splendor. The carved beams, altar, and pulpit have all been stolen or carried away for other purposes, and the modern fittings in use are out of keeping with the spirit of the place.

The patio is still interesting. Bits of the padres' herb garden and twelve arches of the old cloister remain. The magnificent mountains form a splendid blue background for the mission, and the valley itself has great oak trees and two superb olive trees which flank the church.

114

NUESTRA SEÑORA DE LA SOLEDAD
Our Lady of Solitude

Soledad, California

Founded October 9, 1791

S OLEDAD TODAY IS LITTLE MORE THAN A pile of brick and rubble left to the mercy of wind, rain, and sun. Its last remaining, ruined arches look out on a barren country that has a charm of its own; gray and purple lights soften the spring-green or fall-brown vegetation that mantles the hills around.

Our Lady of Solitude—the very words are a little poem in themselves. It is one of the glories of monasticism to seek out the solitude of barren places so that they may be made to bloom like the rose. This was probably Father Lasuen's dream when he established the mission, but it was a dream that never came true.

From its very beginning Soledad endured misfortune. It was begun with gifts from the other missions when the viceroy of Mexico defaulted on his promise to provide the necessary equipment and funds to found the mission. The land was not good; the Indians were a miserable and disheartened group. Soledad was obviously considered a place of banishment and punishment by the Fathers who were sent in to staff the place, for like exiles they did little or no work and the mission failed to prosper.

Father Diego García is responsible for most of the little building and progress that took place at Soledad. In four years, between 1791 and 1795, he achieved wonders with the small group of neophytes at his disposal. A quadrangle of shops, a small monastery, and Indian dormitories of adobe brick were built about the simple adobe church. Later, when the church was carried away by flood in 1832, Father Sarría replaced it with a church still more small and ascetic. Sarría's presence at Soledad was voluntary. He became Father-

115

President after Mexican independence, but he could find no Mexican priest willing to live at Soledad, so he took on the job himself.

With the secularization of church property in 1834, most of the Indians departed. Sarría remained, like the wonderful man he was. While ministering to the few Indians who stayed on at Soledad, Sarría, weakened with age and illness, was struck down with a heart attack. He died there, and his Indians lovingly carried his body to San Diego on a makeshift litter.

The brief glory of La Soledad has long since departed, and no attempt has been made to restore the mission. Lack of interest in a restoration is in a way a pity. True, the mission is off the beaten track and the surrounding land is not hospitable. But the yearning for solitude grows in great souls today as never before, and Soledad might well become a place of quiet and prayer where men and women could go to renew themselves.

SAN CARLOS BORROMEO
Saint Charles Borromeo

Carmel, California

Founded June 3, 1770

CARMEL IS ONE OF THE MOST ENCHANTING places in California. Its wide sweep of bay and intensely blue sea, hemmed in by massive headlands, is a blend of tranquillity and romance. Scarcely less enchanting is the mission from which the town takes its name. Few visitors realize the self-sacrifice, the genius, or the many sorrows that went into its simple beauty and abiding serenity.

When Father Junípero Serra first came to California, in 1769, he and his associates, Fathers Palou and Crespi, planned simultaneous foundations at San Diego, Carmel, and Ventura. This ambitious plan had to be modified because of many adverse circumstances.

The San Diego foundation almost failed and Portolá, the Spanish commander of the expedition that went overland to seek Carmel, found San Francisco and the Golden Gate instead. It was not until a year later that Portolá made a second journey north and this time found Carmel and the cross Crespi had planted there. The ship *San Antonio* came into the harbor at Carmel on June 1, 1770. The unloading of the ship, rudimentary building operations, and other tasks occupied much time, but by July 3, 1770, under the shade of a towering oak, Father Serra and Father Crespi had put up a temporary chapel of woven pine bows. Mass was celebrated and Serra preached a rousing sermon. The chapel was blessed and dedicated to Saint Charles Borromeo.

The original plan made in Mexico had designated San Carlos Mission as the royal mission, the head of the chain, and Serra held to this plan. All supplies from Mexico were sent direct to Carmel

117

for checking and forwarding to the other missions. Serra longed to make San Carlos a thing of beauty worthy of his God and his king, but his generous heart could not refuse appeals of newly founded missions and the great stone church he hoped to see in Carmel remained a dream. When Serra was dead Father Lasuen, who succeeded him as Father-President in 1785, brought the dream into being. The builder Estaban Ruiz was put in charge of planning and superintending the work, and Indian converts cut and hauled great blocks of sandstone from the Santa Lucia Mountains. Father Lasuen laid the cornerstone July 7, 1795; two years later the church was dedicated.

Serra spent most of his active career as Father-President at this mission. When he was dying in his little cell, Father Palou came down from the San Francisco mission to spend the final hours with his friend. The fame of San Carlos Borromeo Mission, the plans made here, and the great deeds done did not help to protect it after Mexican independence. Venal governors filched its revenues, and the Indians suffered an epidemic which frightened them from the spot. So rapid was its decay that San Carlos was begging for a buyer at a time when many of the missions were sold. Earthquake shocks damaged the roof of the church and it gradually sank into ruin.

The restoration was begun in 1870 through the enterprise of Father Angelo Casanova, who identified the graves of Serra, Crespi, Lopez, and Lasuen. Public-spirited Californians who treasured the past raised the money to complete the work. The restored mission is a tribute to the great men who made it and a more stirring tribute to men of all creeds and faiths who restored its haunting beauty to the service of God.

The mission as we see it today is a loving and fairly accurate restoration of Serra's dream and Lasuen's genius. Backed by smoky groves of pines, the mission and its new church stand near the mouth of the suave valley through which the Carmel River runs. The pastoral serenity of the atmosphere is matched by the tranquil atmosphere within the mission walls, where a fountain tinkles in the midst of flowering trees and brilliant beds of flowers. On the left the low, rhythmic line of the monastery leads the eye to the revelation of the church front. The gracefully arched front is broken with false pillars and topped with an ornamental molding, above which a Star of Bethlehem window gleams from the wall of pale pink stucco. Two towers flank the central portion of the front; the tower on the left is massive and is crowned with a somewhat egg-shaped dome, the one on the right is delicate and considerably shorter than the left tower; both towers are broken with arched recesses for the seven

118

bells. This unusual combination of arch and oblong, of balanced and broken rhythms, relieved with the central pattern of the star window, is of a haunting beauty that must be seen to be believed.

An interesting feature of the interior is the gradual curving of the walls toward their meeting with the ceiling arch. The altar is of recent vintage but it blends amiably with the other decorations.

To those who are fascinated by the past, the baptistery is especially interesting. It is of groined sandstone and houses the bronze font brought from Spain by Father Sarría in 1825. Only one of the original windows of Father Lasuen's church remains—that nearest the entrance on the right as one enters the church. The sanctuary contains some of the original candlesticks and paintings, and there are bits of the original Indian decoration along the walls and in some of the carvings.

In the monastery only one room has been restored. It has been made into a museum to house records and mementos of Serra and Lasuen. Jo Mora's fine bronze and stone sculpture of Serra and his friends is the central ornament of the museum. Near at hand you can see Serra's sparsely furnished cell with his Bible laid out on the table as if waiting the flick of his finger to open it to the Psalms he loved so much. Also preserved are the stone Serra is said to have used to beat his breast while praying and the small iron chain with which he scourged himself—relics of an age that believed even the good needed penance, the nemesis of holier-than-thou Christianity.

The tombs of Serra and Lasuen are under the stones of the sanctuary. A bronze plate on the wall commemorates their lives and deeds.

Three miles from San Carlos is the chapel of Monterey Fort, or Presidio, which was called the royal chapel because the government of California was then centered in Monterey. The front of the chapel and its tower achieve a fine balance and movement by means of a mounting series of lessening squares. In the last of these is an excellent statue of Our Lady of Guadalupe against a shell background. The shell motif was used again in niches on either side of the arched entrance. In this chapel the royal governors heard Mass and celebrated saints' days and holy days with all the pomp and gaiety beloved of the Indians.

SAN JUAN BAUTISTA
Saint John the Baptist

San Juan Bautista, California

Founded June 24, 1797

T HE HISTORY OF SAN JUAN BAUTISTA LACKS most of the notes of tragedy and sorrow that distinguish the stories of some of the other missions. From the smiling summer day in 1797 on which Father-President Lasuen founded it in company with Fathers Catala and Martiarena, the mission got off to a good start. The Salinas Valley was rich in timber, stone, and all the other materials the fathers needed to build and ornament their buildings. The little San Benito River made music near by. There was an abundance of supplies and all the tools necessary for a prosperous beginning.

Within a year the establishment had a remarkable growth in building and planting, and the Indians seemed intensely interested in the project. Two years later the Indians went on a rampage and attacked the mission, but Sergeant Castro, who had charge of the soldiers at San Juan, made a few punishing forays and put down the revolt in its early stages. A minor earthquake damaged some of the mission buildings in 1800, but the mission continued to grow, and Indians in considerable numbers continued to present themselves for baptism and training.

The cornerstone of the present church was laid in 1803 and the building was finished and dedicated in 1812. The dedication attracted the attention of both the Indians and the Spanish settlers because the new church was one of the most ambitious buildings of its kind to be erected by ·the Franciscan Fathers in California. It was built to accommodate a thousand Indians and was quite different from the usual long quadrangle of mission churches. The great arch of the central church, rising to a height of 55 feet, was flanked by

121

two lower naves. A central nave with two ambulatories is a common-place in cathedral architecture, but it was a miracle of construction in the mission world, which had to depend upon trampled or baked adobe brick and strong timbers lashed with rawhide. At a later date the two ambulatories proved insecure. Five of the arches that run the length of the central nave were bricked up, providing additional strength for the hand-adzed rafters that support the roof.

122

In its original state the church must have been very splendid. Its great width and height were broken by the rhythm of the irregular arches and their strong square piers marching toward the triumphal arch spanning the sanctuary. A remarkable octagonal pulpit and sounding board jutted from the wall near the left front of the church, and excellent painted Stations of the Cross were ranged in order along the tops of the piers. The altar itself and the reredos behind it were like a huge fan. The central niche of the reredos held a life-size statue of Saint John, carved with great feeling. At the end of each ambulatory were two side chapels, one dedicated to Saint Isidore the Farmer, the other to Saint Anthony of Padua. We can gain some idea of the splendor of the monastery section when we remember that the irregular arches of the cloister covered a distance of 270 feet.

For Indians, visiting celebrities, and Spaniards, San Juan had other attractions. Father Felipe de la Cuesta was a scientist and a linguist of the first order. He spoke twelve Indian dialects and was loved and revered by his neophytes. Scarcely less talented was Father Estévan Tapis, who passionately loved music and spent twelve years of the hardest kind of work organizing a famous choir of Indian boys.

The magnificent days of the mission were all too short. Mexican independence in 1821 and the law of separation quenched the beauty and prosperity of San Juan. Father de la Cuesta, like the good Spaniard he was, refused to take an oath of fealty to the Mexican government, but because there was no one to take his place, he stayed on at San Juan for nine years. Terribly crippled with arthritis, he managed to fulfill his pastoral duties with the aid of faithful Indians who carried him from pueblo to village in a rawhide litter slung between two poles.

For thirty years after the end of San Juan's great days, Father Antonio Anzar, who succeeded Father de la Cuesta, remained in the employ of the Mexican government. About fifty-five acres of church lands were given back in 1859. Father Ciprian Rubio, the next pastor at San Juan, did much to keep the place in repair, but he added a wooden bell tower totally unsuited to the great church and the architectural mode of the period in which the church was built.

Many friendly hands and hearts of all faiths raised the funds for a thorough restoration of the mission, close to the present Route 25. The movement was accelerated in 1928, when San Juan was placed in the care of the Maryknoll Fathers. They have achieved wonders in beautifying the old mission. A museum houses many beautiful relics of the past and a yearly *fiesta,* colorfully costumed, brings alive the happy spirit of mission times after the summit of Pagan Hill was crowned with the cross.

SANTA CRUZ
Holy Cross

Santa Cruz, California

Founded September 25, 1791

T HE MISSION OF SANTA CRUZ HAD A LIVELY and somewhat unsavory history. Father Crespi, the diarist of Portolá's first abortive attempt to find Carmel in 1769, first marked the spot on Monterey Bay because of its fine river and rich grasslands and forests teeming with game. Crespi was also greatly impressed with the giant redwood trees, and it was he who first gave them their name. But the years passed and it was not until the fall of 1791 that Father Lasuen came to dedicate the new mission, the twelfth in the chain. He had only time to raise the cross when he was called to Santa Clara on urgent business, but Indians and soldiers combined to make the actual offering of the first Mass a stirring and festive occasion. Soon the padres had in operation California's first water-powered grist mill.

When the swollen San Lorenzo River rolled in full spate during the rainy season, the fathers discovered the error of founding the mission so near to its bank, and, like practical men, moved the establishment to higher ground. A massive adobe church was built and formally dedicated in 1794.

The history of the mission was anything but happy from that time on. The Indians were quite content with their state of nature: hunting, fishing, gathering the wild abundance of sea and forest. They came to the mission in small numbers and often reverted to their old life after a short stay. A further source of trouble was the pueblo built about the mission by order of Governor Borica. The settlers and the Indians fought and roistered and there was constant strife, much of it caused by the amorous exploits of Spanish men with Indian women. Some of the padres made the mistake of punishing only the women and in this way earned the undying hatred of the Indians. One of the later padres, Father Quintana, is said to have

124

been murdered, but the whole affair is extremely obscure, and it may be that the four Indians punished for the deed were innocent. Pirates, pillage, sacrilege—the mission knew them all between 1812 and 1834. Two earthquakes in 1840 and 1857 completed the ruin of Santa Cruz.

The so-called mission that survives today is not the extensive plant the fathers knew. It is in fact a votive church given by Gladys Sullivan Doyle. Mrs. Doyle, lame from a childhood injury, was cured at Lourdes and in thanksgiving for the cure donated the church as a memorial.

The front of the church is plain except for giant pilasters. An ornamental band breaks the thrust of the pilasters a short distance above the arched entrance and a second band runs the whole length of the front at the top of the pilasters. Over the gable of the red-tiled roof, to the right, the tower rises with its tiled cap and gilded cross. The inside of the church, though it is a complete restoration, is in good taste. Three old statues rank themselves above the altar: Saint Michael, Saint Joseph, and Mary the Mother of Sorrows. The statue of the Virgin is made in the fashion of the wonder-working Virgin at La Soledad, in Oaxaca, Mexico. The beautifully carved wooden statue has jointed arms and legs and was probably once carried in procession on Good Friday. Various changes of costume were made so that the Virgin could be dressed in fitting robes for the changes of the liturgical year. There are dark old paintings and magnificent Spanish vestments in the treasury to the left, and an interesting display of registry books and other documents.

125

California Mission Trails Assn., Ltd.

SANTA CLARA DE ASÍS
Saint Clare of Assisi

University of Santa Clara

Santa Clara, California

Founded January 12, 1777

T HE MISSION CHURCH OF SANTA CLARA DE Asís that is seen today on the campus of the University of Santa Clara has very little to do with the churches built at this mission by the Franciscans. Alterations, rebuilding, and a series of three disastrous fires between 1909 and 1926, in which two of the bells were severely damaged, have combined to wipe out the original character of the mission. The museum, however, has some interesting relics, including a Paschal candlestick lovingly carved and gilded, two carved wooden chairs, a faded daguerreotype of Marcelo, the mission's most famous neophyte, and the original keys and registers. In the university library there are other fascinating items, particularly a vellum-covered choir book and a painting of the mission in its declining days done by Andrew P. Hill. A comparison of the painting with the present church, which is now the university chapel, will show how radically different was the plan brought into being by the mission Fathers.

The first two churches built by the Franciscan Fathers at Santa Clara were not on the present spot. The earthquakes of 1812 and 1818 caused considerable damage to the second church and this was the chief reason that impelled the padres to move to a new site. The third church went up quickly and was dedicated in 1822. At this period Santa Clara, because of the wonderful climate and the fertile lands about it, was one of the most prosperous missions. About a thousand Indians were in residence in the neat pueblos clustered around the church.

127

Scarcely less interesting than Santa Clara's history are stories of some of the padres of the mission. Father José Viader was a rough-and-tumble priest who believed in severe discipline but was just and kindly along with his severity. One night while he was returning from a visit to a sick Indian, Viader was attacked by three pagan Indians, one of them as virile and brawny as the priest. Father Viader gave a good account of himself and was able to put all three of his assailants to flight. Within a day or two the big Indian appeared at the mission, asked to be baptized, and offered to assist Viader in any way with the work about the place. He was baptized with the name Marcelo and it is his picture that may be seen in the museum. Marcelo was eventually given land of his own and lived to be a hundred years old.

Father Réal was equally noted among the Indians. He loved bullfighting and on occasion, if a fighter was injured or failed to appear, Réal sallied into the ring and showed his skill at the ancient sport. The ascetic Father Magin Catala offers an interesting contrast in character. His holiness and discipline were much admired by the Indians. It grieved this good priest that the Indians and settlers at San José pueblo refused to attend services at Santa Clara, and to attract them he planted a fine avenue of willows running from the mission to San José, a distance of three miles. When this failed to draw the people Catala reluctantly granted them their own church.

With Mexican independence Santa Clara Mission declined. It was eventually sold, and was returned to the Church in 1847. Bishop Alemany conveyed the property to the Jesuits in 1851 and from that beginning grew the noted University of Santa Clara of our own day.

SAN JOSÉ DE LA GUADALUPE
Saint Joseph of Guadalupe

18 miles south of San Francisco,

California, on Route 101

Founded June 11, 1797

MOST OF THE TROUBLES THAT WERE VIS-
ited on the various missions arose from the proximity
of the Spanish fort and settlements to the buildings of the padres
and their neophytes. The average Spanish soldier was either an ad-
venturer or a released criminal who spent his free moments drink-
ing and quarreling with the Indian men and doing his best to seduce
the Indian women. The bad manners and bad morals of Spanish
Christians were enough to try the faith of the most naïve neophyte.

Father Serra had often struggled against this abuse, and Father
Lasuen did his best to avoid it by founding new missions widely
separated from fort and pueblo. This was his policy in establishing
San José de la Guadalupe fifteen miles from San José pueblo. The
actual foundation of the mission was made by Father-President
Lasuen, who came up from Santa Clara with a small guard of soldiers. The cross was raised and the first Mass celebrated under a
bower of branches.

Within a short space of time the mission was a growing concern. Ditches were dug, temporary houses were set up, and a few
Indians were in residence in the charming little settlement which
looked out on the blue water of San Francisco Bay.

After 1806, when Father Narciso Duran came to direct San
José, the mission and its *fiestas* became famous. Duran, a talented
musician, made a complicated system of different-colored notes set
down in one great book and patiently taught a group of Indians the
mysteries of counterpoint and harmony. Many visitors came to hear
Duran's celebrated orchestra.

129

California Mission Trails Assn., Ltd.

In spite of the fact that this mission became in time the fourth most prosperous in the chain, its early history was anything but happy. The first serious problem was the warlike character of the surrounding Indian tribes. They made no attempt to attack the mission itself, but they constantly raided the far-flung mission farms, driving off cattle and other livestock. All attempts to punish the raiders were unsuccessful until Mariano Vallejo, a rising young army

130

commander, gathered a strong force and in 1826 went in pursuit of the Indians. His expedition was a brutal success. Many Indians were shot or hanged, not even women were spared. Father Duran, who was still San José's pastor, condemned this outrage in unmeasured language and secured a pardon for the Indian leader Estanislao, a renegade neophyte.

The mission was now secure from Indian attack, but it went from the frying pan into the fire of Mexican independence. Governor Pico sold San José to his brother and their friend Alvarado for $12,000. The United States government eventually restored twenty-six acres of mission property to the Catholic Church.

Of the old mission buildings standing today only a small segment of the monastery remains as it was. The church is a Norman monstrosity built by a French priest who was pastor for a time after the restoration. The old church had a simple beauty. The front of it was broken by a plain pillared doorway with a niche above it to cover a statue. Inside the church the long quadrangle was gay with Indian painting and carving. The simple gaiety of the church was reflected outdoors in the flower-bright patio, where the Indians celebrated their feasts with dances and merriment.

Some interesting souvenirs of the mission age are still preserved in the Norman church today: a hand-hammered baptismal font, beautiful chalices and patens, and the mission bells with their silver tones. The portion of the old monastery remaining was restored with funds provided by the Native Sons of California in 1917. It is a sterling example of the simplicity that made mission architecture a great contribution to American culture. It is only a short walk along the slim-pillared porch to the little chapel which enshrines a small statue of Christ, bleeding and crowned with thorns. The face and hands are exquisitely beautiful. The other rooms of the monastery have become a museum in which is gathered a rather nondescript collection of mission relics. The old olive orchard, the gardens, and the Indian graveyard are worth seeing.

SAN FRANCISCO DE ASÍS
Saint Francis of Assisi
Dolores Mission

16th and Dolores Streets

San Francisco, California

Founded June 29, 1776

THE CHARMING LITTLE CHURCH OF SAN Francisco de Asís has witnessed the heights and depths of human tragedy and romance. When the first plans for a chain of missions were drawn up in Mexico it grieved Father Serra that no provision was made for a station to be named after his patron, Saint Francis of Assisi. When, after the founding of San Diego, Portolá journeyed north in search of Monterey he overshot his mark and found himself on the verge of that great inland sea known as San Francisco Bay. He took possession of land and water in the name of his king, and called it after Serra's patron, Saint Francis. God had given Serra the desire of his heart.

The mission at San Francisco, called Dolores Mission, was not established until 1776. When we remember the almost superhuman energy and loving devotion that went into the founding of the five missions which preceded it in the chain, it seems amazing that Father Serra was able to establish it a mere seven years after his first foundation.

The first temporary chapel was built in 1776. In 1782, Father Palou laid the cornerstone of the present church. The dedication was marked with a tremendous parade and *fiesta* in which Commandant Moraga participated with all the resources of Spanish pomp. The evening was gay with fireworks and the ear-splitting boom of cannons. Nine years after this resplendent beginning the church was finished by Father Cambon, who succeeded Palou. The reign of

132

Cambon ended in 1791 and for several years after that the Fathers in charge were so unworthy of the work that the Indian neophytes fled the place and it fell into temporary decay. This period ended when Father Abella took over the direction of Dolores Mission. He was a born executive, cultivated and tenderhearted. Under his direction an attempt was made to find a sunnier site along the Sacramento River to which the mission could be moved. The attempt was unsuccessful, but a chapel and pueblo were established at sunny San Rafael as a refuge for sick Indians. This mission was fairly successful, but it is no longer in existence today.

At the time when Dolores Mission passed into lay control it was in a half-ruined state. The gold rush of '49 brought a honky-tonk atmosphere to the neighborhood, but somehow the little church survived the loose morals and rowdyism of the period.

In the middle 1860's a Father Prendergast made some unfortunate alterations in the church and its fittings. The building came through the earthquake and fire of 1906 unharmed.

The first serious attempt to preserve and restore the mission was begun in 1916 under the pastorate of Father John W. Sullivan, who collected funds and brought the building to its present excellent state. Its fabric was artfully strengthened with concealed steel beams and the Indian designs on the ceiling and the sanctuary arch were revealed in all their glory of soft reds and yellows. The sanctuary arch itself is notable in that it rests on two square pillars. The old redwood beams, rough hewn by broad-axe, lend an air of massive strength to the composition of the ceiling. The sanctuary is particularly beautiful. Behind the central altar of soft green is a lovely altar screen of gilt and brilliantly colored statues. The niche in the center, marked off from the remainder of the work by two delicate Corinthian pillars, houses an antique crucifix, and ranged in two rows on each side of this niche are carved redwood statues of exquisite beauty. The bottom row has two statues, Saint Ann and Our Lady of the Angels. Above them, in the second row, are Saint Michael, Saint Francis, and Saint Joachim. The whole composition of the screen is marvelously intricate and is finely balanced with a running motif of scrolls and medallions. It is one of the most lovely relics of the mission past.

The two side altars, designed by Father Abella, are scarcely less notable. Each altar has three beautifully carved statues. Altars and statues are all of native redwood. Some of the special treasures of this mission are an Easter candlestick of noble proportions, designed to hold the great candle blessed on Easter Saturday; a number of interesting paintings; a French monstrance; and a silver stand for the Missal.

Outside is the old graveyard bowered in flowers and vines. Graceful trees slant along the prim paths. The graveyard houses the remains of most of the Spanish and many of the American notables who made the history of this part of California. Judges, governors, crooks, and politicians—the green-flecked earth now covers them all like the impartial providence of God which causes the rain to fall on the just and unjust.

134

SAN FRANCISCO DE SOLANO
Saint Francis of Solano

Sonoma, California

Founded July 4, 1823

S AN FRANCISCO DE SOLANO, THE LAST AND most northern of the missions, was founded in conflict, had a short life, and is today merely a museum cluttered with a second-rate conglomeration of mission and Civil War relics.

San Francisco de Solano came into being through the cooperation of Governor Argüello and Father José Altimira, a latecomer to the mission band. Altimira, originally stationed in the decaying grandeur of Dolores Mission, had an ambitious plan to move that mission to a climate more suitable for farming and Indian life. He got the ear of Governor Luis Antonio Argüello, who saw in the Father's plan a twofold gain. First, it would interpose between himself and the Russians at Fort Ross a mission establishment of some strength, and second, the move would create dissension among the Fathers, since Father-President Señan and his advisers were against the move from Dolores.

Altimira selected his dream site at Sonoma and went there to open the mission with a guard of soldiers furnished by the Governor. Father-President Señan rebuked Argüello for overstepping his authority and also wrote a letter of rebuke to Father Altimira that was so forceful Altimira at once stopped all work on the new mission. Eventually a compromise was worked out which provided that Dolores would retain its standing and that both the *asistencia* of San Rafael—used largely as a mission hospital—and San Francisco de Solano would be given full mission status.

Three hundred Indians came up from Dolores Mission, and with the help of a growing band of neophytes the work got under way. The first church was finished in April 1824 and an adobe mon-

135

astery and workshops helped to create the notion of a thriving establishment. But Father Altimira proved a hard master who flogged and abused the Indians for the slightest infraction of discipline and was repaid in kind with hatred, theft, and desertion. The climax came in 1826 when a motley crowd of Indians stormed the mission and drove Altimira and his friends south. The priest was so terrified that he was glad to retire to the peace of San Buenaventura and eventually to Spain.

136

Altimira's place was taken by Father Buenaventura Fortuni, who remained at Sonoma for seven years and did fine work among the Indians. But Fortuni refused to take the oath to the Mexican government, and this brought about his retirement and the advent of the Mexican-born Franciscan José Guitierrez and, following him, the Indian priest Quijas. One was cruel, the other depraved. In the end the mission was looted by General Mariano Vallejo. Under the guise of parceling out the farms to the Indians, Vallejo quietly appropriated both lands and livestock.

For a time the church was kept in some repair, and after the American occupation of California it became a parish church. In 1881 Bishop Alemany sold both land and buildings and the mission was used as a barn until 1903. In that year the Landmarks Club purchased the property and began the work of restoration. Later the state of California bought the property, made it a state monument, and restored the church to its unassuming simplicity.

San Francisco de Solano, started late in an era that brought beauty, civilization, and culture to most of California, today seems a dusty end to the mission story. It was the anticlimax of a divine comedy, and except for the pioneer role it played in the history of California it is not memorable.

SANCTUARY OF
OUR SORROWFUL MOTHER

Sandy Boulevard and Northeast 85th Street

Portland, Oregon

Founded 1926

THE SANCTUARY OF OUR SORROWFUL Mother is one of the most splendid shrines in the world. Surrounded by the busy tides of city life, it is a little island of peace and serenity where men and women go to find themselves. This sanctuary is dedicated to the mystery of sorrow: not the sorrow without hope, but purging sorrow that ends in resurrection and glory.

The sanctuary is unusual in every sense. It is composed of two terraces, an 18-acre one on the street level and a 40-acre one on top of a gigantic cliff. Coming into it from Portland's Sandy Boulevard, noisy with cars, is like coming into a new world of repose and peace. Giant fir trees dusk the air of the little canyon; roses spill out toward the edge of the paths and winding walks of a sunken garden. Dominating the entrance is a crucifixion group in Carrara marble. It sets the theme of the sanctuary in the drama of that moment when Christ said to His Mother from the Cross, "Woman, behold thy son."

To the pilgrim or sightseer several paths offer themselves, two of which lead to the natural amphitheater that holds the center of interest on the lower level. Hollowed out of the granite walls is an arched cavern and under its arch, framed in the serrated walls of the cliff that are half masked in trailing vines and flowers, is a simple white altar. Above it, on a base of tufa stone, is an artful Carrara replica of Michelangelo's *"Pietà"* flanked by two bronze angels with

139

torches held aloft in a gesture of revelation. The mother clasps her son in her arms; He has just been taken down from the Cross. Mary bends above Him with an expression of infinite resignation and tenderness. The exquisite modeling of the two figures catches the winking lights of the votive lamps in their red glasses and refracts the cascade of light falling over the surface of the cliff high above. As if to enhance the drama of the presentation, a heroic bronze figure of Christ carrying the Cross, placed at the west end of the amphitheater, seems to be pointing upward to guide the eyes toward the cliff top 150 feet above where the figure of His Mother stands bathed in light. The whole atmosphere of the shrine is at once artful and artless. The towering trees, the rustic benches, the bursting profusion of falling ferns, and the contrasting light and shadow combine to produce a memorable impression.

The lower terrace has other dramatic moments. Fourteen Stations of the Cross dot the little woodland glade along the base of the cliff and rise gently toward the drama of the Cross. Notable too is the shrine of Saint Philip Benizi. The sculptor has pictured him in a moment of prayer in his hermit's retreat at Montagnata, Italy, to which he had fled to escape being named pope. At his feet is the Papal crown; his eyes are raised to a crucifix that seems to spring from the mossy boulders.

A single rustic chapel on the ground level serves the perpetual congregation on inclement days.

The drama and beauty of the lower shrine amply prepare the pilgrim's mind for the revelation of the upper level. The ascent is made by elevator through a tower that rises ten stories along the left face of the cliff. A bridge-ramp connects the tower with the 40-acre clifftop. Breathtaking views of the Columbia Valley salute the eyes. Far in the distance the top of Mount Saint Helens glitters in the radiant air. Before the pilgrim on the highest face of the cliff, surveying all things from a lofty pedestal of granite, is the heroic statue of the Mother of Sorrows. Here in this world of light the pilgrim meditates on the life of Mary. Looking down on the Way of the Cross below in the valley is the Way of the Mother. Set against this living green backdrop of pines and flowers are seven shrines that tell the story of the seven sorrows foretold by Simeon. These dramatic episodes are visualized in groups of wooden statues all exquisitely carved from linden wood. They are the work of Professor Heider, of Italy, who spent nearly four years making them, and in composition and feeling they touch the highest reaches of the woodcarver's art.

From the towering statue of Mary on the brow of the cliff a straight path leads to a chapel dedicated to Saint Ann, the mother of

Mary. Its simple interior enshrines statues of Saint Ann and of the Virgin and a collection of color prints of famous paintings of the Madonna. Far across the incredibly green expanse of grass is Saint Joseph's Grove. A white marble statue of the saint holding the Child in his arms is fairly bowered in trees and all the floral artifice that goes into a perfect rock garden. It is an ideal spot in which to remember the tender silence of Mary's husband, who speaks no word in the Scriptures.

Behind the lovely firs that bank Saint Ann's Chapel is a magnificent rose garden set in borders of arborvitae. It is like a Persian carpet unrolled before the monastery which houses the Servite Fathers, who look after the shrine. The monastery is a fine building of sandstone, designed in a half-modern style. A dramatic window in the shape of a tremendous cross stands out in the north wall of the chapel.

141

The Servite Fathers are the descendants of those seven aristocratic youths of Florence who, on August 15, 1233, were favored with a vision of Mary. All seven became saints, and the community they founded has persevered in spreading devotion to the Sorrowful Mother. In this sanctuary they have given us a magnificent meditation on the beauty of sorrow that culminates in the joy of light and resurrection.

SHRINES OF THE SOUTHWEST

THE MISSION CIVILIZATION, WITH ITS UTOPIAN
overtones, appeared in the Southwest a hundred and fifty years
before it came to California. The search for the Seven Cities of
Cibola prepared the way, and the encroachment of French explor-
ers westward from Louisiana hastened a series of foundations (1598-
1630) before the Spaniards were properly equipped to make them
in force. The Mexican Indians were at the mercy of their traditions,
which foretold the return of a white god, but the Pueblo Indians
had none of this. Consequently they were tougher and much less
ready for a change of religion and life. They were devoted to their
earth gods and the ceremonial dances that celebrated the annual
rites of fertility.

The Popé Rebellion among the Pueblo Indians in 1680
wiped out most of the original mission work in the Southwest. The
Spaniards, including Governor Don Antonio Otermín and those of
the missionaries who escaped death, were forced back across the Rio
Grande River. Missions were burned, works of art perished, and
precious records went up in flames.

This thoughtless destruction of documents makes it extremely
difficult to tell the early story of the Southwest missions with any
degree of accuracy and completeness. Dates of foundations are vague
and still subject to scholarly debate. Largely missing are the day-to-
day records of the missionaries with their congeries of human-interest
tales that illuminate the California mission story. With the reconquest under Francisco Diaz de Vargas in 1692, the historian is on
surer ground, but a considerable quantity of hearsay and legend has
been woven into the existing records.

No one man dominates the long history of the Southwest
missions as Father Serra does the California foundations. Eusebio
Kino, the Jesuit, is justly fabulous, and the Venerable Father Margil
had both charm and energy, but neither possessed the magnificence
of vision and plan that marked the genius of Serra.

The same causes that operated in bringing an end to the
mission establishments in California worked the downfall of those
in Arizona, New Mexico, and Texas. Mexican independence in 1821
brought an end to the great days of the mission lands. Secularization
soon followed, and much beauty fell into ruin. The work of preservation and restoration of the past also got off to a much later start
than it did in California.

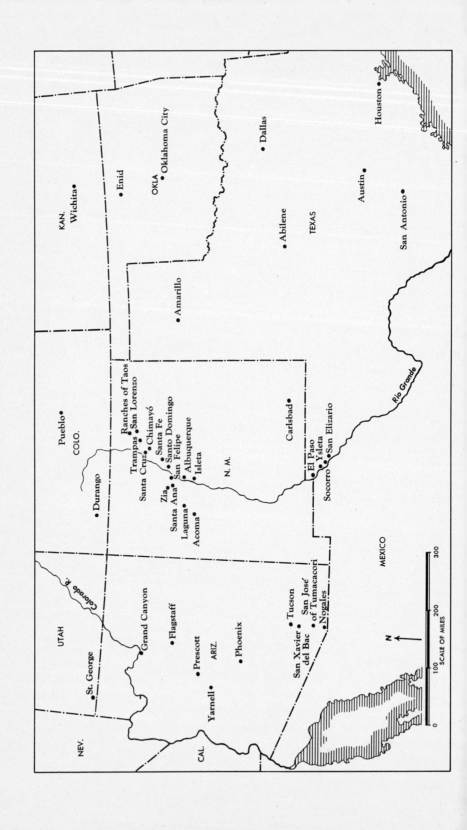

What has been kept or restored is enough to demand admiration of a superb achievement. The vast ruins at San Geronimo de Taos, Jemez Springs, Gran Quivira, Abó, and Quarai are a melancholy commentary on the past, but pilgrims can understand something of the former splendor when they stand before the gleaming beauty of San Xavier del Bac, near Tucson, or lose themselves in contemplation in the patio of San Miguel de Aguayo, at San Antonio.

THE SHRINES

San José de Tumacacori, south of Tucson, Arizona
San Xavier del Bac, near Tucson, Arizona
Shrine of Saint Joseph of the Mountains, Yarnell, Arizona
San Augustino de Isleta, Isleta, New Mexico
Saint Joseph's Mission, Laguna Pueblo, New Mexico
Acoma, Acoma, New Mexico
Church of San Felipe de Neri, Albuquerque, New Mexico
Pueblo of San Felipe, San Felipe, New Mexico
Mission of Santa Ana Pueblo, Santa Ana, New Mexico
Mission of Zia Pueblo, Zia Indian Reservation, New Mexico
Pueblo of Santo Domingo, Santo Domingo, New Mexico
San Miguel, Santa Fe, New Mexico
Cathedral of Saint Francis, Santa Fe, New Mexico
Sanctuary of Christ of Chimayó, Chimayó, New Mexico
Church of Santa Cruz, Santa Cruz, New Mexico
Church of the Twelve Apostles, Trampas, New Mexico
San Lorenzo de Picuris, south of Taos, New Mexico
Church of Rancho de Taos, Ranches of Taos, New Mexico
Mission of Corpus Christi de la Ysleta del Sur, Ysleta, Texas
Mission de la Purisima, Socorro, Texas
San Elizario Mission, San Elizario, Texas
Mission San Antonio de Valero, San Antonio, Texas
San José y San Miguel de Aguayo, San Antonio, Texas
Nuestra Señora de la Concepción de Acuña, San Antonio, Texas
San Juan Capistrano, San Antonio, Texas
San Francisco de la Espada, San Antonio, Texas
San Fernando Cathedral, San Antonio, Texas
Shrine of the Little Flower, San Antonio, Texas

145

Eusebio Francisco Kino, S.J., 1645–1711, as the missionary and explorer is shown in the diorama in the Tumacacori Museum

146

SAN JOSÉ DE TUMACACORI
Saint Joseph of Tumacacori

Near Tubac, Arizona, on Route 89,

40 miles south of Tucson

Founded 1691

F ATHER EUSEBIO KINO OF THE SOCIETY
of Jesus is almost a legendary hero. For years he
practically lived in the saddle, riding the tremendous distances that
spanned the mission empire of Mexico and the Southwest. The Indians called Kino "the Man on Horseback," and they revered the
rawhide-tough endurance of the man whose speech and manner
were as soft and charming as his life was hard.

Kino had wide interests. He was always noting, mapping,
and speculating while his horse trotted through lands unseen before
by the eyes of white men. He noticed particularly the fashion in
which the warlike Indians oppressed the peaceful tribes, and his
compassion made him all the more anxious to organize the pueblos
in such a way as to protect the Christian Indians.

It was at the request of the Indians of Tumacacori that Kino
first came to southern Arizona in 1691. The Indians built him a
brushwood shelter under which he offered the Mass and began his
work of evangelization. By 1698, Kino noted, the Indians had made
considerable progress in the arts of peace; he described an "earth-
roofed house of adobe," fields of wheat, and herds of cattle, sheep,
and goats. Kino and his successors often visited Tumacacori, encouraged devotion, and helped plan advances in farming and ranch-
ing.

The Jesuits were expelled from all Spanish lands in 1767 and
the following year the Franciscan Fathers took up the mission burden. In 1773, when the Apaches were raiding far and wide, Tuma-

147

cacori became the headquarters of the mission chain in Arizona. Under the benign encouragement of the Franciscans, San José continued to flourish. The present massive church, a monument to Indian art and craftsmanship, was begun in 1800 and was in use within two years.

In 1821 Mexico achieved independence from Spain. The anticlerical government gradually took away the power of the missions; the military guard was withdrawn; the financial subsidy was cut off; mission funds were looted and the mission organization scrapped. Mexican priests loyal to the new regime were sent in to take the place of the Spanish missionaries. The result was to be expected: the missions rapidly declined under inexpert management and were again constantly raided by the Apaches.

Tumacacori was sold to a private citizen in 1844. Four years later the disgruntled Indians left the pueblo, carrying with them the furnishings of San José, and settled at Xavier Mission, near Tucson. Vandals, treasure hunters, and the elements swiftly brought the church to ruin, but enough remains to show the fine workmanship. The delightful Romanesque entrance, ruins of the bell tower, the dome, and sections of the patio are nostalgic of an age of faith.

The pueblo was made a national monument by proclamation of President Theodore Roosevelt in 1908. National Park guides take visitors through the church and show them the museum, which is wealthy in its relics of the past. Particularly arresting is the diorama of the interior of the church as it was in the days when the men and women of Tumacacori centered their lives there in a beautiful setting created by native genius.

148

SAN XAVIER DEL BAC
Saint Xavier of the Springs

9 miles south of Tucson, Arizona,

on an unmarked trail

Founded 1700

FATHER EUSEBIO KINO PAID HIS FIRST VISIT to the springs near Tucson in 1692. In the distance everywhere shone the mountain ranges—now purple, now rose, now silver in the changing shafts of desert light.

The spot must have fascinated the priest, for he returned to found a church there in 1700. By 1724 a Jesuit father was in residence at the mission. From that time until 1767, when the royal enemies of the Society of Jesus connived at its suppression, the Jesuits used San Xavier as a base to christianize most of the neighboring tribes.

Father Francisco Garcés arrived at San Xavier in 1768. He enlarged on the Jesuit apostolate and carried the name of Christ to far-distant pueblos beyond the mountains. Father Garcés was martyred by the Yumas in 1781.

The successors of the murdered priest were Fathers Narciso and Baltasar. These two Franciscans were men of vision and had great plans for a church that would vie with the abundant beauty of the mountains. Thirteen years were required for the task, which was carried on under the supervision of the Gaona brothers. By 1783 most of the work was finished, but further improvements and decorations were added between 1791 and 1797.

Built on a stone foundation, the fabric of the church is of kiln-baked brick covered with dazzling white-lime plaster. The Baroque front between the two graceful towers is incomparably beautiful, with its complicated designs in brick and plaster work. A further note of gaiety was the addition of the three balconies,

149

one on each of the two towers, one above the front entrance. From these points of vantage, on the Feasts of Saint Francis and Saint Xavier, distinguished guests and their ladies watched the changing patterns of the Indian dances and the falling stars of the fireworks.

Secularization forced the Franciscans from the mission in 1882 and they did not return again for many years. Today their schools and churches among the Papago Indians are working in the grand tradition of Kino and Garcés.

San Xavier is a living memorial to the mission civilization. In its patio and convent and in the spacious and delightful church we can comprehend something of the sheer poetry of living with which untaught workmen brought San Xavier into existence. It is no wonder the Indians call it La Paloma Blanco del Desierto, White Dove of the Desert.

Photos by "Frashers"—Pomona, Calif.

SHRINE OF SAINT JOSEPH
OF THE MOUNTAINS

Yarnell, Arizona, on Route 89,

30 miles southwest of Prescott

Founded 1939

THE TOWN OF YARNELL IS IN WEST CEN-
tral Arizona at the edge of the Weaver Mountains,
between the towns of Peeples and Octave. Here in a setting of wind-
eroded boulders and mountain trees and flowers, the Catholic Action
League of Arizona erected a Shrine to Saint Joseph in 1939. Laymen
created the shrine, beautified it, and staff it as a center of devotion
and information.

The many statues of the shrine are life-size. They are extraordinary in that their creator, the late Felix Lucero, of Tucson, a
veteran of World War I, made them of reinforced concrete. This
creates an idea of stiffness and roughness, but such is not the case,
for Mr. Lucero managed his material with subtlety and grace. He
achieved a supple naturalism, and the result is deeply affecting.

Christ sitting alone at the table of The Last Supper is im-
pressively beautiful. His figure bent in prayer during the agony in
the Garden of Olives has an instancy of appeal, surrounded as it is
with all the wild beauty of a garden. At his back, from a boulder
in the distance, the empty Cross awaits the coming sacrifice. The
life-size figures of the Way of the Cross are also wonderfully effective in content. They were erected by the Catholic Action Group
as a memorial to all the soldiers of World War I who suffered and
died in the struggle.

The Yarnell shrine is unusual in that it is the work of laymen and their wives who see in Saint Joseph the virtues that ought

151

to characterize the heads of families. Dignity, respect for labor, and a loving sense of command are all exemplified in the statue of Saint Joseph, who at Yarnell greets the casual pilgrim with a grave smile.

SAN AUGUSTINO DE ISLETA
Saint Augustine of the Island

Isleta, New Mexico, on Route 85,

south of Albuquerque

Founded 1621-1630

THE CHURCH OF SAN AUGUSTINO DE ISLETA today has little resemblance to the foundation described by Father Alonzo de Benavides, who delighted in the "very costly and beautiful" *conventos* adjoining it, where the friars directed the teaching of "reading, writing, singing and playing on various instruments." Father Juan de Salas was the founder. The foundation date is not precisely known but it was somewhere between 1621 and 1630, during the period when the Franciscan Fathers were building many lovely churches in New Mexico.

Practically all their work was wiped out in the Indian rebellion of 1680. San Augustino Mission was burned, along with many other missions and their records, but its walls still stood and for thirteen years it was used as a corral by the Indians. After the reconquest the church was restored and continued to be used through the centuries.

Part of the roof was burned a few years ago, and an inept restoration with two squatty spires gave something of the character of a prairie meeting house to a silhouette that was once pure and primitive. The addition of heavy buttresses strengthening the walls accentuated the disastrous effect. The interior of the church, over 150 feet long, was also changed for the worse.

The church is rich in old paintings and hand-carved statues centered in the sanctuary. Saint Augustine's statue is in the middle, behind the altar; Saint Joseph and the Virgin stand on either side of the great Doctor. In the body of the church are four large and

153

ancient oil paintings. The best of the four is a subtle study of Santa Rosalía, which merits special examination. One *convento* has been restored and adjoins the church on the right. Old trees shade its quiet patio and beds of flowers blaze there the whole summer long. The peace and serenity are a pleasant reminder of the men who labored so hard to bring beauty and culture to New Mexico.

Photos by "Frashers"--Pomona, Calif.

SAINT JOSEPH'S MISSION

Laguna Pueblo, Laguna, New Mexico,

on Route 66, west of Albuquerque

Founded 1699

SAINT JOSEPH'S CHURCH IS ONE OF THE most delightful missions in New Mexico and the pueblo of Laguna is one of the largest pueblos west of the Continental Divide. The church is well kept and spacious, but narrow. The massive front is broken above the roof line by two small squares in which the original copper bells hang.

Most of the pueblo churches are constructed of adobe, but Saint Joseph's is of stone. A coat of plaster applied over the surface gives the church and the adjoining convent a pleasant and unusual creamy texture. The use of stone in the fabric of the building is probably due to the fact that Saint Joseph's was built in 1699, a fairly late date in New Mexican mission annals. The neat, square houses clustering about the church are built in the best pueblo style.

The Indians of the pueblo have been unusually progressive. Through the years they have adapted themselves in turn to Spanish, Mexican, and American rule, and when the United States established government schools the Indians attended them and brought back to Laguna the ideas they had been taught. This progressive tendency was furthered, perhaps, by the presence in the pueblo of three American surveyors and their descendants. The three surveyors, who entered the pueblo while surveying for the railroads in 1870, found its atmosphere so delightful that they remained and married Indian girls in the best tradition of the frontier.

155

Photos by "Frashers"—Pomona, Calif.

The Lagunans have continued in the vigorous practice of their faith. The fact that their pueblo was dedicated to Saint Joseph probably made the Indians jealous of the wonderworking portrait of the Saint owned by their neighbors at Acoma, which led to a forced loan of the portrait and an eventual lawsuit to regain it (p. 158).

The inside of Saint Joseph's Church is unusually interesting. A wide band of bizarre red, yellow, and green runs around the wall of the church. The ceiling of the sanctuary is painted with colorful symbols of the sun, moon, and stars. The walls are richly adorned with pictures of the saints, among them a portrait of Saint Joseph painted on elkskin.

From the cliff at the edge of the mesa where the prosperous village stands, the Indians once looked down on a considerable lake formed by the waters of the San José River. It was this lake (*laguna*) that gave the pueblo its name.

ACOMA

Acoma, New Mexico, 16 miles from

Laguna on a secondary road

Founded 1629

T HE INDIAN RESERVATION OF SANTA MARIA
del Acoma lies sixteen miles from Laguna on a secondary road running off of Route 66. The mesa of Acoma is like a
mirage rising from the level floor of the desert. Its perpendicular
cliffs jut upward 350 feet from the plain and a tortuous trail carved
in the rock winds toward the impossible summit, flat as a table,
scoured clean by wind and frost. How the Indians were able to
build a massive church on the top of the rock is one of the mysteries
of faith and human patience that men find hard to understand.

Today the top of the mesa is largely barren, but once upon
a time it was a garden paradise. First came the slow task of carrying
to the top of the rock six feet of rich earth for the gardens and the
cemetery. This was a mere beginning. Generations of Indians
brought up from the plain on their heads the jars and skins of water
that made fruit trees blossom and encouraged vegetables to grow
in the walled garden.

The church came into being by means of the same patient
labor of love. Clay was assembled on the top of the mesa, the bricks
were trodden and dried, and great beams, 40 feet long and a foot
thick, were painfully hauled up for the framework of this house of
God. The whole building is a miracle of Indian toil and ingenuity.

The exterior of the church as the tourist sees it today is like
a great adobe fortress over 150 feet long. Two massive towers flank
the front of the building, which is broken with a square door and
above it the lessening square of a window. The towers have the effect

157

of buttresses, and their strong front walls jut out beyond the façade of the church and taper gently as they rise toward the square arches in which the old bells are hung.

To the right of the church a wall of adobe carries over toward an airy balcony with a carved balustrade and one ionic pillar with its interesting cap. From the porch, the resident father, as Willa Cather has pictured him in that inimitable chapter in *Death Comes for the Archbishop,* could look over his little miracle of flowering green and beyond it to the red and purple desert bathed in light.

The interior of the church, which is dedicated to Saint Stephen, is dark but impressive. An unusual reredos and many statues and paintings ornament the sanctuary. Among the paintings is one of Saint Joseph. Father Juan Ramirez, to whom it had been presented by the King of Spain, brought it to Acoma in the earliest days of the mission, and the Indians ascribed to this portrait their good fortune and continued prosperity.

Saint Joseph was also the patron of the neighboring pueblo of Laguna and the Indians of that pueblo coveted the wonderworking portrait owned by the Acomans. At a time when Laguna was suffering a long drought the Acomans were asked the loan of the picture for a time. They refused, and the Lagunans, a virile people, forcibly carried the picture away. When bloodshed was imminent, Father Mariano de Jesus Lopez made peace by extracting a promise from the Lagunans to return the portrait when their situation improved, but when prosperity returned the Lagunans refused to live up to their promise. Finally the Acomans took their case to the courts, won it, and carried the famous picture back to the "Church of the Sky" in triumph.

Photos by "Frashers"

CHURCH OF SAN FELIPE DE NERI
Church of Saint Philip Neri

West New York Avenue

Albuquerque, New Mexico

Founded 1700-1710

T HE CHURCH OF SAN FELIPE DE NERI, BUILT
in the first decade of the eighteenth century, originally
had the charming simplicity of form and decorations that distin-
guishes all the Indian buildings of the Southwest. The walls and
fabric of the church remain much as they were, but an unfortunate
remodeling of the façade was made in modern times, perhaps to
signalize the elevation of the old mission to the status of a parish
church. The two massive bell towers dwarf the pleasant oblong and
its rather primitive lines, and the style of the towers, with their
Gothic windows and flamboyant points, adds to the incongruity.

The church is rich in paintings and souvenirs of the past. The
parish registers, with their dim old entries that sum up the human
records of San Felipe, are particularly interesting. The staircase to
the choir loft winds about the trunk of a massive spruce tree and
is a fine example of Indian craftsmanship. Interesting too is the
small chapel beneath whose altar lie the remains of Father Gasparri.

Francisco Cuervo y Valdez, a Spanish grandee, was the founder
of the church. Valdez succeeded the great de Vargas as temporary
governor of New Mexico and hoped to perpetuate his name by
founding a church and villa called San Francisco de Alburquerque
(the old spelling of the name), but the Duke of Alburquerque, Viceroy of New Spain, rebuked Valdez for making the foundation without his authority. The church furnishings were forwarded from
Mexico as Valdez had requested, but the title of the new church was
changed to San Felipe de Alburquerque in honor of Philip V of

159

Spain. Eventually both governor and viceroy were edged out of the picture when the church was called San Felipe de Neri.

PUEBLO OF SAN FELIPE
Pueblo of Saint Philip

San Felipe, New Mexico,

on Route 66, 32 miles west

of Albuquerque

Founded 1700-1725

THE PUEBLO OF SAN FELIPE WAS CHRISTIAN-ized by the Franciscans very early in the Spanish occupation of New Mexico. A church was built below the black mesa where from ancient times the Indians had gone to consult their gods and indulge in ritual dances.

No doubt the Fathers were convinced that they had really converted their charges and changed their ways. It must have been a shock to them when the Indians joined Popé in the rebellion of 1680. The pueblo church was completely destroyed, and for thirteen years the Indians went back to worship their gods on the black mesa.

Then came de Vargas in his expedition of reconquest. Once more the San Felipe Indians submitted to Spanish rule and the friars came to reanimate the faith. This time a church was built on top of the mesa and served its small congregation for a hundred years.

As the changing climate made living ever more difficult, the Indians went back into the valley of the Rio Grande, where they could more easily cultivate the corn, beans, and peppers on which they lived.

The present church was built between 1700 and 1725. It is an adobe building with a fine open-work balcony across the front and unusually attractive towers. The pueblo itself is neat and well kept, with a gleaming fence surrounding the patio.

161

MISSION OF SANTA ANA PUEBLO

Santa Ana, New Mexico, on Route 44,

northwest of Bernalillo

Founded about 1600

T HE ANCIENT PUEBLO OF SANTA ANA ONCE throbbed with life. In an age when the climate was kinder and the rivers carried more water, the Indians enjoyed life and had a measure of competence and comfort. Then came years and years of drought. The life-giving Jémez River slowed to a trickle; the plants in the field died; the wind lifted the sand in stinging showers that pocked the adobe of the walls surrounding the church and ancient convent; and little by little the Indians were driven away to seek fertile land.

Today most of the tribe live six miles east of the old pueblo and have built a church there. But the older people, especially the old braves, love to linger on at Santa Ana, and on grand occasions of tribal and religious celebrations the entire clan returns to its revered home.

The exterior church today has a deserted look. Sand has drifted up to the very walls of the ruined convent; walls and roof have an orphan air. Two squat towers ornament the roof. A balcony with primitive carved rails cuts the monotony of the church front and makes a charming shelter above the two asymmetrical doors. There are no benches in the church because the Indians of Santa Ana worshiped as austerely as they lived; they knelt on the smooth adobe floor for Mass and devotions.

Santa Ana has some excellent examples of early religious paintings. The altar screen is significant for its large pictures of John the Baptist and the Saviour.

162

MISSION OF ZIA PUEBLO

Zia Indian Reservation, on Route 44,

west of Santa Ana, New Mexico,

40 miles north of Albuquerque

Founded in early seventeenth century

Z IA PUEBLO, WHICH LIES TO THE WEST OF
Santa Ana, escaped the destructive fury of the Pueblo
Rebellion, perhaps because of its situation on the top of a black lava
mesa overlooking the sandy valley of the Jémez River. Father Bernard de Marta founded the mission early in the seventeenth century.
Mission life, with its dangers and hardships, was an old story to
Father de Marta, who spent thirty years of his priesthood in the
pueblos of New Mexico.

From the mesa where this ancient church stands, the view is
superb in every direction. Far off in the distance are the purple
Sandias and beyond them the iron summits of the Jémez peaks
veiled in silvery haze. Within this vast amphitheater are the colorful
rocks of the mesas and the multishaded green of little valleys, seemingly a stone's throw away in the clear atmosphere.

The adobe church is massive and unadorned except for a
bright coat of whitewash on its fortresslike front. A heavy gallery
that runs across the center of the front breaks the surface of the
façade and gives shade to the square entrance. A slightly lopsided
bell tower, with its inevitable scallop, holds one bell.

The interior of the building is dim and cool. Over the old
altar is a small image of Our Lady of the Assumption, to whom the
church is dedicated. She is dressed in magnificent clothes that
change with the liturgical seasons. Behind the altar is an ornately

carved wooden frame holding a rich picture of the Assumption which was given by the Sandoval family in 1798.

Indians love to linger in the plaza before the church walls. There in the center, in the blinding sun, is a huge wooden cross commemorating the reconquest of de Vargas and a lasting era of peace. Near by is the *campo santo,* where many villagers lie buried in the blessed ground tended by their clan.

Each year on August 15, the Feast of the Assumption, the Indians of the district gather for their annual *fiesta.* The high point of the celebration is a procession in which the Virgin of the Assumption is carried through the pueblo to bring blessings on her people for the coming year.

Church of Saint Dominic

PUEBLO OF SANTO DOMINGO
Pueblo of Saint Dominic

Santo Domingo, New Mexico,

off Route 85, south and west of Santa Fe

Founded about 1886

TWENTY-FIVE MILES SOUTH OF SANTA FE, quite near the Rio Grande, is the Pueblo of Saint Dominic. The first church was built there in 1605 by Father Juan de Escalona, second *comisaro* of the Franciscan missions in New Mexico. The original mission was nearer the river, but a flood completely destroyed it and dictated the move to higher and safer ground.

The present church, with its dazzling white-coated stucco, stands out against a background of low shrub-covered hills. It is built in the mission style but has little connection with the past of the mission civilization. A massive bellcote, off center to the left above the flat roof, has a scalloped design surmounted by a small cross. An open-work gallery casts its shade on a portico notable for its masterful Indian paintings. Those who love pueblo art will find in the gallery an example of the best work of Indian artists, who, though they knew nothing about the classical rules of the academies, managed to charge their work with a joyous life worthy of the best painting.

Photos by "Frashers"

166

SAN MIGUEL
Saint Michael

Saint Michael's High School

Santa Fe, New Mexico

Founded 1621

LITTLE IS KNOWN OF THE EARLY HISTORY of San Miguel. Father Benavides, in his *Memorial* to the King of Spain, records the foundation year as 1621 and the character of the establishment as "a church and monastery." The parish records setting down its early history were burned at the time of the Indian rebellion of 1680, and the roof and interior of the church were burned out at the same time, but the thick adobe walls still stood when the flames had died down.

The Spaniards and missionaries abandoned their settlements in New Mexico for a time, and it was not until de Vargas came with a strong force of soldiers that the territory was reopened and pacified. On his first visit to Santa Fe in 1692, de Vargas gave orders for the repair and refinishing of San Miguel, and the church then served its people for a hundred and fifty years. Its roof was restored in 1830, and the old, beautifully hand-carved beams of the ceiling were replaced with less ornate timber.

In 1872 the triple tower of the church, blown down in a wind storm of cyclonic proportions, was replaced with a single massive tower that detracts from the beauty of the building, and stone buttresses were later erected to strengthen the walls. Though the buttresses deformed the exterior, the interior of the church is a fine example of native workmanship. The nave narrows toward the revelation of the sanctuary. The narrow, deep-set windows soften the fierce sun of the south and drop a rain of radiance on the old paintings and the time-worn ornaments that have helped to make San Miguel a shrine of prayer since the earliest days of our country.

167

CATHEDRAL OF SAINT FRANCIS

Cathedral Plaza

Santa Fe, New Mexico

Founded 1886

IN HER SPLENDID NOVEL, *DEATH COMES for the Archbishop,* Willa Cather told unforgettably the story of John Baptist Lamy, the first American bishop of Santa Fe. It was Bishop Lamy who, as Vicar Apostolic, felt his heart wrung at the state of the faith in the wide, colorful land of New Mexico.

Behind the town of Santa Fe (Holy Faith) were the peaks and slopes of the Sangre de Cristo (Blood of Christ) Mountains red in the glories of sunset. Streets and pueblos, with their saints' names and holy places, and the fallen-down churches told part of the story of the great old days. The new bishop rode the purple distances and gently but firmly brought order and intelligent rule to the warring factions in his vast diocese. When this had been accomplished Lamy determined to build a cathedral in place of the old adobe Church of Saint Francis that had served Santa Fe from the days of the reconquest. In 1875 Bishop Lamy was made an archbishop, and the whole territory rejoiced in the honor conferred upon him.

The Archbishop begged funds in Europe and Mexico, and his friends raised amazing sums of money among the Spanish families of New Mexico. French architects and masons were imported to superintend the vast work of building and stone-cutting in the neighboring quarries. Slowly the work went on, often interrupted by changing contractors or lack of funds. The walls of the cathedral were erected about the old Church of Saint Francis, which during

169

the building carried on undisturbed—except for the noise of hammers and trowels—its long service to the Catholics of Santa Fe.

In 1884, when the old church inside the golden shell of the new building was torn down and hauled away through the dirt streets of the town, the citizens of Santa Fe cooperated in the work without pay. The old bells were blessed and hung in the north tower of the cathedral the same year.

By 1886 the cathedral was finished as far as the communion rail. Archbishop Lamy blessed the building and pontificated at a temporary altar placed before a huge sheet of canvas that covered the unfinished sanctuary.

After Archbishop Lamy's death in 1888, his successors finished the handsome Romanesque building that many pilgrims visit today and decorated it with Moorish and Gothic touches. The ponderous steeples, originally designed for the towers, have fortunately never been finished.

The church has many important relics of its past history dating from the earliest conquest of New Mexico and later territorial times. The cathedral once possessed the superb choir screen taken from the military chapel of the Spanish commandant. This screen, which dates from some time after 1761, was carved in New Mexico of native stone and is a marvel of intricate art in the Aztec style. For years it stood almost unnoticed in the darkness of the unfinished cathedral sanctuary. In 1940, however, Archbishop Gerken transferred the treasure to the newly built Church of Christo Rey (Christ the King), in Santa Fe, where it may be seen in all its refurbished glory. Only the stone ornamental border at the top, shown in old photographs, is missing.

The little statue of La Conquistadora (Our Lady of the Conquest) is, so tradition says, a lovely remembrance of de Vargas' gratitude to Mary for her aid in the reconquest of New Mexico. Each year on the second Sunday after Trinity it is carried in procession from the cathedral to the Rosario Chapel, where it remains for nine days, and is then returned to its shrine with appropriate pomp.

The Rosario Chapel, built in 1816, is itself a shrine of sorts. It replaces the votive chapel which de Vargas promised La Conquistadora for his success in storming the Pueblo of Santa Fe. De Vargas was successful and paid his debt to the Virgin, but his chapel fell into ruin. The present Rosario Chapel marks the spot, and that is why La Conquistadora goes there once a year to be fêted.

SANCTUARY OF CHRIST OF CHIMAYÓ

Chimayó, New Mexico, 24 miles

north of Santa Fe on Route 64

and east on a secondary road

Founded 1816

C HIMAYÓ, NEW MEXICO, IS ON THE WEST
slope of the Sangre de Christo Mountains. The climate is delightful for both the cold and the heat are moderated, and wide-flung orchards of apricots and sweet Mexican apples make spring glorious with blossoms and autumn tawny with fruit. The people of the district are gentle and happy. Money plays almost no part in their lives.

Since the beginning of the Spanish settlement of New Mexico men have come to the holy earth of Chimayó for health and special favors. The place attained continental fame when Don Bernardo Abeyta in 1816 built at Chimayó a little chapel to Christ the Lord. Don Bernardo erected his votive offering in memory of the good health and prosperity he and his family had enjoyed for generations. When Don Bernardo died he left the shrine to his daughter Carmen. She enlarged and embellished it to the delight of the many Spanish and French priests who visited Chimayó. Then a young priest came as chaplain, and he tried to force the Abeyta family to give up control of the shrine. Doña Carmen refused, and unhappy days at the shrine ensued. Finally the young priest was removed by the Bishop and peace was restored.

From early days the chapel focused attention on Chimayó and attracted men of all sorts to the holy place. Sick children in the arms of their parents, incurable cancer patients, men and women of all classes and faiths came to Chimayó—and still come. Briefly they

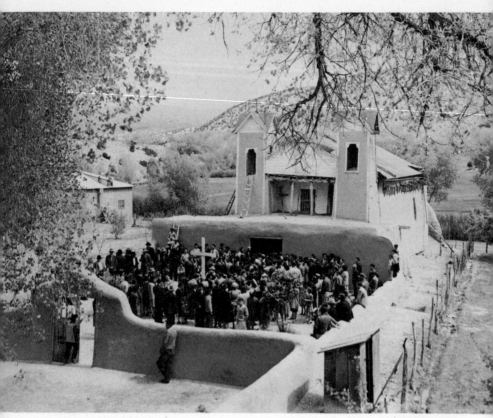

Wide World Photo

pause in the simple adobe chapel after entering under the naïve gallery supported on its two plain pillars.

The dusk of the church is perfumed with incense and the altar is illuminated with hundreds of votive candles. In their light the rich old Indian designs above the altar are muted to beauty, and the artful carving of the ceiling beams and communion rail become marvels of primitive artistry.

It is customary for the sick to take some of the blessed earth of the sanctuary to use as medicine, a pinch at a time taken with a glass of water. Extraordinary cures have been claimed, some of them by people of little or no faith. The Church has not made any pronouncement on the virtues of the shrine, and no record of cures has been set down.

Today the Church controls the shrine and ministers to the thousands of people who come to pray in the chapel. The air of primitive innocence has a tremendous charm of its own, but not the drawing power of the holy earth of Chimayó.

CHURCH OF SANTA CRUZ
Church of the Holy Cross

Santa Cruz, New Mexico,

on Route 64, northwest of Santa Fe

and north of Pajuaque

Founded about 1700

SANTA CRUZ, ONE OF THE LARGEST OF THE early churches of New Mexico, strictly speaking, is not a mission church.

Two ugly towers with heavy bases cast a shadow across the large door and the one undistinguished window which break the front of the church. The parts of the tower that hold the bells are stepped back at the line of the eves and have pleasant, rounded arches but their beauty is somewhat marred by the exaggerated pyramidal tower caps crowned by large crosses.

What the exterior of the church lacks in beauty and interest is more than made up by its interior, which is the repository of a fine collection of paintings, some of them brought all the way from Spain to New Mexico in the earliest days of the reconquest. Many of the paintings of saints were done in Mexico, and there is a possibility that some may be the work of New Mexican artists. In addition to the art collection there are rare books and ancient parish registers and letters. The historical-minded pilgrim will be especially interested in a letter from Charles IV of Spain, which comments on the administration of Indian affairs in New Spain. The collection housed at Santa Cruz helps pilgrims to reconstruct something of the romance and danger that attended the spread of Christianity in New Mexico.

The mission of the padres was more than a mere attempt to convert the Indians. Viceroys and governors might seek to use the Indians to further their official interests and the glory of the King of Spain, but the Fathers who worked and lived with the Indians desired to lift them out of squalor into a better mode of life than they had ever known. Planting, animal husbandry, and the making of beautiful buildings and ornaments were all initiated to provide a better and happier way to Christ.

CHURCH OF THE TWELVE APOSTLES

Trampas, New Mexico, 35 miles

north of Santa Fe on Route 64

and east on Route 76

Founded 1580

T RADITION HAS IT THAT THE CHURCH AT Trampas, built in honor of the Twelve Apostles, was entrusted to twelve native builders who were expected to be of blameless life and to keep themselves unspotted by the world if they hoped to build a church worthy of the special friends of Christ. When the twelve had been found, they set to work fashioning the great carved *vigas* that would hold the ceiling and treading out adobe for the walls. It is not astonishing to learn that the church was exactly twelve years in the building. It was begun in 1580 and dedicated in 1592. The twin towers flanking the narrow front with its inevitable balcony are like great buttresses protecting the entrance. The tower tops are finished with a kind of latticework base on which are slim pillars crowned with delicate caps.

The bells hung in the towers were worthy of the ambitious undertaking, being mostly of gold and silver with a small mixture of copper. One bell called Maria del Refugio, hung in the right tower; the second, Maria del Gracia, hung in the tower on the left. The centuries went by while the mellow old bells called the Indians to prayer and the worship of God. Several years ago, however, thieves attracted not by the rich sound of the bells but by their precious metals came in the night and took away Maria del Refugio along with its latticework frame. Today Maria del Gracia tolls alone, perhaps for some Judas who disgraced the Twelve Apostles.

SAN LORENZO DE PICURIS
Saint Laurence of the Picuris

On Route 64, 20 miles south of

Taos, New Mexico

Founded 1630-1680

T HE PICURIS INDIANS WERE A SAVAGE AND hostile people when the Spaniards first came to New Mexico. Regardless of their intransigent attitude, a small mission church and convent were built in the tribe's pueblo center some time between 1630 and 1680. At the time of the pueblo rebellion of 1680, Father Ascensión Zarate, the mission priest, was imprisoned and then put to death. The church and friary went up in flames while the Indians danced in triumph.

The second church building, erected after the reconquest, has remained much as it was in early times. The little front, with its uneven scallop above the roof, is topped with a cross. The arch below it holds one small bell. Seen in its setting of mountains and thick forests, the tiny mission has the memorable beauty of some primitive shrine in the Swiss Alps.

The church is dark inside, like most churches built under the blazing sun of the Southwest, but it houses many lovely relics of the past. The rudimentary stone altar is in sharp contrast to the paintings in the altar screen and the many statues of native workmanship. A glowing canvas depicting Saint Laurence on his way to martyrdom on the gridiron is one of the great treasures of the mission. Beautifully carved beams in the musicians' gallery and in the roof give travelers a telling insight into the patience and artistry of the Indians. This insight is deepened and enlarged by a careful examination of the colored decorations in which the gridiron plays an important part. Each year on August 10 the Festival of Saint Laurence is celebrated with unique ceremonies and dances.

The mission is fairly well off the beaten track, twenty miles south of Taos, N. M., but it is well worth a visit because its atmosphere and religious feeling are a spur to faith and the enduring fortitude fostered by the friars. The body of the martyred Father Zarate has been moved to Santa Fe and is buried in the Saint Francis Cathedral.

Church of Rancho de Taos

Photos by "Frashers"

CHURCH OF RANCHO DE TAOS

Ranches of Taos, New Mexico

Founded 1772

T HE CHURCH AT RANCHES OF TAOS IS ONE of the most beautiful churches in New Mexico. Adobe houses cluster around it like chickens around a mother hen, and the fertile lands of the Taos valley, dotted with small ranches, surround it on every side. Great buttresses supporting heavy twin towers make a massive frame for the central part of the façade. The wide single door is topped with a fanlike arch that is very beautiful.

The church was built in 1772, at the period when Father Junípero Serra was planting the mission civilization in California. The comparative lateness of its founding probably explains its ambitious design. The adobe walls are very thick, the shape is cruciform, and the length is more than 120 feet.

The faintly lighted interior contains many souvenirs of the past. The altar is a fairly modern replacement, but the screen behind it is Baroque in style and frames eight oil paintings of various saints. A large hand-carved statue of Christ and the ornamental altar screens bring many tourists to the church.

To the right of the wooden cross in the patio is the old Indian burial ground.

MISSION OF CORPUS CHRISTI DE LA YSLETA DEL SUR

Mission of the Body of Christ of the Island of the South

Ysleta, Texas

Founded 1682

T HE ANCIENT MISSION OF CORPUS CHRISTI founded in 1682 in the westernmost corner of Texas is almost entirely a restoration. A disastrous fire on May 14, 1907, destroyed the church and its treasure of ancient statues, paintings, and gold and silver plate. After the fire only the walls of the sacristy remained standing, but one famous statue of Christ, brought from Spain long ago, was rescued from the interior of the building. Also saved was the mission bell, which outdates the mission itself and is probably of Mexican origin.

Father Juan Córdova, a Jesuit, who was pastor of the church at the time of the fire, hired a competent carpenter from Socorro and with a kind of holy fury soon had the mission rebuilt. Father Córdova did most of the work himself, and the present mission gives ample testimony that he did it well. The church front has simplicity and balance. The old, uneven, and rather primitive line of the gable was rebuilt in an artfully graduated scallop; the square door became an arch; the plain bull's-eye window above it was surrounded by an ornamental molding; and the two asymmetrical niches in the gable were reduced to one. The greatest change of all, however, was made in the bell tower. The oldest available photographs of the mission, taken about 1880, show a square base of naked adobe brick, with tall bell arches crowned with a kind of beehive cap broken by one arch and one bull's-eye opening. This tower was replaced with a modern variation suggesting a hint of Moorish influence.

One of the most interesting sights of the place is the mission farm, which has been in continuous operation since 1682 and is prob-

180

ably the oldest farm in the United States. Its fruitful soil still bears a rich crop every year.

The land on which the mission was built was given by the Tigua Indians, who sought refuge in the valley of El Paso del Norte after the Popé Rebellion of 1680. The founders of the mission were Father Francisco Ayeta, a Franciscan friar, and Don Antonio Otermín, Governor of New Mexico. In Spanish, *ysleta* or *isleta* means "little island," and the mission was named Corpus Christi de la Ysleta del Sur because at the time of its foundation it was on an island made by the channels of the Rio Grande. The Tigua Indians, who were both proud and faithful sons of Spain and of the Church and who often donned their war paint to fight the just battles of their white friends, later requested that the name of the church be changed to San Antonio de la Ysleta because Saint Anthony was the favored patron of the Tigua Nation. The change, however, was not made.

The last Franciscan left Ysleta in 1852 and for a time the mission was staffed by diocesan priests. When the Jesuits took over the care of the mission in 1881 they altered its title to Nuestra Señora del Monte Carmelo (Our Lady of Mount Carmel), and in deference to the long-continued demands of the faithful Indians, a compromise was effected and a statue of Saint Anthony was finally restored to the niche over the church door.

181

MISSION DE LA PURÍSIMA
Mission of the Most Pure Virgin

Socorro, Texas, on Route 80,

south of Ysleta

Founded 1683

A HEAVY OX CART WITH WIDE WOODEN wheels was lumbering through the dusk of the desert of western Texas. Along the sandy banks of the Rio Grande it went as the shallow water caught the last of the light. Several Indians walked beside the cart. They walked in silence, which was their way, but a special gravity shone in their faces because of the carefully wrapped bundle in the cart. It was a statue, hand carved in Mexico and brave with fresh color—a statue of Saint Michael, the great archangel. To the Indians a *santo* in the sky was not half so desirable as a *santo* on earth, one they could see and touch, one to whom they could pray.

Suddenly the creaking wheels of the cart sank into the sandy soil. Now the Indians bestirred themselves. Uttering sharp cries, they beat the oxen with switches of thorn trees and heavier limbs of cottonwood. The great beasts strained and snorted but the cart refused to budge. In the darkness the Indians held a long consultation and decided that Saint Michael obviously did not wish to go further. He had chosen a site for his chapel.

This story is the popular legend of the founding of Socorro Mission. Remaining records indicate that the mission was founded by Father Francisco Ayeta and Governor Don Antonio Otermín in 1683, a year after they had founded the mission at Ysleta. The mission was large and was built in the form of a cross. It was called originally Nuestra Señora de la Purísima Concepción, then San Miguel del Sur, and finally La Purísima.

182

The original church was swept away in a flood in 1776 and a new site was chosen about a mile from the old church. The work of building was begun at once but was not finished until 1840; sixty-four years went into the building and carving that made the church an exceptional achievement in a frontier community.

Its massive walls and unusual bellcote high above the main door are in the best tradition of the austere mission style. The ceiling beams are a marvel of carving. The miraculous statue of Saint Michael stands proudly in its own shallow arch above the altar at the left of the sanctuary. Indians still come to light their candles to the Commander of the Lord's Armies, for they are convinced that the *santo* selected his own resting place and that he continues to look after his people.

SANCTUS

SANCTUS

SANCTUS

184

SAN ELIZARIO MISSION
Saint Elzéar Mission

San Elizario, Texas, on a secondary road

off Route 80, south of Socorro

Founded 1683

THE TOWN OF SAN ELIZARIO WAS ONCE THE county seat of El Paso County. Spanish families of means lived on great estates, and the new Americans adapted themselves to the slow-moving pastoral civilization about them. Vineyards, vegetable gardens, and groves of pecan and fruit trees gave to the fertile valley the atmosphere of a little paradise. The center of the town was the Church of San Elizario, with its quaint buttresses and graceful bellcote. Then the railroad came. It passed by San Elizario, and the once lovely town gradually declined.

The original mission was a military chapel dedicated to Our Lady of Pilar and Saint Joseph. The present church, dedicated to Saint Elzéar, was built in 1773 on the site of the old fort. Since that time many changes and reconstructions have radically altered the original appearance. It is finished in the authentic mission style with a dash of the modern spirit.

The inside walls of the church, the altars, and the statues have been modernized, and the decorative stencils on the walls are a far cry from the bright designs once popular with the Indians.

San Elizario Mission, like the town to which it gave its name, lives mainly in the past. Only on the feast days of its saint—a Frenchman and a great general—does the old plaza come alive with a faint flash of color worthy of a splendid past.

185

MISSION SAN ANTONIO DE VALERO
Mission of Saint Anthony of Valero
The Alamo

San Antonio, Texas

Founded 1718

THE ALAMO IS FAMOUS IN SONG AND STORY. Here behind the stout walls built under the supervision of the padres, a little band of frontiersmen struck a blow against the dictator Santa Ana and prepared the way for the independence of Texas. Travis, Davey Crockett, Bowie, and their peers—those names are almost legend. Santa Ana stormed the Alamo after three days of furious fighting and barbarously slaughtered the remaining heroes, but the terrible wounds inflicted on his forces at the Alamo gave the Texans and their allies time to regroup and the sacrifice of the Alamo insured the victory at San Jacinto. Protestants, Catholics, and men of almost every religion, working together, had written in their blood a glowing page for freedom.

Many well-informed people know the story of gallant sacrifice but there are few outside Texas who can recall the earlier chapters of the San Antonio story. The town was actually founded in 1718, although it had been authorized by the viceroy two years earlier. Father Olivares, who had founded a mission at Solano in 1716, moved his mission to the new center. Originally called San Antonio de Padua, the mission was rechristened San Antonio de Valero in deference to the King's viceroy, the Marquis de Valero. The establishment began with ten families and a guard of Spanish soldiers.

Olivares labored mightily to convert the Indians of the neighboring tribes, but the mission and its padre were plagued by a series of disasters culminating in a hurricane which destroyed the buildings in 1724. A new beginning was made at the present site of the Alamo, "two gunshots away" from the first foundation, and by 1727 considerable progress had been made in the construction of a

186

Ford Green

convento and an irrigation system. Already seventy families of Indians were in residence. Smallpox and sickness slowed the mission's growth for the first twenty years. A report dating from the year 1761, however, indicates that the mission was in a flourishing condition.

A regrouping of influence among the different groups of Franciscans led to a changing of the guard at San Antonio Mission, and from this point on the fortunes of the establishment persistently declined. The mission records were transferred to the Church of San Fernando in 1793. The mission church was still incomplete, though a great part of the work had been done on the cloisters and walls.

Religious services again took place in the Alamo during the time when the Flying Company of San Carlos Parras was quartered in the enclosure during the Mexican War of Independence. The company officially left the mission in 1813, but they returned and again took up residence until some time between 1820 and 1830. Soldiers of Texas took over in 1835 and used the Alamo as a strong point of defense in the famous battle which was the birth pangs of Texas freedom.

Texas has remembered the whole story. The men who suffered and died to found a civilized outpost in a strange country far from the pieties and orange groves of Andalusia, or the red-slashed clay of the high plains where olive trees are heavy with fruit, have much in common with those who hated tyranny and wanted to bring a better world into being. Sacrifice, discipline, and hope are the qualities pilgrims find at the Alamo.

188

SAN JOSÉ Y SAN MIGUEL DE AGUAYO
Saint Joseph and Saint Michael of Aguayo

Pyron Road, off Route 281

San Antonio, Texas

Founded 1720

THE FOUNDER OF SAN JOSÉ, THE VENER-
able Father Antonio Margil de Jesús, was an unusual
man even when compared with the many giants of the Franciscan
tradition in America. Learned, ascetically handsome, cultured,
Father Margil had the simplicity of a child and the manners of a
grandee. His life was one long pilgrimage. Scorning all easy modes
of travel, he traversed deserts and mountains in the service of the
King of Kings, becoming a familiar figure in all the mission lands
of the Southwest. He was dignified and graceful in his brown robe
and strong cowhide sandals and his only weapons were the Word of
God and the strong oak pilgrim staff clasped by a muscular brown
hand. A native of Valencia, Spain, Father Margil had the easy, light-
hearted ways of his province, which is famous for beauty, dancing,
and music.

Mexico provided the first field for the exercise of his zeal and
talents. With a Spaniard's love of order and system, Margil saw that
a rigid course of training was necessary for all missionaries who
hoped to preach to the Indians. With this thought in mind he
founded the Missionary College of Guadalupe, in Zacatecas. This
college eventually rivaled the eminence of the Querétaro College,
which, more thoroughly Spanish in its sympathies and tradition,
sent a long line of illustrious missionaries into the Southwest and
California.

Father Margil had long wished to found a mission empire
dependent on the Querétaran chain, and when the Marqués Miguel
de Aguayo succeeded Governor Alarcón, the friar applied for per-

189

The Alamo Register, Joe Bacon Photo

mission to establish a center to serve the Pampoas Indians, near San Antonio. The proposed mission was to take as its name San José y San Miguel de Aguayo, a title which no doubt did much to move the Marqués to speedy action.

Aguayo commissioned his lieutenant general, Captain Juan Valdez, to select the proper site and convey ownership to Father Margil. The place, selected in 1720, was a spot three leagues from San Antonio Mission. Plans for a walled presidio and a village in the center of the mission were drawn up at once and carried out with a magnificence worthy of the large-visioned founder.

A word picture written in 1768 describes the mission in detail. Nowhere in New Spain did the Indians fare better than at San José y San Miguel. Their quarters were light and airy. The weaving rooms furnished fine white goods for clothing and thick woolen blankets and sheets for the beds, an astonishing innovation for the Indians.

The irrigation ditch was like a little river, and was plentifully stocked with fish. The fields about the pueblo were fenced in and bore a rich yearly crop of corn, sweet and Irish potatoes, lentils, brown beans, cantaloupes, watermelons, sugar cane, superb olives, and mouth-watering peaches that weighed as much as a pound apiece. The patios were garden paradises heavily scented with the compounded fragrances of all the gardens of Valencia.

The Indians were well versed in religion and most of them spoke Spanish, at least in the pueblo under the watchful eye of the padres. The musical talents of the Indians were developed to a high degree. They played the harp, violin, and guitar, and they especially loved singing; on great feast days they chanted the rosary in four voices accompanied by musical instruments. Each Indian was given two suits of clothes for work days and one for Sundays and feasts. The dancing at *fiestas* was a marvel of Spanish intricacy, but many Indians still had a fondness for furious Indian dances and often sneaked away to pagan pueblos to indulge it.

On ranchos and in workshops the entire establishment throbbed with life and achievement. All this activity came to full flower in the comely church finished shortly after 1778. It had been some fifteen years in the building.

The Mexican Revolution brought an end to the great days. Secularization of church property speeded the decay, and a hundred years after the cornerstone of the church was laid the dome and north wall toppled into ruin.

Benedictines, Holy Cross Fathers, and Redemptorists in turn tried to awaken interest in the old mission. It was not, however, until several bishops and the San Antonio Conservation Society became interested in the work that it made distinct progress. Dr. Carlos Casteñada, of the University of Texas, prepared the way for the restoration by his translation of available Spanish records. Old foundations were cleared of rubble, and little by little the many buildings were faithfully and carefully restored. The property was then given to the state of Texas and later became a national historic site.

Pilgrims to this shrine can spend hours examining the various parts of the restoration—the old grist mill, cloisters, beautifully arched granary, and workshops. But it is the church itself that is the real marvel. The superb stone tower with its massive cap, the high walls, and the subtle dome are like a salute of trumpets to the fathers and Indian workman who built them with crude tools and a fully perceptive love. The carvings about the main entrance and the rose window of the baptistery are exuberantly beautiful.

In 1931 the Franciscan Fathers returned to San José. Once again there is the tap of sandals on the flags of the cloister and a flash of brown robes in the chapel. Old Indian crafts have been revived and flourish. Something of Father Margil's spirit seems to hover over the spot in the revival of his dream.

191

NUESTRA SEÑORA
DE LA CONCEPCIÓN DE ACUÑA
Our Lady of the Immaculate Conception of Acuña

Mission Road

San Antonio, Texas

Founded 1731

M ISSION CONCEPCIÓN WAS FIRST FOUNDED in 1716, east of the Angelina River. In 1731 the mission was moved to the west bank of the San Antonio River, one league south of San Antonio Presidio. The move was made to insure more protection against marauding Apaches, for the infant mission had the usual troubles with disease and raiding Indians. In time, however, a great church was built in strong Renaissance style. Its two solid towers and the dome were topped with graceful stone lanterns. Perhaps at Concepción the Querétaran Fathers hoped to rival the magnificence of San José. They were largely successful, for the descriptions that have been preserved indicate that the church was richly endowed with gold and silver plate and paintings and that a lovely statue of the Immaculate Conception was enthroned over the main altar.

The Indians at Pueblo Acuña were particularly well instructed. Morning and evening they recited in chorus their lessons from *Ripalda's Catechism*, to which the Fathers added explanations and problems designed to impress their stolid charges. In 1785, Concepción was rated the best mission in the province. This would seem to indicate that the Querétaran Fathers had finally achieved their goal of surpassing San José in wealth and importance, though not in architectural loveliness and exuberance of invention.

192

Revolution and secularization brought inevitable decay. The mission declined; the Indians left the security of their pueblos; and their lands were filched by the career men of the new Mexico.

193

SAN JUAN CAPISTRANO
Saint John Capistran

Mission Road

San Antonio, Texas

Founded 1731

ORIGINALLY FOUNDED UNDER THE NAME of San José, this mission was moved to San Antonio in 1731 from its location east of the Angelina River some twenty miles northwest of Nacogdoches. To avoid a confusion of titles, the mission was renamed in honor of Saint John Capistran, a fifteenth-century reformer of the Franciscan Order and a preacher of a great crusade against the Turks.

San Juan Capistrano never attained the importance of San José or Concepción. The lands allotted to the Indians of the pueblo were never sufficient to feed the cattle, sheep, and horses which the mission seemed particularly successful in raising. The chapel was never large enough to contain its congregation, and a large room in the convent was turned into an additional church, decorated with bright altars, carved statues, and oil paintings.

Father Morfi, reporting on the mission in 1778, speaks of a "spacious clean and decorated church." Morfi also noted that the church was of different style than the other missions of San Antonio because it did not stand out distinctly in its own patio but was incorporated into the pueblo wall. Apache raids may account for this radical departure from accepted principles. Capistrano and La Espada (p. 196) were farther away from the protection of the soldiers quartered in the Presidio.

San Juan had begun to decline before the Mexican Revolution. Disease and raids had cut its population to about a hundred by the year 1792 and the following year there were less than fifty inhabitants in the pueblo.

194

Pilgrims today will gain some idea of the mission civilization of San Antonio from the ruins of the massive aqueduct near San Juan which once furnished water for the ranches of near-by Espada Mission.

SAN FRANCISCO DE LA ESPADA
Saint Francis of the Sword

Espada Road

San Antonio, Texas

Founded 1731

AFTER SEVERAL EARLIER FAILURES DATING from the very beginning of Texas, San Francisco de la Espada was established a short distance below San Juan Capistrano in 1731. The bell tower was built in the shape of a short Roman sword and this, tradition asserts, gave the mission its name. Perhaps its exposed position and the constant assaults of Apaches also had something to do with the title.

The mission in its heyday was noted for its green, well-watered pasture lands, which supported some four thousand head of cattle. These were the constant prey of the Apaches, whose continual raids discouraged the Indians of the mission and caused them to desert in considerable numbers. Father Bartolomé García of Espada made a great contribution to Indian solidarity by preparing a grammar in the most common language of the many tribes living in the vicinity of San Antonio. This manual, published in Mexico on October 15, 1760, played a tremendous part in breaking down tribal divisions and old prejudices and helped the padres in teaching religion and the arts.

Espada was secularized in 1773 and its lands were divided among the Indians living there at the time. No resident priest remained, but the fathers from San José ministered to the Indians of the mission for many years afterward.

In the melancholy ruins of the missions of the South Loop today there is little remaining to indicate the beauty and culture that once flourished there. The civilization brought by the padres was

196

one of discipline and duty, but these qualities were burnished with the joy and gaiety of Saint Francis, who loved the birds and flowers and all the natural loveliness of the world. Often the looms in the workshops were quiet and the mills ceased their grinding, while the Indians danced and sang in the plaza and made processions with their flower-crowned *santos* preceded by lights and smoking censers.

Mission vied with mission in splendor of worship and joyous celebration. The mission civilization failed, but it did not fail because of any major fault of the missionary Fathers.

197

198

SAN FERNANDO CATHEDRAL

The Plaza

San Antonio, Texas

Founded 1734

S AN FERNANDO WAS THE PARISH CHURCH of the Villa San Fernando. It was named after Don Fernando, Prince of Asturias, who later became King of Spain.

The first small group of families at the villa attended Mass in the presidio chapel. In 1734, three years after this initial contigent of settlers from the Canary Islands had arrived in San Antonio, the cornerstone of San Fernando was laid. The King of Spain had authorized an appropriation to cover the cost of building, but, because the royal grant was slow in coming, the first work on the church was financed by donations from colonists and soldiers. Finally the viceroy contributed 5000 pesos.

Apparently the building proceeded at too slow a pace, for in 1746 all the residents were ordered to help with the work. The viceroy sent a further contribution of 12,000 pesos. On November 6, 1749, the church was blessed, along with a small cemetery in the churchyard.

San Fernando was placed strategically at the very center of San Antonio. The principal entrance opened eastward on the town plaza, the west door faced the plaza of the presidio. The church was seriously damaged by fire in 1828, and repairs were not completed until 1841.

The present cathedral contains part of the old building and parts that are new. Its interior, in spite of renovation and change, has kept the spirit of Old Spain. In its shrines and soft colors it tells

199

something of the story of frontiersmen hungry for beauty in an alien land.

Photo by PFC. Bill Clark and PFC. Gene Bournique, USAF

SHRINE OF THE LITTLE FLOWER

North Zarxamora Street and Kentucky Avenue

San Antonio, Texas

Founded 1926

THE CARMELITE CONVENT AT LISIEUX, IN France, is the mother shrine of Thérèse Martin, popularly known as the Little Flower. There her body rests in the atmosphere of prayer and simplicity so dearly loved by this unusual child. Thérèse was born at Alençon on January 2, 1873. At the age of fifteen she entered the convent at Lisieux against the wishes of all who wanted her to wait and spent nine years there in prayer and suffering. Loving God as a child loves a good father, she made this love and trust the foundation stones of her heroic virtue. Thérèse died in 1897, and a series of brilliant miracles led to her early canonization.

This child saint completely captured the heart of Americans, and when Father Raymond, the Carmelite Provincial, went to France in 1931 he was given the rare privilege of a visit with the two living sisters of Saint Therese, cloistered nuns of Carmel like their famous sister. Their memories of the saint so fired his imagination that he determined to build an American shrine in honor of Therese.

Slowly, with funds contributed by non-Catholics and Catholics from every state in the Union, the National Shrine of the Little Flower was built in San Antonio, Texas. The consecration of the shrine on September 27, 1931, attracted many notable people.

Built in a combination of Romanesque and mission styles, the Indiana limestone church is a beautiful tribute to the "Saint of the Little Way." A tall bell tower in three pillared tiers houses six great bells that at intervals during the day strike the opening

201

chords of the *Gloria* and the *Te Deum;* a smaller tower on the left of the front bears a bronze statue of Saint Therese. With one hand she holds aloft the crucifix, with the other she scatters her rose leaves of good for souls.

The interior of the church is gay with bright marble and mosaic work. It typifies the joy in religion that marked the entire life of Thérèse Martin and led to the many favors she has granted to her devoted followers.

SHRINES OF THE SOUTH

ST. AUGUSTINE, NEW ORLEANS, ST. MARY'S CITY IN Maryland, Bardstown, Kentucky—much of the early Catholic history of the South clusters about these centers.

From St. Augustine, Spanish Jesuits and Franciscans fanned out northward and began the evangelization of the Indians. One group of Jesuits, led by Father Segura, built a log chapel near what is now Fredericksburg, Virginia, and was martyred by hostile Indians in 1570. Today the approximate spot of the martyrdom is marked with a giant crucifix that dominates the landscape near Acquia Creek, twelve miles north of Fredericksburg. It is not a shrine in the narrow sense of the word, but it well deserves to be a place of pilgrimage.

It was English Jesuits who, in 1634, played the chief religious role in the establishment of St. Mary's City, Lord Baltimore's original foundation in Maryland. This once-impressive town is today a complete ruin, and though it is worth a visit because of the important part it played in the development of religious freedom in our country, it is a historical rather than a religious shrine.

The site of the first Carmelite monastery in America, founded at Port Tobacco, Md., in 1787 by Bishop Carroll, the first American Bishop, is also an interesting historical shrine that owes much to Jesuit influence. It may in time become a widely popular shrine, especially since the revival of interest in the contemplative life has brought it into the spotlight of public attention.

The Jesuit contribution to the making of New Orleans is an inspiring story of heroism and ceaseless activity that carries through to our own times. The development of minds rather than shrines seems to have been the chief Jesuit preoccupation, but the Chapel of Our Lady of Prompt Succor, in New Orleans, and the Oratory of Saint John Berchmans, in Grand Couteau, came into being largely through the prudent advice of Jesuit spiritual directors.

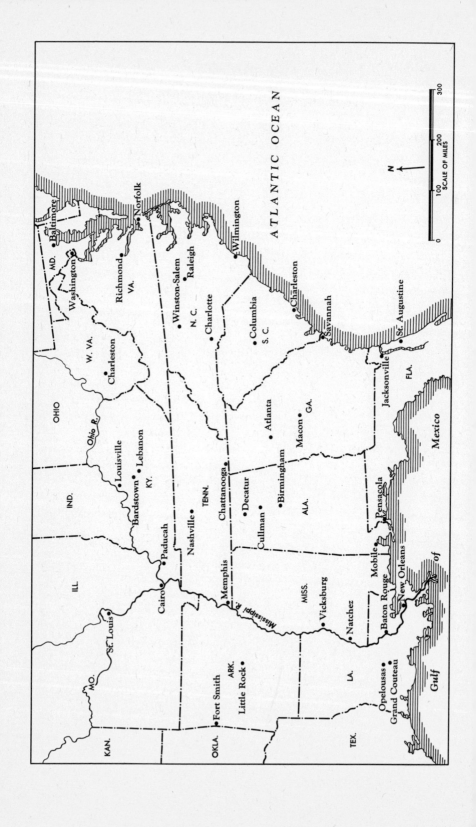

ATLANTIC OCEAN

N

SCALE OF MILES
0 100 200 300

Baltimore
MD.
Washington
Norfolk
Richmond
VA.
W. VA.
Charleston
Winston-Salem
N. C.
Raleigh
Charlotte
OHIO
Ohio R.
Columbia
S. C.
Charleston
Louisville
Lebanon
KY.
Bardstown
IND.
Atlanta
Macon
GA.
Savannah
St. Augustine
Paducah
Nashville
TENN.
Chattanooga
Decatur
Birmingham
ALA.
Pensacola
Jacksonville
FLA.
Cullman
Mobile
ILL.
Cairo
Memphis
Mississippi R.
New Orleans
Gulf
St. Louis
MISS.
Vicksburg
Natchez
Baton Rouge
of
MO.
OKLA.
Fort Smith
ARK.
Little Rock
LA.
Opelousas
Grand Couteau
Mexico
KAN.
TEX.

THE SHRINES

Shrine of Saint John Berchmans, Grand Couteau, Louisiana
Saint Louis Cathedral, New Orleans, Louisiana
Shrine of our Lady of Prompt Succor, New Orleans, Louisiana
National Shrine of Saint Ann, New Orleans, Louisiana
Saint Roch Chapel, New Orleans, Louisiana
Ave Maria Grotto, Cullman, Alabama
Nuestra Señora de la Leche y Buen Parto, St. Augustine, Florida
Monastery of the Holy Sepulchre, Brookland, District of Columbia
National Shrine of the Immaculate Conception, Brookland, District
of Columbia
Minor Basilica of the Assumption of the Blessed Virgin Mary, Balti-
more, Maryland
Saint Joseph's Church, Bardstown, Kentucky

SHRINE OF SAINT JOHN BERCHMANS

College of the Sacred Heart

Grand Couteau, Louisiana

Founded 1867

J OURNEYING EASTWARD FROM SAN AN-
tonio, the pilgrim will come upon Grand Couteau
in southwestern Louisiana, not many miles south of Opelousas.
There, at the College of the Sacred Heart, is the Shrine of Saint
John Berchmans.

Saint John Berchmans entered the Belgian community of the
Society of Jesus when he was scarcely more than a child. Like Saint
Therese of the Child Jesus, he had enough determination to leap
the barriers set up against such an early entry. Within the society,
John amazed his confreres. He was completely detached from worldly
things and devoted himself to the observance of the rule and the
deepening of his spiritual perceptions. He particularly loved to serve
Mass and to decorate the altars. John went to Rome for his philos-
ophy course and died in the Holy City at the hour he himself had
foretold. Behind him the young man left an enduring memory of
unusual devotion, which grew with the years and led to his beatification in 1865 by Pius IX and his canonization in 1888 by Leo XIII.

Shortly after the beatification a biography of Blessed John
came into the hands of Mother Martinez, Superior of the Sacred
Heart Academy at Grand Couteau. At that time a postulant of the
convent was Mary Wilson, who was born of Protestant parents in
western Canada on September 20, 1846. Mary went to visit in St.
Louis, Mo., in 1862 and during her stay met a Catholic woman who
often took her to church, where the ceremonies of the Mass made a
deep impression on the young visitor. Little by little the girl studied

207

the doctrine of the Catechism and prepared herself for baptism. Finally she wrote the news to her parents, who replied in a furious letter filled with threats and reproaches. The letter was a shock, but in spite of it Mary persisted, was baptized, and entered the Convent of the Sacred Heart, in St. Louis.

In the first steps of her religious training, Mary, never physically strong, was sent to a milder climate—first to Baton Rouge, next to New Orleans, and then to Grand Couteau. The change of climate failed to achieve the desired effect and Mary's sickness increased from day to day. The two physicians who examined her pronounced her illness an inflammation of the stomach and found symptoms which promised little hope of recovery. The opinion of the doctors seemed borne out: the girl's chest became inflamed; her tongue was swollen, and her gums and lips were also alarmingly inflamed. At times she was unconscious.

Mother Martinez, the Superior, was so moved by the biography of newly beatified John Berchmans, that she decided to urge the entire community to make a novena to the young saint in the hope of effecting a miraculous cure for Mary Wilson. On the last day of the novena Mary appeared to be dying and Holy Communion was given her at about 6:30 in the morning. After the Conventual Mass, Mother Martinez came to visit the girl and found her sitting up in bed, completely cured. Many people came to see the young postulant, but none was more amazed than the two doctors, who could give no explanation for the sudden change.

In a torrent of speech, Mary told Mother Martinez what had happened. While the community was at Mass, John Berchmans had appeared to the girl to tell her that she would be cured and that she would soon receive the habit. Mary later amplified her story in a sworn statement which was forwarded to Rome and eventually played a part in the canonization of Saint John Berchmans.

Later, in the following year, a second vision foretold Mary Wilson's death before the year was out. So it happened. The young novice, after a three-day illness, died quietly on August 17, 1867.

Pilgrims came to visit her grave, and in time the infirmary was turned into a chapel. Two scenes from Mary's cure are painted on the wall of the sanctuary and a boyish statue of Saint John dominates the altar.

SAINT LOUIS CATHEDRAL

615 Pere Antoine Alley

New Orleans, Louisiana

Founded 1727

S AINT LOUIS CATHEDRAL STANDS IN THE
Place d'Armes, the central square of the city of New
Orleans. With its patina of holiness and history that attracts innumerable pilgrims, it is one of the most venerable and interesting
churches in the United States.

The first parish church of Saint Louis was dedicated in 1727.
Because it was the principal church in the French colony of Louisiana, official documents were read from its steps or posted on its
doors, and the great French and Creole families of those days made
it the center of their social and civil life.

When Louisiana was ceded to Spain in 1762, a new life and
rule came to the infant settlement. Consequently it was Don Andres
Almonester, a Spanish philanthropist and official, who came forward
with the offer of funds when the Church of Saint Louis was burned
in the disastrous fire of 1788 that wiped out half of New Orleans.
The Saint Louis Cathedral that tourists visit today is substantially
the rebuilt church that was dedicated, December 23, 1794, in the
presence of the Governor and all the Spanish notables of the city.
Although there have been many enlargements and a long series of
improvements and changes, the cathedral crystallizes, as it were, the
span of history that has known French, Spanish, and American rule.
The pomp and circumstance of three empires and the devotion of
generations have given it a character at once unusual and charming.
Here General Andrew Jackson came the day after the historic battle
of New Orleans to participate in a great *Te Deum;* here Spanish
grandees and French aristocrats, Cardinals and the colored folk of
the city and bayous have come to pay homage to the Lord.

The exterior of the church is like a tiered cake in three layers. A great central panel of stuccoed pillars is topped with a historic clock. A tall Gothic spire rises from the central tower above the clock, to be flanked by well-balanced side towers capped with spires.

The interior of the church, with the subdued classical feeling of its pillared balcony and high altar, is lighted with splendid stained-glass windows. Famous murals add touches of opulent and historic color. Of particular interest is the tremendous mural in the arch above the main altar that pictures Saint Louis of France, surrounded by the clergy and barons, announcing the Seventh Crusade from the steps of the Notre Dame Cathedral in Paris.

Almost as interesting as the Cathedral is the old Ursuline Convent, at Chartres and Ursuline streets. The oldest remaining building in the Mississippi Valley, it is famous as the site of the first woman's *college* in the United States, the first Catholic school within our boundaries, and the first Indian and Negro school. The convent has been a center of culture and holiness since that eventful day in July 1727, when the first Ursulines arrived in New Orleans.

210

SHRINE OF
OUR LADY OF PROMPT SUCCOR

2635 State Street

New Orleans, Louisiana

Founded 1851

I N 1792 THE FRENCH REVOLUTION FORCED all French religious orders from their houses. Many cloistered nuns went to the guillotine; others returned to the dubious security of their families. Among the latter was Madame Saint Michel, an Ursuline nun born Frances Agatha Gensoul, who returned to her home in Pont St. Esprit. Later, when the persecutions had somewhat abated, she went to Montpellier and opened a boarding school for girls, a school that was brilliantly successful and brought many women into the religious life of her Order.

When a letter from a friend invited her to join the Ursuline convent in New Orleans, the Bishop of Montpellier, Monsignor Fournier, was unwilling to lose this splendid worker and forbade Mother Saint Michel to leave. Only one avenue was open to her, she could write a letter to the Pope and she knew the hazards of such a stratagem. The Pope was already a prisoner of Napoleon and the mails were slow and unsafe. How could she hope for an answer? But Mother Saint Michel did hope, and she dared even beyond that. Kneeling before her own matronly statue of the Virgin and Child, she asked for a *prompt* and *favorable* answer to her letter. If both conditions were met, Mother Saint Michel promised to popularize devotion to Our Lady of Prompt Succor in New Orleans.

Her letter was sent on March 19, 1809. An answer from the Pope written by Cardinal di Pietro arrived in Montpellier on April 29. The Pope granted Mother Saint Michel's request and gave her his Apostolic Benediction. Considering the slowness of stagecoaches,

the upset condition of Europe, and the red tape of Papal procedure, it was truly an amazing response to Mother Saint Michel's plea.

Mother Saint Michel left at once for her new field of labor, taking with her the statue of the Virgin and Child and several faithful companions. On New Year's Day 1810 the little group arrived in

New Orleans, center of the vast territory that had been settled by French Catholics and six years earlier had passed to the United States as a part of the Louisiana Purchase.

The burdens of the new life were many, but Mother Saint Michel, radiantly happy, found them trifling. Her first concern was the propagation of devotion to Our Lady of Prompt Succor among the Catholics of New Orleans and especially among her students at the convent, then at Chartres Street between Hospital and Ursuline streets. Mother Saint Michel also wished to establish a feast day for her Lady, but how could she hope to do so without some signal event to reinforce her own private experience?

The signal event presented itself in the Battle of New Orleans, January 8, 1815. The Americans protecting the city were outnumbered; the landing force was made up of the finest troops of England. Once again Mother Saint Michel made a vow to the Virgin: if she granted victory to the American troops Mother Saint Michel promised a Solemn Mass each year to celebrate the Feast of Our Lady of Prompt Succor.

The battle fought on the field of Chalmette turned into a resounding victory for the Americans. When, the following year, a great service of thanksgiving was held in Saint Louis Cathedral in New Orleans, special tribute was paid to the Virgin under her new title. Year after year the anniversary was kept, and in 1851 formal approval of the new feast and of the title of Our Lady was given to the Ursulines in a rescript of Pius IX.

The devotion soon spread over the United States and the world and a confraternity of Our Lady was established at the convent in order to propagate it. When the Ursulines moved to their new convent at 2635 State Street, the lovely statue went with them. The statue of Mother and Child was solemnly crowned in 1894, and Our Lady of Prompt Succor became the patroness of Louisiana.

Today Our Lady has a new chapel on the grounds of the Ursuline Convent. It is a faultless Gothic building, as serene and lovely as devotion and art could make it. Here Mother Saint Michel's statue is enthroned under a stone canopy. Through the openwork of the altar screen shine the ruby and sapphire lights of the huge stained-glass window in the wall behind it. The statue itself is charming: Mary holds the child on her hip; Mother and Child have a look at once commanding and benign; and both heads are crowned with magnificent golden circlets shining with jewels.

Pilgrims are always at Our Lady of Prompt Succor—asking favors, showing their love—and Mary's answers to many have been as astonishing as the favors granted to Mother Saint Michel which first gave rise to a new devotion for the Universal Church.

213

214

NATIONAL SHRINE OF SAINT ANN

2117 Ursuline Avenue

New Orleans, Louisiana

Founded 1852

DEVOTION TO SAINT ANN HAS BEEN POP-
ular in New Orleans since the beginning of the city.
With the arrival of many settlers from Brittany it received added
impetus, for those people loved "good Saint Ann" and had a profound devotion to her.

In 1852, Archbishop Antoine Blanc erected a new parish
church "in rear of the old city of New Orleans" and placed it under
the patronage of Saint Ann. The brick church in Gothic style attracted a diverse congregation: haughty Creoles, aristocratic French,
and many humble Negroes "from the *faubourg* back-of-town." Each
year on the Feast of Saint Ann noted preachers came to the city
and the church was jammed to the doors with pilgrims from the
district.

Both French and Creoles, however, were strongly infected
with Jansenism. Their spiritual life and practice would revive briefly
each Saint Ann's Day; the remainder of the year was given over to a
somewhat lackadaisical performance of religious duties. But in 1901,
with the arrival of a new pastor of Saint Ann's, the Very Reverend
John Baptist Bogaerts, the atmosphere of the parish changed almost
completely. On the fiftieth anniversary of the parish Father Bogaerts
established in the church a beautiful shrine to Saint Ann. He took
a further step forward in founding Saint Ann's Confraternity on
August 13, 1902. From that time forward solemn novenas to Saint
Ann and special devotions in her honor brought crowds of people
to the shrine. Many special favors were reported.

215

Saint Ann's Church was moved to its present location on Ursuline Avenue in 1920. Cardinal Gasparri, Secretary of State to Pius XI, in a Papal Brief of May 18, 1926, made the New Orleans shrine the National Shrine of Saint Ann for the United States. The following year the Archconfraternity of Saint Ann was legally incorporated and the National Shrine Bureau was established. *Saint Ann's Herald* became the official magazine of the society. Today funds are being collected for the building of a basilica-style church which will be the national center of devotion to Saint Ann.

In addition to the lovely shrine in the church, a grotto of Saint Ann has been built on the grounds in the general style of the grotto at Lourdes. Our Lady looks down from her niche in the rock, as Bernadette saw her, but in this case Mary's eyes are bent toward the chapel of her mother, Saint Ann, whose altar and statue shine out from the cave below. The grotto is surmounted by a crucifixion group, and it also has a replica of the Holy Stairs and a cave of many shrines.

Seventy thousand letters asking for prayers and favors were received during the solemn novena of 1953. They came from every state in the Union and from most of our island possessions. Thousands of pilgrims carried candles in the street procession and were individually blessed with the relic of Saint Ann.

SAINT ROCH CHAPEL

New Orleans, Louisiana

Founded 1874

N EW ORLEANS IS A CITY OF SURPRISES,
with its charming vistas in the old quarter, unex-
pected parks, drifts of magnolias framing pillared porticos, gusta-
tory delights at Antoine's, and high-jinks of carnival time. Most
surprising of all is none of these. One would not expect to find hope
and love springing out in a graveyard, but this happens in New
Orleans.

On August 16, thousands of people move toward the *campo
santo,* the old walled cemetery of the Germans. The crowd is full
of contrasts: old women hobbling along on canes; young and middle-
aged people in wheelchairs; a woman with a haunted face and deep
shadows under her eyes; young girls smartly dressed, their heads
bound up in colorful scarves; athletic-looking boys. They all troop
past the folded iron gates, past the life-size angels at the entrance
—wingless angels who lost their wings in a hurricane. The central
aisle of the *campo santo* is lined with marble tombs in which the
past sleeps—hopes and desires, evil and good—the quiet dust of men
and women. The stone slabs of the aisles whisper with shuffling
footsteps. A great cluster of heads is bowed before a gigantic cross
on which a figure of bronze hangs in an attitude of loving resignation.

The crowd is thickest before the triple arch of a small Gothic
chapel, the clean thrust of its narrow front like a tall peaked hat
against a blue sky flecked with cotton-ball clouds. No one shoves
or pushes; order is here, and voices are muted in respect. In and out
of the small chapel the people go in quiet files, catching for a moment a glimpse of a narrow interior, a small, railed-in Gothic altar,
and a kindly statue of a pilgrim saint under its central canopy.

217

Swiftly the priest offers a little golden reliquary to be kissed by the thousands passing before the sanctuary rail. It is the Feast of Saint Roch, and his clients have come from all the suburbs and neighboring towns to pay him honor.

The story of this cemetery and chapel is fascinating. Both are the work of Father Peter Thevis, who came to the United States from the Rhineland in 1867. In New Orleans a yellow fever epidemic was then at its height. All day the bells tolled and men with muffled faces manned the wagons that carted bodies out of the gloomy houses.

Father Thevis was a man of steady nerves. The German Church of the Holy Trinity, to which he was assigned as assistant, was sorely hit, and the priest threw himself into the work of healing and consolation. When the next year brought a return of the dreaded yellow jack, the pastor of Holy Trinity was one of the victims and Father Thevis succeeded to the burden. From the pulpit he preached hope. "Turn to Saint Roch. He will protect you." Candles were lighted until the whole church was ablaze. The soft sift of rosaries between the fingers was like a sigh of hope. When the plague had departed, tradition says, not one member of Holy Trinity had perished.

Father Thevis told his people of the vow he had made to erect a cemetery and a chapel to Saint Roch if the plague spared them. His listeners were more enthusiastic than the city authorities, who did not give permission for the work until 1874.

The men's societies fell on the project with German vigor and thoroughness. The ground was leveled, the aisles laid out, the walls raised. Within a year, on September 6, 1875, thousands of men and women sang the Rhineland hymns at the dedication ceremony and the laying of the cornerstone of Saint Roch's Chapel. A year later it was finished and the Feast of Saint Roch was given over to the blessing of the chapel and the cemetery.

From that time forward, while generations of men and women entered the vaults of the dead, three feasts were widely celebrated in the chapel and burial grounds: the Feast of Saint Roch, All Souls' Day, and Good Friday. Beautiful Stations of the Cross were erected on the walls, and in contemplating the sorrows of Christ, men and women learned the path to resurrection. On Good Friday and All Souls' Day the air pulsed with prayers for the dead. Chrysanthemums were everywhere, like trailing stars drooping from vases and tins and boxes. The marble fronts of the tombs were banked with bronze and white and yellow.

People came now nine days before the Feast of Saint Roch, some asking health, some asking to preserve it. Young girls were

there looking under thick lashes at boys in the crowd, for it was said that Saint Roch was skilled in finding a good husband. Vows were made and fulfilled. Every year young and old painfully walked along with beans in their shoes for penance and beautiful girls made their pilgrimage with bare feet.

In time the whole chapel was paved with stones marking favors received and the walls of the sacristy were covered with *ex votos* that may be seen today: crutches, braces, shoes, canvas and iron girdles, casts of hands and feet and faces on which Saint Roch had worked his healing.

That is why the *campo santo* with its little chapel breathes out a perfume of love and hope. That is why people journey past the wingless angels at all hours. Even at night the windows glow red with votive lights: for love found, and in thanksgiving for the candles of hope lighted in dark hearts.

219

AVE MARIA GROTTO

Saint Bernard's Abbey

Cullman, Alabama

Founded May 27, 1934

BROTHER JOSEPH ZOETTL WAS BORN IN Bavaria on January 24, 1878, and spent his early life in the Catholic schools of Landshut. Two things marked those years: a talent for mechanics and, not less important, a vocation for the order of Saint Benedict. When in 1892 a new monastery, Saint Bernard's Abbey, was established at Cullman, above Birmingham in the north central part of Alabama, Brother Joseph came to the United States and entered the abbey as a lay brother.

In his spare time Joseph developed a hobby of making mechanical toys from odds and ends of metal and cardboard. Next he enlarged his interests by creating rock and marble miniatures of famous buildings and placing them as ornaments at the edge of the Brothers' recreation ground at Saint Bernard's. Soon his miniature panorama of Jerusalem in the time of Christ was so much admired that visitors came at all hours to view it.

These interruptions began to disturb the monks in their orderly round of prayer and work, and, in consequence, a more public location for the development of Brother Joseph's hobby was sought. In 1932 the long hill at the front of the monastery was made available to him by the Father Abbot.

With amazing speed Brother Joseph, working alone, brought into being a whole miniature fairyland. Little Jerusalem was recreated and to this were added amazing small replicas of architectural wonders famous in Benedictine history and of noted shrines in Christendom. Little pools and streams of water began to add to

220

Brother Joseph and his miniature of the Temple of God of Jerusalem

the illusion of reality; wide beds of flowers made borders of beauty. Finally Brother Joseph fashioned a large grotto which, by his ingenuity, became his finest tribute to the Mother of God.

The Mary Grotto is a cave twenty feet deep in the hillside from which the stone for Saint Bernard's was quarried. The ceiling and walls are decorated with artificial stalactites that glitter in the light. An ample altar of intricately patterned small stones is crowned with a life-size marble statue of the Virgin. Saint Benedict and his sister Scholastica kneel at Our Lady's feet in an attitude of supplication.

Bishop Toolen of Mobile, Alabama, formally blessed the shrine on May 27, 1934, assisted by many priests, students, and a great crowd of people.

Brother Joseph's shrine is an invitation to prayer, but it is also an education in Bible history. Like the Juggler of Notre Dame, the humble lay brother has earned Our Lady's smile with his simplicity and skill.

221

222

NUESTRA SEÑORA
DE LA LECHE Y BUEN PARTO
Our Nursing Mother of Happy Delivery

St. Augustine, Florida

Founded September 8, 1565

S T. AUGUSTINE, FLORIDA! THE NAME CON-
jures up the first white settlement in America. The
settlers were Spaniards, but unlike Ponce de Leon, who hoped to
find youth in the Land of Flowers, these settlers expected to spend
their lives founding a new outpost for God and their king. On
Saint Augustine's Day in 1565 the little fleet in command of Pedro
Mendez de Aviles stood off the coast and named the city they proposed to found for the great doctor of the early Church.

It was not until September 8, the Feast of the Nativity of Our
Lady, that the colonists ventured ashore. With Spanish *punctilio,*
they wore their best clothes, so that the glancing light caught the
rich tones of velvet and silk and made sunbursts on the casques and
polished mail of the soldiery. Banners were unfurled—the flags of
royal Spain and the standard of the Virgin. So Pedro Mendez took
possession of the land in the King's name. Working speedily, the
colonists set up an altar of palmetto logs on the point of land
looking out on the bright blue water of the inner channel. Then
the chaplain, Father Grejales, vested himself and offered Mass in
honor of Mary. Silence fell under the trees, and the silver chime of
Mass bells first rang out on the shores of the United States.

The plot of land given to the first mission was called *Nombre
de Dios* (Name of God). From this mission, for two centuries, Jesuits
and Franciscans carried the faith among the Indians to the north
and west. Some of these missionaries were martyred, but the work
went on. Father Blas Rodriguez, one of the missionaries, was cap-

223

tured by pagan Indians while he was offering Mass. Foreseeing his eventual martyrdom, he begged to be allowed to finish the Sacrifice. His request was courteously granted, and at the end of Mass he was hacked to pieces.

About 1620 the chapel of Nombre de Dios was dedicated to Nuestra Señora de la Leche y Buen Parto (Our Nursing Mother of Happy Delivery). A lovely little statue of the Nursing Mother was enshrined in the small stone building—the Virgin cradles the Child in her arms and offers Him her breast; she looks down upon her Child with a look of brooding tenderness, a smile hovering on her lips.

It is easy to understand how in early days this devotion to Our Lady was so popular in the Spanish colony of Florida, often decimated by plagues and Indian raids. The devotion had first grown up in Madrid about 1602, when a Spaniard saw a German mercenary soldier making off with a stolen statue of the Nursing Mother and by force or bribe gained possession of the statue. It seemed a heaven-sent chance, for the man's wife was dangerously ill in a prolonged pregnancy and it appeared inevitable that mother or child, or both, would die. The man took the rescued statue home, enshrined it there, and offered burning prayers for his wife's delivery. His petition was granted. The sick woman gave birth to "a beautiful boy" and her strength returned so swiftly that she was able to nurse her own child. This episode gave rise to the devotion to Nuestra Señora de la Leche y Buen Parto.

The shrine at St. Augustine, which was some distance north of the city walls, suffered in the varying fortunes of the infant colony. In 1728 it was pillaged by Colonel John Palmer's men during a British raid; in a later raid Governor Benavides ordered it destroyed to prevent the British from capturing it. A temporary shrine was set up within the fortified walls, but this in turn was dismantled in 1763 and its furnishings were carried to Cuba and South America when the British assumed control of Florida. In 1875 the old site of Nombre de Dios was repurchased, and Bishop Verat almost immediately began the rebuilding of the Shrine of the Nursing Mother on the old foundations.

Today the shrine is loved and venerated by a whole continent and Nombre de Dios has reassumed something of its antique charm. It is quiet under the ancient trees with their trailing pennons of Spanish moss, where blue skies and shining waters work their magic. A palmetto-log altar stands on the point where the first Mass was offered. There are Stations of the Cross and rosary shrines along the sanded paths. The little stone chapel stands at the heart of this peace.

224

Inside, set on the plain stone altar backed with fluted rose draperies, the Nursing Mother smiles down on the face of her Baby. Expectant mothers come here to ask a happy delivery, families to petition for health and concord. Many a rapt young bride on her honeymoon looks on the face of the Mother while the beads of the rosary tell a story that never dies. The chapel has many souvenirs, among them the headboard and coffin of Captain General Mendez, the founder of Saint Augustine.

On the birthday of Our Lady a great pilgrimage comes to the shrine. Little girls in gauzy veils, parish societies, priests and bishops return to celebrate pontifical Mass on the palmetto altar under the trees. On this day Nombre de Dios takes on much of its old splendor, and the Nursing Mother, with that same delicate smile, looks down on the children who flock about her altar.

225

MONASTERY OF
THE HOLY SEPULCHRE

Brookland, District of Columbia

Founded 1897

THE FRANCISCAN ORDER HAS PLAYED A wonderful and exciting part in laying the foundations of our country. In California, Arizona, Texas, and Florida, and in the vast reaches of the Northwest, the story is well known to students of history. Hennepin, Serra, Hobart, Margil, and Padilla (martyred in Nebraska) are among the many Franciscan names remembered with gratitude. And it should not be forgotten that it was Father Juan Perez who influenced Queen Isabella of Spain to finance the voyage that led Columbus to the discovery of America.

The love and courtesy exemplified in Saint Francis is found in his sons, who carry on his spirit among us. A fine distillation of those qualities shines forth from the Franciscan shrines and may be found in particular abundance at the Monastery of the Holy Sepulchre, in Brookland.

This memorial of the Holy Land was founded by Father Godfrey Schilling in 1897. The site was the old Meehan estate in Brookland, a suburb of Washington. Two years after the land was purchased the great church and monastery were dedicated. They are built of vitreous buff brick ornamented with white stone, and their architectural style is in general a modified Byzantine, although the church front is more in keeping with the classical rules of Palladio. Church and cloisters cover a huge expanse of ground, and the effect is enhanced by fine gardens, and trees surrounding the buildings.

The Church of the Holy Sepulchre roundly lives up to its name. It enshrines many replicas of famous places in the Holy Land

226

which were sacred in the life of Our Lord and His Mother. They
are displayed with a telling drama which makes this holy spot
memorable in the minds of all those who are fortunate enough to
see it. The first impression of the interior of the church is one of
light and radiance. Amber windows in the clerestory surrounding
the arching dome pour in a flood of light which is refracted from a
wealth of colored marbles, giant frescoes, and gilded bronze. Under
the great dome is set the simple, white-pillared altar with a graceful
baldachin of bronze above it. The columns are fretted with a pattern
of American birds and flowers in high relief. From the interior of
the square columns the bronze statues of the Twelve Apostles shine

227

down on the altar, taking a rosy glow from the richly colored likeness of Mary, *mediatrix* of all graces, which forms the ceiling of the baldachin.

The main entrance of the church is flanked by two shrines, one commemorating the crowning with thorns and the other, on the right, the scourging of Christ. Our Lady's Chapel is the first on the left, the Chapel of Saint Anthony on the right. In the opposite corners are the chapels of Saint Francis and Saint Joseph. Between these points are the most unusual chapels. The one on the east is the Shrine of the Transfiguration, where a great wall plaque in high relief depicts the exaltation of Christ on Mount Tabor. Rayed with glory, Christ is suspended above the earth, where Elias bends in prayer and Moses exhibits the Tablets of the Law. The whole scene is intensely dramatic and alive in the movement of the drapery and the uprush of lines toward the resplendent figure of Christ.

At the other end of the church is the altar of the Crucifixion. Here in life-size and lifelike perfection is the whole somber drama of the Crucifixion: the soldiers, Christ's enemies, the three Marys, the good thief, and the bad thief, realistically portrayed, and Christ hanging between them at the first moment of descending darkness as the Crucified bends to drink the gall and vinegar. In sheer visual power the scene is better than a whole book of meditations on the Cross.

The north and south ends of the church contain the altars of the Holy Ghost and the Sacred Heart. These chapels, like those of the Transfiguration and the Crucifixion, are raised one story in the air and are approached on wide staircases worn smooth by the feet and knees of pilgrims. In the north and south chapels the Holy Spirit and the Sacred Heart find symbolic representation in the center of murals that portray scenes from Christ's life and the life of Saint Francis. The symbolic meaning of the four raised chapels is obvious; the hills of Calvary and Tabor are like the spiritual mountains of Christ's love and the inspiration of the Holy Spirit.

For many pilgrims and tourists the most interesting parts of the Monastery of the Holy Sepulchre are the faithful replicas of places in the Holy Land. There are five of these: the Grotto of the Holy Sepulchre, the Stone of Anointing, the Altar of Calvary, the Grotto of Nazareth, and the Cave of Bethlehem. Outside in the beautiful garden are the Grotto of Gethsemane, the Tomb of the Blessed Virgin, and the Chapel of the Ascension. All are careful reconstructions of the originals as found in Palestine today. From them it is possible to absorb something of the exact atmosphere surrounding Christ's life and death. To these shrines the Holy See has

228

granted the indulgences accorded to the same places in Palestine. Thus in a sense the Catholic pilgrim is able to gain many of the indulgences that otherwise may be obtained only through a long journey to the Holy Land.

Scarcely less interesting are the catacombs in the deep crypt of the church, copies on a smaller scale of the Roman Catacombs, which show the exact way the Christians worshiped underground and the way they were buried. The naïve art of those early Christian days is amply evident, and few pilgrims will be untouched by the dramatic chapels of Saint Benigus, Saint Cecelia, Saint Philomena, and Saint Sebastian. Here are moving murals of saints being consigned to the beasts of the Roman circus. Also underground is a purgatory chapel which, in its realism, may spur the careless to holy respect.

The grounds of the monastery are laid out in opulent style. Scattered among the beds of brilliant flowers are artful shrines and chapels that call the heart to prayer. A visit to this shrine is an unforgettable experience. It has many beauties, many strange and wonderful things that are no less beautiful than they are inspiring to the mind and heart.

NATIONAL SHRINE OF
THE IMMACULATE CONCEPTION

Brookland, District of Columbia

Founded 1914

THE PATRON SAINT OF THE UNITED STATES
is Mary the Mother of Christ, under her title of the
Immaculate Conception. The promulgation of the dogma in 1854
gave world-wide popularity to Mary and materially increased devotion to her, especially in the United States. Up and down our
land churches and cathedrals were built in her honor.

Beautiful as these tributes were, they lacked the splendor
of Chartres or any of the other magnificent European cathedrals
into which grateful Continental nations had poured their best love
and the finest flower of their artistic genius. So, under the leadership
of Bishop Shahan, the first rector of the Catholic University of
America, a plan gradually took shape for a national shrine worthy of
Our Lady and the riches and destiny of our nation.

A plot of land for the building was set aside near the southwest corner of the Catholic University campus in Brookland, D.C.
In May 1914, Cardinal Gibbons presented Bishop Shahan to Pius X,
then in the last year of his life. The saintly Pope expressed great
interest in the national shrine, blessed the project, and as a sign of
his interest promised to give the shrine a mosaic of Murillo's painting, "The Immaculate Conception." Pius X died before the project
could be completed, and his successor, Benedict XV, had the pleasure
of presenting the gift to the shrine five years later. Pius XI granted
many favors to the shrine, and when his successor, Pius XII, came
to the United States in 1936 as Papal Secretary of State he visited
the present crypt. Many people can recall the memory of that spare
figure bent in prayer before the Blessed Sacrament.

230

Bishop Shahan might well have been overwhelmed by the vastness of the undertaking before him, but he was a man of strong faith. He began by interesting groups of women in the shrine and commissioned the distinguished architectural firm of Maginnis & Walsh to draw up a comprehensive plan. The Byzanto-Romanesque dream that took shape on their drawing boards is the splendid church now under way. On May 20, 1920, Archbishop Bonzano, the Apostolic Delegate, offered a field Mass on the site of the main altar, and in September, Cardinal Gibbons laid the cornerstone of the church, assisted by Cardinal O'Connell and most of the Archbishops and Bishops of the nation. The scene was of medieval splendor such as this country has seldom seen. Ten thousand people thronged the green slopes of the campus to watch the procession, in which all the religious orders participated. (The architect's sketch of the completed shrine is the frontispiece in this book.)

Since 1920 the shrine has moved slowly forward toward completion. The northern crypt was opened for services in the Holy Week of 1926; the southern crypt and the two huge sacristies were finished in 1931. These crypts and the great vestibule between them are 458 feet long and 320 feet wide at the point where the sacristies jut out from the line of the wall. A mosaic floor of colored marbles collected from all over the world heightens the effect of the whole composition. The gently arched ceilings of the crypts and vestibule are to be lined with gustavino tile, which will cast a soft golden glow like muted sunshine. Marble pillars of great variety and opulent splendor will make this one of the most beautiful churches in the world.

At this juncture the northern crypt is the only fully ornamented part of the building. The gustavino ceiling is inset with rich ceramic tiles picturing the Eternal Father, the child Jesus, the Holy Ghost, the Four Evangelists, and various scenes and symbols from the Roman Catacombs. The whole effect is remarkably colorful and splendid. The main altar, set in the exact center of the northern crypt, is a lovely creation of semitransparent golden onyx from Algiers. In gilded panels about its base are the statues of Christ, Saint Paul, and the Twelve Apostles. Gilded candlesticks set with precious stones and a large, burnished gilt crucifix are the only adornments of the table.

Ranged about the altar in the arms and end of the Greek cross are fifteen chapels. The group in the north apse is dedicated to God the Son. It is flanked by the two arms of the cross, the west dedicated to God the Father and the east to the Holy Spirit. Each of the three recesses is ornamented with five altars matching the Algerian marble of the central altar under the dome.

Each altar is spaced off by pillars of gorgeously colored marble and is backed by a mosaic of the saint to whom the altar is dedicated. Above the mosaics are the lunette windows of stained glass which carry out the proper symbolism of the whole unit and integrate it with the special background of each saint. The execution of the plan is rhythmical and splendid like a tissue of gold cloth picked out with patterns of bright silk threads.

The chapels of the west arm memorialize Saint Agnes, Saint Agatha, Saint Cecelia, and Saint Anastasia. The chapels of the east arm are dedicated to Saint Brigid of Ireland, Saint Margaret of Antioch, Saint Catherine of Alexandria, Saint Susana of Rome, and Saint Lucy of Rome. Here around the splendor of the central Mary altar, the women of the first ages of the church cluster. They

232

formed themselves in her likeness for the greater glory of God.

The central altar in the north apse is dedicated to the Good Shepherd. It is the altar of the Blessed Sacrament, and here the pilgrims of the world come to spend a quiet hour: seminarians and priests, nuns and pious women, men of all races carrying their Holy Hour books. It is fitting that this central altar should be flanked by chapels named after those most intimate with Our Lord and His Mother. Saint Elizabeth and Saint Joseph are on the left; Saint John, the beloved disciple, and Saint Ann, holding the Virgin, are on the right; the family of the Good Shepherd comes to worship Him in His family atmosphere.

233

Aside from the north crypt, there are many interesting things to see at the national shrine, not least of which is the mosaic of Murillo's "Immaculate Conception," which may be found in the west sacristy. It is a superb piece of work which took five years of labor by the best mosaic workers of our time before it was presented by Pope Benedict XV. The delicate shading of the stones is a miracle of artistry, and the picture is one of the the great treasures of the national shrine. The Lourdes Grotto is beloved of all pilgrims; the iron work in the door of this chapel and the grille in the interior are considered particularly good.

The south crypt of the memorial chapel, with its hundreds of memorial tablets, will eventually have a frescoed ceiling, showing funerary art from the days of the Catacombs to our own time. In the middle of the chapel is an effective Carrara statue of Mary Mother of Men standing with outstretched hands as if to welcome saints and sinners, the joyous and the brokenhearted. The south crypt also contains a chapel to Pius X, still not entirely completed, and the mortuary chapel of Bishop Shahan. This chapel, Celtic in feeling, is dominated by a Celtic cross over the altar. The Bishop's tomb is in the best medieval style, and the effigy on the top of the tomb is a faithful likeness.

The National Shrine of the Immaculate Conception is widely known even in its unfinished state. At every hour of the day great buses disgorge crowds of pilgrims in the drive near the east entrance. During May, noted preachers give courses of sermons in honor of Mary and the great reaches of her church are packed with crowds of people. Processions to her statue make the arches ring with song. This is as it should be, for a shrine, however beautiful, is an empty shell unless it calls to the hearts of men and tells the beauty of holiness.

In future years we may well envision this shrine as a center of pilgrimage for national groups of Catholic women and men. Then the bells in the campanile will play the hymns of Mary and surging crowds will carry from her shrine some of the tenderness and love she came to kindle among men.

MINOR BASILICA OF THE
ASSUMPTION OF THE BLESSED VIRGIN
Baltimore Cathedral

Cathedral and Mulberry Streets

Baltimore, Maryland

Founded 1775

T HE TRIUMPHANT CLOSE OF THE AMERI-
can Revolution at Yorktown, Virginia, in 1781
brought religious freedom to nonconformists, Jews, and Catholics.
In the infant nation the greatest group of Catholics was to be found
in and around Baltimore, Maryland, and in consequence Baltimore
became the first seat of a bishop in the United States. The Carroll
family, outstanding in the colony, had been prodigal of service in
the struggle for independence, and it was not astonishing that John
Carroll became the first bishop of Baltimore. His diocese embraced
groups of Catholics scattered over the eastern seaboard and a wide-
flung frontier.

The building of the Baltimore Cathedral is a story of hope
and of interfaith cooperation. The first Catholic congregation, a
body of refugee Acadians, came to Baltimore Town in 1756-1757
and purchased an abandoned building, where Jesuit priests from
Maryland and Pennsylvania ministered to them. In 1764 land for a
new church (the site of the present city courthouse) was bought from
the Carroll family, but various quarrels and difficulties prevented
the opening of the Church of Saint Peter until 1775. In that year the
plain red Mass-house was dedicated, and in 1782 Father Charles
Sewell became the first resident pastor. Enlargements in 1784 and
again in 1790 were providential, for Bishop Carroll was consecrated
in the chapel at Lulworth Castle, in Dorsetshire, England, in 1790
and the Church of Saint Peter became his residence and cathedral.

In this venerable building the first American Synod was held and the first American priests were ordained: Fathers Stephen Badin and Prince Demetrius Gallitzin (p. 75). Here, too, many famous bishops were consecrated: Leonard Neale, Michael Egan, John Cheverus, Ambrose Marechal, giants of the early American church.

In 1790 the temporary cathedral was already somewhat too small for its purposes and plans and subscriptions for a more commodious and dignified building soon got under way. Property was first acquired in "Old Town," but by 1805 the lightning growth of the city had made the site undesirable and in 1806 a new piece of land just outside the city limits was bought from General Howard. Many difficulties had delayed its purchase. Howard wanted $25,000, a huge sum which at that time seemed far beyond the means of American Catholics. When the Sulpician Fathers threw their weight behind the project, however, enough money to begin the work was raised among merchants and friends. General Howard then lowered his price to $20,000.

The church, first designed by Dr. William Thornton, was improved and modified by Benjamin Harry Latrobe. The working drawings, completed by Latrobe in March 1806, embodied a cruciform church in Classical style. Latrobe was apparently inspired by the Pantheon in Paris, and he may have taken many suggestions from the design of Lulworth Chapel, where Bishop Carroll had been consecrated.

Bishop Carroll laid the cornerstone of the new building on July 7, 1806. Delays attended the first work. Latrobe changed his plans seven times in the course of building—always for the better— and his seventh plan is very largely the fine cathedral pilgrims see today.

The War of 1812 halted the construction. Bishop Carroll had become an archbishop in 1808, but up to the time of his death, in 1816, his cathedral remained unfinished. Archbishop Marechal, the third archbishop of Baltimore, raised sufficient funds to complete the building, which was dedicated on May 31, 1821.

Slowly, over the years, the Baltimore Cathedral was furnished and adorned. Today its interior is rich with the patina of history and it is known and loved for its grace and strength. Three plenary councils of the United States have been held here. Six archbishops and twenty-four bishops attended the first full Council of 1852; President Andrew J. Johnson attended that of 1856 with seven archbishops and thirty-eight bishops present; and the third, in 1884, prepared in Rome and attended by twelve archbishops and fifty-nine bishops, was the largest council assembly held outside the Eternal City since the Council of Trent in the sixteenth century.

236

The long and profitable rule of Cardinal Gibbons, who was in the van of many forward-looking movements, brought to the Baltimore Cathedral distinguished guests and prelates from all over the world.

Pope Pius XI raised the cathedral to the rank of a Minor Basilica in 1937. This act gave the mother church of American Catholicism rich indulgences that can usually be gained only by a visit to the Seven Churches (Basilicas) of Rome.

SAINT JOSEPH'S CHURCH

Bardstown, Kentucky

Founded 1819

O THE SOUTH AND SEVERAL HUNDRED
miles west of Baltimore lies Bardstown, near the
center of Kentucky and almost due south of Louisville. Today it is a
thriving little metropolis but once it was part of a vast, unexplored
wilderness.

In the years just before the Revolutionary War, the colonies
experienced their first growing pains. Frontier after frontier was
explored, and adventuresome men and women began to enter the
wilderness in the hope of making their fortune. One of the first
regions to be opened up was Kentucky, which became a province of
Virginia in 1776 and long was famous in folk songs and stories about
the exploits of its founder, Daniel Boone.

Among the members of the early and somewhat cohesive
groups that loved the free spirit of the frontier were many Catholics.
Bardstown soon became a pioneer metropolis, and in 1808 at the same
times that the Dioceses of New York, Philadelphia, and Boston were
created, it was made a Diocese. Benedict Joseph Flaget was named
the first Bishop of the Bardstown See, and such was his force and
genius that eleven years later he dedicated his new cathedral—an
extraordinary achievement, considering the meager resources of the
frontier. Flaget must have taken great pride in the work, for until
then the only Catholic cathedrals in the United States were those in
the cities of Baltimore and New Orleans.

The building of Saint Joseph's Cathedral was a genuine community achievement. Frontiersmen quarried the limestone, kilned
the bricks, felled the timbers, and made the hinges, even the nails, by
hand. The result was a little masterpiece of ingenuity.

238

From the outside the church is impressive. It has the balance of neoclassical Colonial, combined with graceful hints of Greek, Roman, and Romanesque architecture. Four soaring Corinthian columns support a fine pediment and above it looms a square clock tower surmounted by an octagonal bell chamber. From this paneled and domed cap a fine spire fingers the sky. The interior is in basilica style. The main altar is particularly fine because of its graceful arch which incorporates an effective painting of the Crucifixion by Van Bree.

Most notable of the church treasures are the paintings presented by Louis Philippe, King of France from 1830 to 1848. Bishop Flaget had met the future king and his brother while they were exiles in Havana, and before he left Cuba presented to Louis the collection which the Royalists of Havana had taken up. When the prince came to the United States among the places he visited in 1797 was Bardstown. It was in remembrance of this visit and of the Bishop's kindness that Louis Philippe gave the paintings to the cathedral. All are supposed to be the works of such great masters as Van Dyck, Reubens, and Murillo. There was some discussion about their authenticity, but not enough to discredit the claim. In fact, so widely were the pictures known and valued that in 1950 a gang of thieves slashed them from their frames. The treasures were recovered in Chicago by the FBI.

Saint Joseph's was a Cathedral and then a Proto-Cathedral, but today its correct title is Saint Joseph's Church. It is a historical and religious shrine of great importance.

239

SHRINES OF CANADA

MOST OF THE FAMOUS CANADIAN SHRINES DATE FROM the very beginning of French Canada. The first settlers who came to New France shortly after 1600 were men of childlike faith, and they wove that faith into the fabric of their lives. Wolfe's victory on the Plains of Abraham in 1759 and the resulting British domination of Canada brought a temporary halt to the normal development of French devotion, but by the middle of the nineteenth century French Canadians had firmly consolidated their cultural and political position.

Shortly after that La Salette and Lourdes, in France, became the focus of world attention and world-wide pilgrimage and the inspiration found abroad turned the minds of deeply religious men toward the ancient holy places of their homeland. Once again they began to enlarge and beautify their shrines. Pilgrims today will be forced to admire the achievements and the deep faith from which such beauty springs.

The shrines described in this section are widely known to even casual travelers. In addition to the noted shrines, the historic churches and chapels of Montreal and Quebec City are worth more than a passing glance. They are of great historical and artistic importance, even though they are not shrines in the popular and narrow sense of the word.

The Church of Notre Dame was the first parish church of Old Montreal and as a parish dates back some 300 years to the founding of the walled Ville-Marie. The first church was built in 1656. The present one, built in 1829, accommodates twelve thousand people and is one of the largest churches on the North American continent. Carved wood and stained glass glorify the story of early Montreal; valuable paintings and a rich church museum add further luster to the past.

The Basilica Cathedral of Saint James, in Montreal, is also important. Inside and out it is a half-size copy of Saint Peter's, in Rome, of particular interest to pilgrims who may never have the pleasure of seeing the masterpiece of Michelangelo.

Saint Patrick's Church, set amid stately elms in the heart of Montreal, is a center for the English-speaking Catholics of the great city. This church, which dates from 1841, is of purest twelfth-century

240

Gothic, and its soaring interior, rich in delicately carved stone and marble, is widely admired.

Of much greater antiquity is the sailors' church of Montreal, Our Lady of Good Help. For over three hundred years it has been a beacon and a place of pilgrimage for men who sail the seven seas. The first chapel was built in 1657, the present church in 1771. It, too, is crammed with French-Canadian history.

Quebec City is even richer than Montreal in its wealth of ancient churches and chapels. First among these is the Cathedral of Our Lady of Quebec, which once served a diocese that stretched from Canada to Mexico. The first Mass was sung here in 1650. Since that time the historic church has suffered bombardment (1759) and several disastrous fires. Part of its walls were built in 1647, the façade in 1844, and the interior, elegantly Baroque in style, in 1922.

Historical-minded pilgrims will be enchanted with Our Lady of Victories, which stands at the top of the Place Royale, the old seventeenth-century market place. This little church, founded in 1688, was dedicated to Our Lady of Victory as a thank offering for victory over the British in 1690. In 1711 a second victory changed its name to Our Lady of Victories. The church is a storehouse of ancient treasures and paintings, carvings, and mementos of the past.

Almost equally beloved is the chapel of the Ursuline Convent. The convent is famous throughout Canada and the United States as the first institution of higher learning for women in Canada and the United States. The present chapel, part of which dates from 1720, is severe in style except for the sanctuary, which is a jeweled masterpiece. Montcalm is buried there, and his tomb draws many visitors. The chapel is rich in relics; among them are a piece of the True Cross, a portion of the Crown of Thorns, and the body of Saint Clement, which was presented to the Ursulines in 1687.

The Island of Orleans, in the St. Lawrence River just north of Quebec City, has many eighteenth-century churches, among which are Sainte Famille (Holy Family), Sainte Petronille (Saint Petronilla), and Saint Jean (Saint John). In them may be found fascinating examples of painting, carving, and the creations of goldsmiths and silversmiths famous in the history of Quebec.

The parish churches along the shore between Quebec City and Beaupré and on the Island of Orleans have served French Canadians since the first days of New France. They are too numerous to mention, but pilgrims who travel to Beaupré by car or bus will see their tall steeples flashing out above the clustering trees.

French Canada is a land of faith, and its evidences are everywhere in the landscape: in towers, in steeples, and in great shrines that compare in splendor to the holy places of Europe.

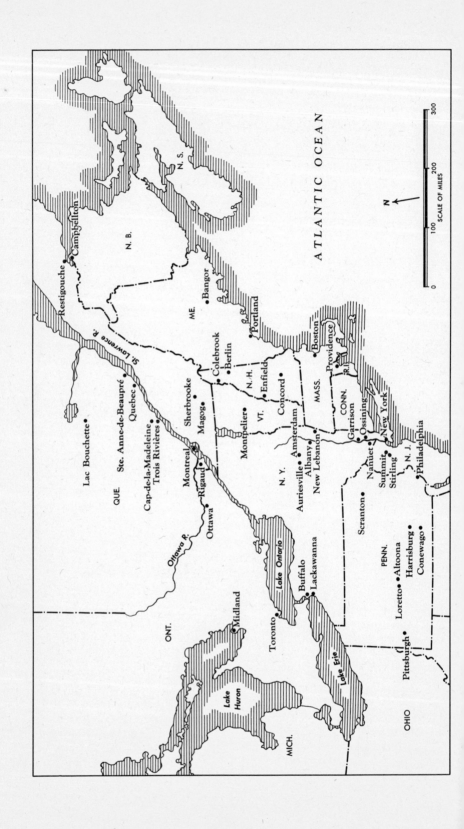

ATLANTIC OCEAN

N

SCALE OF MILES
0   100   200   300

Restigouche
Campbellton

N. B.

N. S.

St. Lawrence R.

Lac Bouchette

Ste. Anne-de-Beaupré
Quebec

Cap-de-la-Madeleine
Trois Rivières

QUE.

Sherbrooke
Magog

Montreal
Rigaud

Ottawa R.

Ottawa

ONT.

Midland

Lake Huron

MICH.

Toronto

Lake Ontario

Buffalo
Lackawanna

Lake Erie

ME.

Bangor

Portland

Colebrook
Berlin

N. H.

Montpelier

VT.

Enfield

Concord

Boston

MASS.

Providence

R. I.

CONN.

Amsterdam

Auriesville
Albany
New Lebanon

N. Y.

Garrison
Ossining

New York

Nanuet
Summit
Stirling

N. J.

Philadelphia

Scranton

PENN.

Loretto
Altoona
Harrisburg
Conewago

Pittsburgh

OHIO

THE SHRINES

Sainte Anne-de-Micmacs, Restigouche, Quebec
Sainte Anne-de-Beaupré, Sainte Anne-de-Beaupré, Quebec
Our Lady of the Holy Rosary, Cap-de-la-Madeleine, Quebec
Hermitage of Saint Anthony, Lac Bouchette, Quebec
Saint Joseph's Oratory, Montreal, Quebec
Chapel of Atonement, Pointe-aux-Trembles, Quebec
Our Lady of Lourdes, Rigaud, Quebec
Saint Benoît-du-Lac, near Magog, Quebec
Martyrs' Shrine, near Midland, Ontario

SAINTE ANNE-DE-MICMACS
Saint Anne of Ristigouche

Restigouche, Quebec

Founded 1745

RESTIGOUCHE IS A VILLAGE IN THE INDIAN reservation of that name, on the Gaspé Peninsula on the north shore of the Bay of Chaleur, just across the water from Campbellton, New Brunswick. The mission (which retains the old spelling, Ristigouche) dates from the earliest days of New France, soon after the coming of the French in 1600.

Champlain brought with him from his home town of Brouage, in France, several members of the missionary Franciscans known as Recollects. They went first to colonize the Micmacs, along with their confreres the Jesuits. Their labors were successful, and in 1610 Membertou, the high chief, was baptized. Gradually the whole tribe followed their chief into the Church.

The Recollects were devoted to Saint Anne (as the name is spelled abroad), and in a somewhat naïve fashion the Fathers instructed the Micmacs to look on her as their grandmother. The Indians found the suggestion entirely to their taste and followed it with such faith that they customarily dedicated all their churches and chapels to the Grandmother of the Saviour. The original mission, Chigouk (Old Mission), was abandoned in 1745, and the inhabitants crossed the narrow strip of water to Mission Saint Anne that same year.

The mission at Ristigouche was particularly beloved by the Micmacs and continued to be after the English conquered New France, though much of the surrounding property was appropriated by British settlers. The last battle of the struggle for Canada was fought at Ristigouche in 1760—a sea battle between the ships of Admiral Colville and Commander John Byron. The French were

244

assisted by shore batteries, but in spite of this aid the victory went to the English, who, in revenge, deported the Recollects and French settlers. Longfellow has told something of this heartrending story in *Evangeline*.

After many vicissitudes and many pastors, some of gigantic spiritual stature, the mission passed into the hands of the Capuchins in 1894. The present church, built after a long series of churches had been destroyed by fire, dates from 1927.

Sainte Anne-de-Micmacs is off the beaten track. For the persevering pilgrim it is a worthwhile journey because the roads wind through the most unspoiled villages of French Canada, which are like some glimpse of a lost and gracious world. The scenery about the mission itself is superb. The church is not particularly notable, but it has in its treasury a relic from the arm of Saint Ann given to the mission by Bishop A. A. Blais of Rimouski, Quebec, in 1895. The relic is exposed for veneration during the whole month of July.

The monastery gardens are charming, and there are many historical souvenirs to attract the merely curious. To the Micmacs it is the center of their land and history and the hospitable home of their grandmother, Sainte Anne.

Charles E. Bernard

Photo Moderne, Quebec

SAINTE ANNE-DE-BEAUPRÉ
Saint Anne of the Meadow

Sainte Anne-de-Beaupré, Quebec

Founded 1658

THE FRENCH WHO FIRST SETTLED CANADA were largely from Brittany and Normandy. They knew the sea and loved it; they also respected its moods of fury and storm. In their fishing boats they roamed the green reaches of winter waves, and always before setting out they prayed at the shrine of Mary or of her mother, Saint Anne. Miracles of devotion and rescue were commonplace among these men of faith, who carried the old devotions to the new and dangerous land of French Canada where they took deep root.

Some time before 1658, a group of sailors finding refuge from a storm, it is said, set up a tiny chapel to Saint Anne on the small cape that juts out into the St. Lawrence, some twenty miles from the walled city of Quebec. The place selected was a quiet spot and a charming one in a pretty meadow (*beaupré*) sloping down from the circling hills of the Lorentides, one of the oldest mountain ranges in the world. By 1658 the parish required something more than a rudimentary shrine, and a new church was begun. In this operation Saint Anne showed her love of the beautiful meadow by working her first miracle. Louis Guimont was a cripple, so deformed in fact that he could not participate in the serious work of building the new church, but with great effort he managed to place three small stones in the foundation. Instantly he was cured, to the great joy and wonder of the villagers.

Strange to say, the chapel begun in 1658 was never completed. It was too close to the shore, and the mountainous ice floes of spring swept it away. Meanwhile Father Thomas Morel had arrived in New France, and Bishop Laval placed him in charge of the parish of

247

Beaupré. Father Morel chose a safer site for a church under the edge of a lofty hill to north of the shining meadow. This building, finished in 1662, was of stone and timber and had a little belfry with one bell. A small statue of Saint Anne and her child, brought from France, was enthroned in the humble building. Once again Saint Anne showed her approval by performing significant miracles: a crippled woman of the village was cured and a paralyzed soldier from the Quebec garrison was restored to full health. Bishop Laval paid formal tribute to these cures, and that remarkable woman Venerable Marie de l'Incarnation, writing of Beaupré in 1665, from the quiet of her Ursuline convent in Quebec, said of this shrine: "Seven leagues from here there is a village called 'Petit Cap' where there is a church dedicated to Saint Anne, in which Our Lord vouchsafes to work great prodigies by the intercession of the Blessed Virgin. There the paralytic are made to walk, the blind receive their sight, and the sick, no matter what their ailment may be, regain their health."

Soldiers, sailors, noblemen, workmen—everyone felt impelled to make a pilgrimage to Saint Anne. In the warm dawns of summer, when the great river was rosy with the first light, a fleet of as many as eighteen birch-bark canoes would be seen sweeping over the water. The Christian Indians would run their light craft ashore and in dignified silence walk in procession to the shrine. Then the air would resound with prayers and songs in the Indian tongue while the beauty of the Mass unrolled.

When Father Filion became the new pastor of Beaupré, in 1676, his first concern was the building of a church which might be worthy of Saint Anne. Stone was cut and the work soon brought to completion. The people of the whole valley who had joined in the building rejoiced in the work of their hands. It was this church, twice enlarged, that served pilgrims for two hundred years, surviving the furious raids of the Indians, the French and English wars, and all the ravages of storms and turmoil. Its altars were of lovely native workmanship, its walls ornamented with votive paintings of rescues and tablets of gratitude. In gilded wood and thrilling color, it was a minuscule refraction of the French art and splendor at Versailles. Its very stones seemed saturated with prayer and faith.

Through some miscalculation of sentiment this stone shrine was torn down in 1876. Its stones were saved and went into a much smaller reconstruction which remains today as a memory of great faith and a splendid past.

Shortly after the perpetration of this mistake, the shrine at Beaupré, which had begun to attract pilgrims from all over North America, was given into the care of the French Redemptorist Fathers. Through their efforts, and a generous rain of funds from the whole

248

continent, a spacious and beautiful Basilica was erected. The exterior was Gothic and the interior Corinthian; the long rows of fluted pillars and the white marble altar with its elegant baldachin were much admired. The wonderworking statue of Saint Anne stood on its marble pillar before the center of the altar rail.

Saint Anne proved to be a grateful mother, for she showered healing on many who came to ask her help. The rear pillars of the church were lost in a rising phalanx of canes and crutches. The blind left their black glasses behind them, and grateful clients sent *ex voto* tablets and rich rings, bracelets, and necklets of gold and jewels for favors received.

In 1922 the Basilica burned to the ground but many treasures escaped the flames, among them the copper-covered statue of Saint Anne which had stood so many years above the front entrance. A temporary church was hurriedly built, but this too was destroyed by fire in 1926. Fortunately, many treasures of the shrine which had been rescued from the first fire were still in storage.

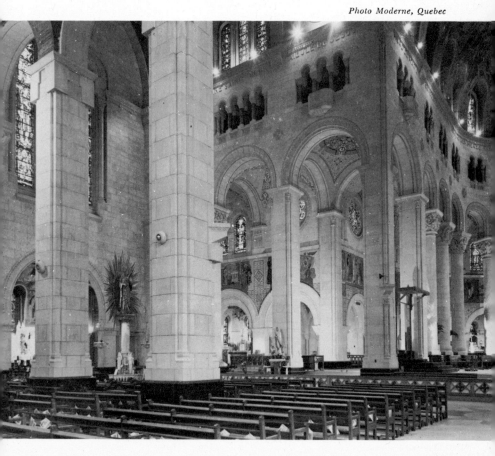

The devotees of the saint met the challenge of fire with an equal fire of generosity. Beginning in 1923, they erected to Saint Anne a splendid stone Basilica. Though it is still unfinished, its beauty is amply evident. The church is in the Romanesque style and its interior is like some lovely *Book of Hours*. The ceiling, painted with scenes from the life of Saint Anne, has a pale-green background, the color of the midsummer night sky in Canada, and flames with the golden story of Saint Anne. Noble pillars with unusually beautiful carved capitals carry the roof of the nave toward the triumph of the apse. Here bright marbles from all over the world and magnificent colored windows patterned after the stained glass of Chartres are like superb colored illuminations on the gray vellum of the stone. Light, color, line—the combination is dazzling.

The wonderworking statue stands within its marble rail in the north transept. The face of Saint Anne is maternal but stern. At her back is the shrine of the large relic, where the galaxy of precious onyx pillars and the subtle carving of the altar statue—Saint Anne surrounded by angels with lifted wings—make this chapel very beautiful indeed. It houses the opulent golden reliquary containing a bone from the wrist of Saint Anne. In all, the shrine possesses seven well-authenticated relics of the Saint, of which the wristbone is the most important.

It would take a volume to catalog the various chapels and riches of this great church. It is enough to sum up the achievement in a paragraph from the official guidebook.

The new Basilica stands *where the sailors landed* after their escape and where, toward the middle of the seventeenth century, the first settlers erected a wooden chapel in honor of their Benefactress. But what a change! The 10 settlers of 1658 who worked at the first chapel have been replaced, two and a half centuries later, by millions of heirs. Granite, marble and costly materials take the place of the squared timber of the virgin forest; the primitive building, 40 feet long, has grown into a sumptuous Basilica 325 feet in length, 200 in width; two spires of stonework, raising their lofty heads 300 feet in the air, replace the little wooden belltower; the primeval simplicity of a timber building has developed into an elaborate monument of architecture.

There are other buildings of note besides the Basilica: the series of chapels built about a copy of the Holy Stairs; the charming replica of the first stone shrine that houses pictures, statues, and carvings, including some of the oldest relics in Canada; the life-size bronze Stations of the Cross running along the edge of the hill that appeal to the devotion of every pilgrim; and the Fountain of Saint Anne, which is always thronged with pilgrims seeking help or dipping up the waters for sick friends and relatives at home: a mother and her child crippled by polio; a lame man hunching himself along on two canes; a blonde young girl riddled with tuberculosis.

An interesting group of buildings has grown up about the shrine. The superb Gothic convent of the Redemptoristines—cloistered nuns who ceaselessly pray for the pilgrims and all the sinners of the world—and the Redemptorist monastery and Juvenate find their proper atmosphere in this holy place. In the fine hospital at the end of the plaza before the church, religion and science live side by side. The latest therapy and healing keeps pace with the spirit of hope and faith found at Beaupré.

A small pamphlet, "Land of Miracles," is available at the shrine. In this pilgrims will find set down some of the major cures and the testimony of doctors concerning them. The crutches and canes and all the other paraphernalia of illness bear out the testimony of the doctors.

The cures listed in "Land of Miracles" are divided into four sections: those certified by the Canadian hierarchy of the early years; cures supported by medical testimony; cures with testimony of reliable witnesses; and cures related by the beneficiaries themselves. They cover a wide variety of diseases; cancer, blindness, tuberculosis, ulcers, arthritis, epilepsy, asthma, meningitis, and almost every other ailment to which the body is subjected.

One example from the mass of affecting testimony will suffice.

Dr. Simard, of Sainte Anne-de-Beaupré, declared, on July 17, 1948:

"I testify that Mr. Evariste Langevin, aged sixty years, came to consult me early in February, 1947, for severe digestive troubles, which had a serious effect on the state of his health. The patient vomited all food, even the lightest, and he was emaciated and pale.

"A clinical diagnosis of stomach cancer was made and confirmed by radiography. The surgeon consulted advised an operation in an attempt to save the patient's life. This the patient refused."

The cure   It was on the advice of Father Louis Gosselin, C.SS.R., that the patient refused the operation counselled by the doctors. The good Father urged him to place all his trust in Good Saint Anne. This took place in the beginning of February, 1947.

The invalid made several promises, among them that of saying three Hail Marys morning and evening in the honor of Saint Anne, and of always carrying with him a splinter of wood from the miraculous statue which stands on top of the Basilica façade.

Two days after his decision to refuse the operation and to trust in Good Saint Anne, Mr. Langevin felt no further pain, was very well and very hungry. He was to have no further trouble with his digestion.

251

Dr. Arthur Simard on July 17, noted the following findings.

> "Since then, I have seen Mr. Langevin fairly often. He can now eat practically whatever he wishes, and does his work with an energy he has not felt for many years. I have noticed an increase of weight of twelve pounds, and a remarkable improvement in his general health.
>
> "I would have preferred to wait two years before signing a certificate testifying to a definite cure. Nevertheless, I have had Mr. Langevin under observation for seventeen months, and his physical state appears to me so striking that I willingly give this testimony at the present moment."

On December 28, 1948, the same doctor experienced no hesitation about replying definitely to the question relative to the supra-natural nature of this return to health.

> *"There is no doubt that this cure is above all medical interpretation.* The necessary conditions for such cures are found in their integrity in this case."

The beautiful meadow is beautiful still. Like the Pool of Probatica at which the sick and the blind awaited the visitation of the healing angel, so too at the shrine of Christ's grandmother, Saint Anne, numberless pilgrims await the healing hand of Christ. More numerous than the healings of the body are the mental cures in which sinners long steeped in sin find resurrection and a new life; the worried and the warped walk into an atmosphere of peace; enemies are reconciled, and lukewarm faith takes on the ardor of first conversion. Many weary feet walk the beautiful meadow, but seldom indeed do they walk in vain.

252

OUR LADY OF THE HOLY ROSARY

Cap-de-la-Madeleine, Quebec

Founded 1659

W HEN THE FRENCH FIRST COLONIZED CAN-
ada they established a chain of missions and trading
posts in the vicinity of Quebec and Montreal. Among these, the post
at Three Rivers assumed an early importance. Sheltered as it was
by the three islands at the point where the St. Maurice River flows
into the St. Lawrence, the little settlement soon became a beehive of
activity. Fleets of canoes set out from this point on journeys to the far
lakes and rivers of the St. Lawrence network as *voyageurs* and missionaries wrote history with their lives.

The first church to be erected in this vicinity, in 1659, was
a simple wooden structure dedicated to Saint Mary Magdalen. It was
built on the little cape that juts out into the St. Lawrence east of
Three Rivers, and eventually the cape took the title of the saint and
today is known as Cap-de-la-Madeleine. This first church was founded
by the Jesuits, men of the stature of Marquette, Brebeuf, Daniel,
and Lallement, and Jesuits remained in charge of the parish until
1680, when it was placed in the care of the diocesan clergy. In 1694 a
Confraternity of the Rosary was established, the first to be founded
in Canada. The present exquisite stone shrine was begun in 1714 by
Father Paul Vachon. Completed in 1720, it is the oldest building of
its kind in Canada.

When French Canada was taken over by the English the glory
of Cap-de-la-Madeleine subsided. In 1854 a new pastor was appointed,
the first in nearly a hundred years. Father Leandre Tourigny found
his parish irreligious and disaffected, and to encourage devotion the
priest enthroned over the altar in the fieldstone chapel a statue of
Our Lady, which in time became known as Our Lady of the Cape.

253

With the advent of Father Luc Desilets in 1864, the parish slowly entered a new period of fame and prosperity. The ten families Father Desilets found there refused the Sacraments and seldom came to church. One evening Father Desilets found a pig in the chapel champing his teeth on a rosary dropped on the floor by a careless parishioner. The scene so shocked the good father that it kindled in him a fury of zeal, and "The people drop the rosary and the pigs pick it up," became his constant sermon. It was not long before Father Desilet's zeal had remade the lives of his people.

As the parish began to grow a larger church was needed, so for two years the men of the parish cut stone on the opposite side of the St. Lawrence, planning to haul it across the river on the ice in the middle of winter. Perversely, the winter of 1879 proved to be a mild one and the freezing weather never came. By mid-March the parish had almost given up hope, but Father Desilets had not. He promised the Virgin of the Rosary that if enough stone could be brought over to build the lower walls of the church he would leave the Rosary shrine standing.

The faith of the priest found immediate response. On the night of March 15 a violent wind drove the ice floes from along the shores to the center of the river. These islands of solid ice were held together by chains of sleet and snow and formed, as it were, a bridge. This crust hardened in the bitter weather and the men, bundled in furs, praying as they went and testing each step of the way, drove their sledges across and hauled over the requisite amount of stone. Buoying them up was the knowledge that the whole village had gathered in the little chapel to storm heaven with the prayers of the rosary. The story is a favorite in the district, and there are witnesses who ventured down to the shore that night to see the wonderful ice bridge.

A further extraordinary circumstance marked the spot. Going beyond his promise, Father Desilets renovated the shrine chapel and moved the statue of Our Lady of the Cape to a niche above the main altar. The chapel was rededicated to Our Lady of the Holy Rosary. On the evening of the dedication day, in 1888, Father Desilets, a visiting Franciscan priest, and a sick man, Pierre Lacroix, saw the statue open its downcast eyes. They continued open for some time, and though the three moved about the church to test the evidence of their senses they were in the end convinced of what they saw. Their sworn testimony remains.

Rosary pilgrimages come to the little shrine on all days and at all hours. Mary's joys, sorrows, and glories are continually on the lips of the hundreds of thousands who come to her tiny chapel in the full bloom of summer or the white loveliness of winter.

254

255

A visit to the shrine of Our Lady of the Holy Rosary is a memorable experience. Once you have entered the gates you will find yourself in a climate of peace and faith. The center of the shrine is the ancient Rosary Chapel, made of fieldstone and enchanting in its simplicity. Here the miraculous statue is enthroned, garlanded with a great rosary and crowned with a superb crown made from the family jewels and gold that were the gifts of the Irish families of the district. In a tiny niche over the front door of the chapel is a small but memorable Baroque statue of Our Lady of the Assumption. The hands are outstretched and the drapery is agitated by the wind of her ascent.

The beautiful Way of the Cross is a favorite with every pilgrim. The Stations are laid out in the same general position as in Jerusalem and the last Station, the tomb of Our Lord, enshrines a white marble statue of the dead Saviour. To the right of the Rosary Chapel is a little lake in the center of which is a tall pedestal supporting a statue of the Virgin. From the feet that crushed the serpent little fountains jut out and fall like twinkles of rain on the calm water. Zigzag paths wind down to the shores of the lake. Here on the Feast of the Assumption or the Nativity of the Virgin a hundred thousand pilgrims wind in and out chanting Mary's praises. The candles they carry and the pattern and swirl of light make the whole shrine into an illuminated rosary. Most visitors linger on the Bridge of Rosaries that spans a little brook. Built of ornate stone, seemingly suspended on a gigantic rosary, it recalls the bridge of ice on that long-ago night of faith and accomplishment. Equally beloved is the Way of the Rosary, which memorializes the fifteen mysteries of the Mother of God.

Many cures are recorded in the archives of the shrine, and plans have been made for a superb basilica in modern style. But no building, however magnificent, could compare with the little fieldstone chapel of 1714. To this reservoir of prayer pilgrims are drawn irresistibly, and from it tranquility and hope breathe out upon the whole landscape. Many a pilgrim is heard to exclaim, "Here I could be happy. Here I could find peace."

256

HERMITAGE OF SAINT ANTHONY

Lac Bouchette, Quebec

Founded 1907

FATHER ELZÉAR DE LAMARRE, THE SU-
perior of Chicoutimi Seminary, was educated in
Italy. During his studies he cultivated ardent devotion to Saint
Anthony and upon his return to Canada worked incessantly to spread
devotion to his patron. First Father De Lamarre set up a shrine to
Padua's saint at the hospital in Chicoutimi; next he started a magazine, *The Messenger of Saint Anthony,* to honor his patron; and then
he founded a new congregation of nuns, the Sisters of Saint Anthony
of Chicoutimi, to assist him in prayer and the work of his apostolate.

In 1907 Father De Lamarre purchased a tract of land on the
north shore of Lake Bouchette, which lies 130 miles to the north of
Three Rivers and Cap-de-la-Madeleine. The zealous priest wished to
establish a little center to which the seminary professors could retire
in the summer and renew themselves in body and spirit.

The chalet was built, flanked on the right by a simple chapel
in the Gothic style. At his retirement Father De Lamarre went to
live in the chalet at Lake Bouchette, and there he moved the headquarters of his magazine in order to edit the little paper with greater
convenience.

In the course of improvements on the property a natural
grotto was discovered in a ridge of rock and Father De Lamarre saw
in this a sign that the Virgin favored his work. A statue of Our Lady
of Lourdes was set in a niche above the grotto, an altar was placed
in the cave, and the new shrine was dedicated to Mary. A great crowd
of pilgrims and notables witnessed the ceremonies.

For the remainder of his life Father De Lamarre spent happy
hours in prayer at the grotto. Many religious men and women from
towns near by began to follow the example of the priest and soon by
popular will the hermitage became a regular place of pilgrimage.

Father De Lamarre died in 1925 and was buried in the chapel. According to his wish the Capuchins took over the shrine the same year. The simple chapel and chalet still stand against an inimitable backdrop of pines and birches. Below them the Lourdes Grotto, with its outdoor pulpit and ranked benches, follows the slope of the hill to the border of the glittering lake dotted with mist-green islands. The wide bowl of the hills in which the lake nestles is dark with pines.

Father De Lamarre's small chalet has grown into a great pilgrim center. A monastery and a new church for pilgrims, a gem of modern architecture set in the primeval forest, have been built, the Catholic Action groups come with their emblazoned banners to honor their patron, Saint Anthony. These are young and vigorous pilgrims, but the aged and the sick come too, for it is said that Our Lady's spring has qualities of healing in its waters. Young and old follow the beautiful Way of the Cross and venerate on their knees a replica of the Holy Stairs. Saint Anthony draws his thousands of devoted followers, but Our Lady of the Saguenay, as she is called today, draws tens of thousands to her little paradise in the wilderness.

258

SAINT JOSEPH'S ORATORY

Montreal, Quebec

Founded July 20, 1896

C HAMPLAIN'S MONT ROYAL DOMINATES
the skyline of Montreal. Near its summit, seeming in
its great mass and thrust almost a part of the mountain, shines a
tremendous egg-shaped dome crowned with a tall lantern. It is the
Oratory Shrine of Saint Joseph, a splendid monument to a man and
his faith.

The man was Brother André, of the College of Notre Dame
of Holy Cross, who for forty years was the doorkeeper of his monastery. Born of a poor Quebec family, Alfred Bassette was twenty-
five years old on that day in 1870 when he entered the Congregation
of Holy Cross as Brother André. He had tried many trades in
Canada and the United States before he discovered his true vocation,
and wherever he went he had carried with him an intense devotion
to Saint Joseph, the patron saint of Canada since March 19, 1624.

In his new life, in spite of many time-consuming duties,
Brother André somehow found opportunities to intensify his devotion. In his mind a dream slowly took shape—a dream of a great
shrine to the patron of Canada which would make the name of Saint
Joseph shine before men. Because Notre Dame College looked up
from level ground toward the top of Mount Royal, each time
Brother André went to the door he saw the summit of the mountain,
and he felt that Saint Joseph's shrine must rise there. It seemed an
impossible dream, but did not the Scriptures say that faith could
move mountains? Brother André smiled at the thought. It was the
smile of a child, a smile of confidence.

It was some time before the desired land could be acquired
near the top of Mount Royal. When it was bought, on July 20, 1896,

259

Brother André at once began to collect funds to build a small wooden chapel, which was authorized in 1904. Soon the word went around that this was a wonderworking shrine where the sick were healed and the confused and reprobate found new purpose and peace of mind. The slight, unassuming lay brother had healing in his hands. His light laugh and merry ways gave no clue to his long fasts and penances or to the austerity of his life.

Soon the little wooden chapel was too small for the crowds of pilgrims. It was enlarged three times, and many lovely touches were added, but the crowds were always larger than the space available. Mounds of crutches and votive tablets told an ever enlarging story of faith and healing. The innumerable cards on crutches and glasses, written by those cured, are touching in their simple faith:

"Thanks to Saint Joseph who made me walk."

"Cured of infantile paralysis, November 10, 1936. Thanks to Saint Joseph."

"I was troubled with sore eyes, condemned by two specialists, but now I can see. Thanks to Saint Joseph and Brother André."

When Brother André was asked about his part in such cures he would laugh and make his characteristic reply, "It was not I but God Who is responsible. All this comes through Saint Joseph's prayers. I am only Saint Joseph's little dog."

The unassuming brother knew very well that the miracles of healing ascribed to Saint Joseph and himself would have to await the final approval of the Church. It was the healing of the soul that engrossed Brother André's attention—the necessity of planting hope and love in hearts that were arid and desolate.

When his work at the shrine was over for the day, and that was usually very late, the little brother would put on his shabby coat and hat for his daily visits to a large circle of shut-ins. He brought them laughter and little jokes; he poured out on them endless resources of prayer and faith. The sick and the unhappy came to him from all over the world and learned to see that it was Brother André himself who was the miracle.

Through these years Brother André's great plan came into being. Gardens were laid out at the foot of the hill, massive granite steps began to climb the slopes, and in 1918 the crypt of Saint Joseph's Shrine was completed. With its four arched doors and powerful buttresses, it makes an admirable entrance to the shrine. This crypt holds two thousand people, and its low arches ring continually to the hymns and prayers of pilgrims: crowds of school children, Bishops, Cardinals, workmen and their wives, Seminarians

260

and Sisters, and always the thousands of sick and lame and blind. For the convenience of the sick and aged, elevators and escalators have been installed to carry them to the various levels of the shrine. Hardier pilgrims walk up the endless cascades of stone steps.

The upper church is a glorious temple. Outside, its style is classic Renaissance, but the interior, styled under the direction of Dom Bellot, is modern in feeling. Great clusters of decorative arches spring from the piers that support the dome. A clear, unimpeded view of the altar is possible from any spot in the edifice, and the parti-colored brick facing refracts the abundant light from the clerestory windows.

When Brother André died, in 1937, his funeral was a triumph. Endless queues of people—two hundred thousand of them on that last Sunday—came to look at him and touch his hands and feet. His tomb is in the lower church, and the low frescoed arch above it has the modesty of his own life. His cause has already been introduced in Rome.

Pilgrims will find this shrine of extreme and varied interest. The Holy Stairs leading to the crypt, which pilgrims ascend on their knees; the lower church, with its superb marble statue of Saint Joseph; and the Shrine of Saint Joseph itself, with myriads of winking red lights—these are a prelude to the beauty of the upper church. Crutches, canes, glasses, and thousands of written testimonies are signs of towering faith, apostolic in its evidence of healing.

Today Saint Joseph's Oratory whirrs with endless prayer and activity. A library has been collected containing every important book and document ever written about Saint Joseph and thoughtful readers may be seen there at all hours of the day. The shrine has its own radio station and distributes color films which multiply the work and fame of Canada's patron.

On feast days the children come to Saint Joseph's by the thousands. With a great rush of pure melody they sing the chants of the Mass and the lilting hymns loved for long years in the old villages of Quebec. A Cardinal will preach a flawless sermon, and then, when Mass is over, he will walk among the youngsters with the superb dignity and the laughter of a child. Pictures will be taken, and the Prince of the Church will be jostled a bit by youngsters eager to touch him or kiss his ring. The whole atmosphere takes on the simplicity of that Father who walked through a house in Nazareth.

Brother André lives on in the glory of his patron, Saint Joseph, and the shrine created by the humble lay brother has become a powerful place of prayer for innumerable pilgrims.

CHAPEL OF ATONEMENT
National Shrine of the Sacred Heart

Pointe-aux-Trembles, Quebec

Founded 1886

EVERY YEAR, IN PREPARATION FOR THE Feast of the Sacred Heart, a novena of prayers and sermons is broadcast to Canada and the United States. The broadcasts are beamed from the Canadian National Shrine of the Sacred Heart, at Pointe-aux-Trembles, in the outskirts of Montreal.

The Sanctuary of Atonement, as it is called in Canada, began with a modest chapel in 1886. The Franciscan Fathers first inaugurated an unusual pilgrimage, and the saintly reputation of Father Frederic Ghyvelde, the pastor, attracted many people. In 1898 the shrine was given into the care of the Dominican Friars, who were succeeded a year later by the Blessed Sacrament Fathers. Father Jean of this community threw himself into the crusade of atonement for eighteen years. It was under his supervision that replicas of the Grotto of the Agony of the Garden, the Holy Stairs, the Lourdes Grotto, and many other shrines were erected on the grounds surrounding the simple chapel. The original Chapel of Atonement was burned in 1905 and a new and more splendid building replaced it and was blessed in 1910.

The Capuchin Fathers took over the direction of the sanctuary in 1921, built a monastery, and cultivated the work in the grand spiritual style that is traditional among these austere sons of the great Saint Francis. The year 1927 saw the beginning of pilgrimages from many parts of Canada—societies of men and women who came in a body to make atonement for the sins of men.

263

Today the gray stone chapel of the Sacred Heart stands like a beacon light on the main highway between Montreal and Quebec. Sunday Mass in the fieldstone Shrine of the Sacred Heart draws great crowds from the neighboring towns and cities, while the numerous other shrines are thronged with quiet people praying for sinners. Particularly inspiring is the Way of the Cross. At each Station one of the Fathers preaches a fervent exhortation to an attentive and often sorrowful crowd which is led to savor the connection between sin and the intense suffering of Our Lord.

The Archconfraternity of Prayer and Penance has its headquarters here, and the shrine is affiliated with the glorious world shrine of the Sacred Heart, on Montmartre, in Paris. Popes and Cardinals have blessed the work and many indulgences have been granted to the Chapel of Atonement.

264

OUR LADY OF LOURDES

Rigaud, Quebec, on Route 17,

between Montreal and Ottawa

Founded 1874

THE TOWN OF RIGAUD IS IN THE PROVINCE of Quebec, not far from the border of Ontario. Rising from the rich alluvial plain of the Ottawa River is a hill about a thousand feet high, and near the foot of this hill, on the banks of the Ottawa, the clerics of Saint Viator in 1850 established Bourget College, named for Bishop Bourget of Montreal.

In 1874, Brother Ludger Pauzé of the college conceived the idea of spreading the devotion to Our Lady of Lourdes in the vicinity of Riguad. With this thought in mind he set up a small statue of the Virgin on a pinnacle of rock on Rigaud Mountain. Brother Pauzé's statue aroused considerable interest among the people, and Father Chouinard, his Superior, saw in this growing devotion a sign of Divine approval. He selected a new location, and in a solemn procession of teachers and students Brother Pauzé's statuette—it was but ten inches tall—was carried to a more accessible spot, a niche carved in the abrupt face of the cliff. Below it is a natural amphitheater hemmed in by close ranks of pines and maples.

On October 17, 1886, the first organized pilgrimage from the town of Rigaud took place. On this occasion a large statue of Our Lady was blessed, and, at her feet, a kneeling statue of the little Bernadette. A year later a small domed oratory, just large enough to contain an altar and a small group of pilgrims, was erected on the highest point of the hundred-foot cliff. Mass was first offered there on October 9, 1887.

Devotion to the shrine at Rigaud has grown steadily, and

265

L'office Provincial de Publicité, Quebec, Driscoll Photo

today it is thronged throughout the summer months. The face of the cliff is crossed by primitive switchback paths and flights of steps that lead to an arcaded shelter for the aged and the sick. A rustic pulpit on the right faces the congregation. Mary and Bernadette shine out from the next level of the rock, with the domed octagon of the simple oratory above them.

The pilgrim at Lourdes, in France, is first of all struck with the peaceful atmosphere of the place. The same is true of the shrine at Rigaud. Under the thick-ranked trees, the air is still and little brooks make quiet music. Mind and heart are soothed, for there is healing in the very atmosphere. The sick and the blind drink from a fountain as they do at Lourdes, and in time a thanksgiving chapel with a lofty tower will stand on the top of the rock. Memorials to all the shrines of Our Lady—such as La Salette, Lourdes, and Fatima—will speak to the devotion of the faithful from the various levels of the cliff.

One of the sights near the shrine is the Devil's Garden, a wide field on top of the mountain covered with thick layers of stones arranged in precise rows as if they had been washed in by a powerful tide. The storytellers of the region have their version of the phenomenon. On winter nights they love to tell the story while the wind whistles outside and the thick-falling snow lashes the windows. The field, they say, was once owned by a prosperous farmer who was more greedy for gain than he was for the good of his soul. One Sunday, against the express command of the village priest, the farmer decided to stay away from Mass and plow his field. His wife watched him depart with the plow and the horses and in the course of the morning heard his voice raised as if in a scream. When nightfall came and her husband failed to return, the anxious wife, accompanied by her neighbors, laboriously climbed to the field and found that husband, horses, and plow had all been spirited into the ground by the devil and the once rich field was thickly covered with stones.

Long told and believed in the district, this story is, of course, a legend. Rigaud Mountain was once covered by a glacier, and the field of stones is the remains of a glacial moraine in which the great boulders chewed off from the tops of mountains were ground into their present shapes and sizes and deposited in precise waves as the glacier receded. This scientific explanation of what happened millions of years ago is scarcely less astonishing than the storytellers' legends about the meaning of the place.

In any event, the field of stones offers a rich contrast with the peace and beauty of this Canadian Lourdes where pilgrims find peace and healing.

SAINT BENOÎT-DU-LAC
Saint Benedict of the Lake

Near Magog, Quebec

Founded 1912

THE BENEDICTINE RULE AND DISCIPLINE has had a perennial attraction for men ever since Saint Benedict transferred his small group of monks to Monte Cassino, in Italy, in the year 529. From this early foundation the Order has spread over the world. It has carried with it a love of quiet, of scholarship, and of all those arts which recivilized Europe after the fall of Rome. Meditation, painting, sculpture, architecture, the great art of plain song—these are achievements of primary value, but Saint Benedict held them of no more worth than manual labor. "To labor is to pray" was the way he phrased it, and since man at prayer sums up and crowns all his other activities we can see a profound beauty in the picture of Thomas Merton at work in the hay fields. The lesson of the dignity of labor is one our age needs to learn if it is to emerge from the vicious snobbery of the bourgeois mind.

In 1912 the Benedictines selected a 600-acre farm near Magog, in the Province of Quebec, for their first foundation in Canada. The farm is at the north end of Lake Memphremagog, which runs through the border down into Vermont. The monks built a simple chapel and for some years were content to occupy the enlarged frame buildings of the farmland. The singing of the Divine Office seven times a day kept pace with farming and dairying. Soon the monastery was self-sufficient, and the establishment of its cheese factory made Ermite cheese known all over the North American continent.

Dom Paul Bellot, a monk from the parent monastery of Solesmes, in France, and one of the world's outstanding architects,

gave special distinction to the infant monastery. The churches Dom
Bellot built in Holland established his reputation, but his masterpiece is Quarr Abbey, on the Isle of Wight, in which the monks
from Solesmes took refuge during the persecution of the religious
orders in France in the early part of the twentieth century. During
a visit to Canada in 1938-39, Dom Bellot drew up a comprehensive
plan for the new monastery of Saint Benoît. It is a five-sided building of warm white Stanstead Vermont granite, crowned with a
mansard roof. Towers of varying height break the monotony of the
mass and are capped in a way reminiscent of French château and
Romanesque styles. So far only the south and southeast sides of the
monastery, which face toward the quiet mirror of the lake, have been
finished. In autumn the sheaves of grain march up the hill to the
very doors of the lovely chapter tower.

The interior is of variegated brick. All the ornamentation
grows from the fabric of the building, a trick of style in which Dom

269

Bellot excelled. Near the entrance to the monastery, on a little knoll, the square stone tower of a delightful shrine to Saint Benedict beckons from the road. Inside is a modern statue of the saint who remade the face and civilization of Europe. Many pilgrims stop to venerate the relic of Saint Benedict enshrined there.

Bishops, priests, Catholics, Protestants, and unbelievers—all come to Saint Benoît for retreat and prayer. The great sweep of lake and mountains has a tranquilizing effect on the mind, and the grave chant of the Divine Office and the prayerful atmosphere do much to satisfy the hunger for contemplation which is in the soul of every man.

The present resources of the monastery are insufficient for the demands upon them. Pilgrims, retreat groups, and pious associations need a noble abbey church and a guest house in keeping with their spiritual aspirations and animal needs. They will have them when the completion of Dom Bellot's plan brings into being one of the most beautifully original monasteries in the world.

O. Allard

MARTYRS' SHRINE

Near Midland, Ontario

Founded 1907

THE WESTWARD MARCH OF CHRISTIANITY through Canada was astonishingly rapid, and by 1615 the Recollect Father Le Caron was working among the savage Huron Indians of Georgian Bay on Lake Huron, ninety miles north of the present city of Toronto. But the Recollects had insufficient numbers of missionaries to cover the field and soon asked the Society of Jesus for help.

Under the leadership of such men as Jean de Brebeuf, the Jesuits were not long in building up a thriving missionary enterprise. Knowing the country and the dangers from the raiding Iroquois, they were quick to sense the need of a fortified center to which the Christian Indians could retreat in times of trouble. To meet this need, Fort Sainte Marie came into being about 1625. Its brick and stonework bastions enclosed some fifteen hundred square feet of ground and a log palisade connected the strong points of the redoubt. Within this island of safety were a chapel, a hospital, a house for the Fathers, and extensive storerooms. Here the missionaries periodically returned to renew their spiritual life after the cruel hardships of savage existence. Fort Sainte Marie proved to be a sound investment. It was first a strong fortress, but it was also a center in which Indians were taught the arts of building, agriculture, and sanitation. The Hurons were docile people and were willing to learn. Had it not been for the furious hatred of the Iroquois, Fort Sainte Marie would have achieved wide and lasting good.

Today we remember the place because of the lion-hearted priests and laymen who in their work among the Indians suffered the immortal martyrdom that led to the canonization of this group of

271

Field plan of Fort Sainte Marie, 1639–1649

Jesuit martyrs on June 29, 1930, whereby they became the first North American saints.

The martyrdom of Brother René Goupil, Father Isaac Jogues, and John La Lande has already been described in the account of the North American Martyrs' Shrine at Auriesville, N. Y. (p. 54). Father Jean de Brebeuf and Father Gabriel Lallemant, another Jesuit priest, also suffered incredible tortures before they were burned at the stake at Saint Ignace, a mission of Fort Sainte Marie, on March 16 and 17, 1649, in celebration of a triumphant Iroquois raid.

Earlier, in 1634, Anthony Daniel had accompanied Father Brebeuf to the Huron mission on Georgian Bay. Two years later Daniel returned to Quebec and founded a school for Indian boys, the first of its kind in Canada. Some time afterward he returned to Huronia and was placed in charge of Saint Joseph's Mission, about fourteen miles from Fort Sainte Marie. In 1649 the Indians also descended on that mission. Father Daniel was killed, and with obscene shouts the Iroquois hurled his body into the burning chapel.

Reluctantly the Jesuits decided to abandon Fort Sainte Marie for a more secure spot. They destroyed their fort and returned to Christian Island, in Georgian Bay, which could be more easily protected against surprise attack. From this new center they ventured forth on journeys to the converted Hurons. On one such trip Fathers Charles Garnier and Noel Chabanal were caught by raiding Mohawks, tortured, and killed.

From 1649 until 1907 Fort Sainte Marie was forgotten. Occasionally scholars and priests examined the holy ground of the old

272

273

fort and its environs, but not until 1907 was a small chapel erected on the supposed site of the martyrdom of Brebeuf and Lallemant. In 1925, with the impending beatification of the Jesuit martyrs in Rome, the site of the martyrs' shrine was returned to Fort Sainte Marie, and in 1926 an imposing church was erected.

The church is of gray stone with two lofty spires that may be seen for miles. The exterior of the church looks rather like a fort and the interior, though not distinguished, has a noble simplicity.

A dining room and hostel for pilgrims can care for about a hundred guests. In the grounds are bronze Stations of the Cross and little shrines where pilgrims can meditate on these lions of God who feared neither death nor torture. The old fort has been partially restored, and an interesting museum contains historical relics found during the careful work of restoration.

SHRINES OF THE MIDWEST

THE SHRINES OF THE MIDWEST TELL PART OF THE
spiritual story of the various national groups that made our country
the rich and inventive nation it is. In the early colonial period
French missionaries came down the lakes and rivers from the north.
Like the intrepid Marquette, they were often geographers as well
as priests, so that both mapmakers and religious men owe them a
great debt of gratitude. Soon too the Jesuits came from the south,
making their way up the Mississippi, and the story of the early
settlement of St. Louis is as inspiring as that of New Orleans.

To these early contributions must be added the influence of
the strong German, Polish, Belgian, mid-European, and south European groups which established centers on the expanding frontier in
Ohio, Wisconsin, Minnesota, and Illinois. These groups, long suspect
because they jealously guarded their languages and cultures, brought
with them a wealth of particular devotions and many artistic skills.
So profound has been their influence on national life that the
thoughtful American may question whether the contents of the
melting pot has not melted the pot itself. The answer to that question will be the work of some future historian when the whole record
has been tested by time.

The religious record as it stands today is a rich one. In addition
to the shrines listed in this section, there are many smaller ones too
numerous for inclusion in a book of this kind. Among them may be
mentioned the Lourdes Grotto at Annunciation Church, in Aurora,
Illinois. Since 1918 it has been a place of summer pilgrimage for
many German and Polish groups from Chicago and Milwaukee.
The Franciscan monastery at Cincinnati, Ohio, has a shrine to Saint
Anthony which attracts pilgrims from the city and suburbs. Of
wider interest is the Shrine of the Holy Rosary, in Parma Heights,
Ohio. These and many other small shrines attached to churches and
monasteries are rich in religious atmosphere.

For those who venture far afield, the old mission church at
Cataldo, Idaho, is an interesting souvenir of the past.

275

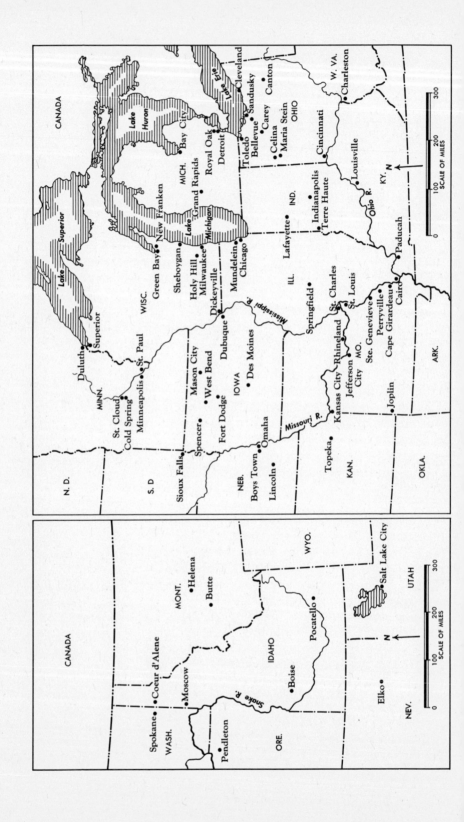

THE SHRINES

Holy Cross Monastery, Cincinnati, Ohio
Chapel of Relics, Maria Stein, Ohio
Our Lady of Consolation, Carey, Ohio
The Sorrowful Mother Shrine, Marywood, near Bellevue, Ohio
Saint Paul's Shrine of Perpetual Adoration, Cleveland, Ohio
National Shrine of Our Lady of Lourdes, Euclid, Ohio
Sainte Anne-de-Detroit, Detroit, Michigan
Shrine of the Little Flower, Royal Oak, Detroit, Michigan
Church of Our Sorrowful Mother, Chicago, Illinois
Shrine of the Little Flower, Chicago, Illinois
Shrine of Saint Jude, South Chicago, Illinois
Benedictine Sanctuary of Perpetual Adoration, Mundelein, Chicago,
*   Illinois*
Holy Hill, Hubertus, Wisconsin
Chapel of Our Lady of Good Help, New Franken, Wisconsin
Dickeyville Shrine, Dickeyville, Wisconsin
Assumption Chapel, Cold Spring, Minnesota
Grotto of the Redemption, West Bend, Iowa
Old Cathedral of Saint Louis, St. Louis, Missouri
Shrine of Blessed Philippine Rose Duchesne, St. Charles, Missouri
Our Lady of Sorrows, Rhineland, Missouri
Shrine of the Miraculous Medal, Perryville, Missouri
The Children's Shrine, Boys Town, Nebraska
Old Coeur d'Alene Mission, Cataldo, Idaho

HOLY CROSS MONASTERY

1055 St. Paul Place

Cincinnati, Ohio

Founded 1861

THE CHURCH OF THE IMMACULATE CONception, on Mount Adams, in Cincinnati, was blessed in 1861. Bishop Purcell had furthered the erection of the building as a permanent memorial to the promulgation of the dogma of the Immaculate Conception on December 8, 1854. Ten years after the church was blessed, the Passionist Fathers were given charge of the property, which they enlarged considerably through purchase of the old Cincinnati Observatory. On these extensive grounds the frame Church of the Holy Cross was built.

Almost immediately the church became a place of pilgrimage. In 1895 a larger church was blessed, and in 1898 a Lourdes Grotto was built. Especially on Good Friday, great throngs of people came to the mountain to pray and to venerate the Cross. On their knees they ascended the 180 steps to the top of Mount Adams, saying a Hail Mary on each step and an Our Father on each of the five landings. Arriving at the top, the pilgrims visited the wayside Shrine of the Cross, next the church, and at the Lourdes Grotto received an individual blessing with a relic of the True Cross. Often as many as fifty thousand people made this Good Friday pilgrimage. Soon the shrine became became well known to the residents of Cincinnati and the surrounding towns. Pilgrimages grew more frequent, and people began to come every Sunday to the Lourdes Grotto.

Crutches and trusses have been left at the shrine, and many speak of favors obtained, but no effort has been made to record the cases. Mary's mountain remains a popular place of pilgrimage and the grotto is crowded every Sunday of the year.

279

CHAPEL OF RELICS

Maria Stein, Ohio, south from

Celina on Route 127 and left on Route 119

Founded 1875

THE YEAR WAS 1872. THE REVEREND J. M. Gartner, Vicar General of the Diocese of Milwaukee, was in Rome for several months. It was a time of injustice and the pillage of churches, when the House of Piedmont had just taken over the Papal States and established a unified monarchy for the whole of Italy. The uncontrollable followers of the new regime had plundered the Papal States and looted the churches and convents of the Holy City; pawnshop windows in Rome were filled with chasubles, sacred vessels, and jeweled reliquaries.

Like many other foreign visitors, Father Gartner was horrified at what he saw, and whenever possible he redeemed some of the sacred articles. Seeing how little value the people of Italy placed on them, the Vicar General sought to gather up what he could in order that he might take the sacred articles to the United States for safe-keeping and honor.

Cardinal Patrizi, the Prefect of Apostolic Custody, helped Father Gartner and encouraged him in his plan. The Assistant General of the Jesuits was also helpful, urging the Milwaukee priest to include the city of Venice in his work of ransom. Father Gartner went to Venice and, with the help of the Baron of Pilat and the Cardinal Patriarch, redeemed many precious reliquaries which he added to his magnificent collection from Rome.

Upon his arrival in New York City, Father Gartner exhibited the relics in the Holy Redeemer Church, on East 3d Street. Thousands of visitors, among whom was Cardinal McClosky, came to venerate them.

"Don't separate them," the Cardinal advised Father Gartner. "You can do more good by finding a church for them that will draw many pilgrims."

The Cardinal's idea appealed more and more to Father Gartner as he exhibited the relics to eager throngs in Baltimore and Cincinnati. He wrote an enthusiastic letter to Piux IX, telling him of the wonderful reception of the relics in the United States, and the Pope responded by adding many more relics that Father Gartner had wanted. All the relics of the collection were sealed with the Apostolic Seal and had papers guaranteeing their authenticity.

After consultation among many priests and bishops, the relics were placed in the Chapel of the Sisters of the Precious Blood in Maria Stein, Ohio, who keep perpetual vigil before the Blessed Sacrament. Little or nothing was said about where the relics were, but somehow people found out and pilgrims came to honor them and to ask favors. Twice the chapel had to be enlarged, and finally in 1889 a new monastery was built with a large chapel for Father Gartner's collection.

When the relics were placed in the new chapel, in 1892, Archbishop Elder preached a sermon explaining the meaning of relics and the honor paid them. In the magnificent procession thirty priests carried *ostensoria* with relics, eight priests bore the body of Saint Victoria, and the Archbishop with bent head held the relic of the Holy Cross. Young girls in white scattered flowers. Societies and sodalities came with flying banners and resounding music.

Today the center of the shrine is the high altar of the chapel. It is clothed in hundreds of relics rayed by precious reliquaries: relics of the Cross, of the life and death of Our Lord and His Mother, and of Apostles, martyrs, confessors, doctors, virgins, and widows. The wealth is truly staggering.

The monastery at Maria Stein is on the top of a great hill, and its spire twinkles above the tops of giant trees that hide the red-brick walls. It is a magnet of faith and devotion that has drawn endless pilgrims to a shrine unique among the holy spots of the world.

OUR LADY OF CONSOLATION

Carey, Ohio

Founded May 24, 1875

T HE PARISH OF OUR LADY OF CONSOLATION was organized by the Reverend Edward Vatmann in 1868 under the title of Saint Edward. Father Vatmann's successor, the Reverend Joseph P. Gloden, obtained his Bishop's consent to change the name of the church to Our Lady of Consolation and secured from the mother shrine in Luxembourg a replica of the image of Our Lady. Along with the image Bishop Adames of Luxembourg sent relics taken from the wood and the cloth of the statue of the mother shrine.

The statue finally arrived at Father Gloden's house in Berwick, Ohio. On May 24, 1875, a thousand people gathered at Berwick where the image was enthroned on a lavishly decorated portable platform. Then, singing hymns and chanting prayers, they carried it on foot seven miles to the Church of Our Lady of Consolation in Carey.

For thirteen years Father Gloden fostered devotion to Our Lady. His successors kept up the devotion, and one of them, Father Mizer, made ambitious plans for the erection of a magnificent shrine church. Before he could put his plans into effect the Order of Friars Minor Conventual was given charge of the parish.

A succession of ardent Superiors spread the devotion to this shrine far and wide through Ohio. Pilgrims came until the walls fairly bulged on feast days. In 1907 a new site for a large church was selected. The crypt was completed in 1909, but the revered image remained in the simple old church until carried in triumph to the main altar of its new home on Christmas Eve 1918. The dedication

283

of the upper church took place in June 1925, with Bishop Samuel Stritch officiating.

The shrine, as it stands today, is in modified and somewhat severe Romanesque style. A soaring bell tower lends variety to a façade broken only by a huge rose window and generous triple-arched doors. The inside of the church is decorated in a combination of Byzantine and Romanesque. Bright marble and ornamental tiles artfully reinforce the symbolisms of the fine windows, which are modeled after the jewel glass of Chartres.

The shrine altar of Our Lady of Consolation is on the right of the main altar, and no pains have been spared to make the background worthy of the delightful old statue. The brilliant marbles employed in the decoration are heightened with blue and gold mosaic work. The statue is charming. The Virgin and Child have frank, doll-like faces. The Virgin carries the scepter in her right hand and with her left hand holds out the Child, who, with the orb cradled in His left hand, raises His right hand in a gesture of blessing. Both Mother and Child are clothed in beautiful robes that are

284

changed with the liturgical seasons and both wear superb crowns. A veil of exquisite lace falls from under the Virgin's crown and ripples about the hem of her dress.

Most pilgrims come to the shrine in the good months of the year. Trains and buses bring thousands of visitors, and many cures of mind and body have been reported. For the convenience of pilgrims the Franciscan Sisters have opened a hostel. In 1930 thirty acres, two blocks west of the shrine, were added to the church property. They have been beautifully landscaped and an outdoor shrine to Our Lady and Stations of the Cross have been built. On any summer afternoon the scene, in movement and religious fervor, resembles one of those thronged tapestries of the Middle Ages.

Hughes Photo Service

285

THE SORROWFUL MOTHER SHRINE

Marywood, near Bellevue, Ohio

off Route 2, near Flat Rock

Founded 1850

FATHER DE SALES BRUNNER, IN 1850, ESTABlished a shrine of the Sorrowful Mother in a little woodland south of Bellevue, Ohio. Father Brunner had been attracted to the place because of its resemblance to a famous Marian shrine in the Black Forest, in Germany.

The small red-brick building that rose soon became a center of attraction for Catholics in the Cincinnati district. Pilgrimages were organized, and crowds came to pray and ask favors. The devotion was centered about a beautifully carved statue, brought from the Black Forest, depicting the dead Christ in the arms of His Mother after being taken down from the Cross. The statue had been raised above the altar, and so ardent was popular devotion to it that a flight of steps was built to enable pilgrims to touch it with rosaries, scapulars, and other religious articles.

From the beginning numerous cures were reported at the shrine, and by 1870 Father Brunner's chapel had become too small. Consequently a larger church, which came to be much beloved because of the fine chime of bells in its narrow tower, was built in the German Gothic style.

The Feast Days of the Assumption in August and of the Seven Sorrows in September were always celebrated with special pomp. The voices of pilgrims from neighboring towns echoed in the little woodland as groups carrying bright banners chanted hymns to the Mother of God. But in 1912, when a large number of pilgrims converged on the shrine to celebrate the Feast of the Assumption, they found only a heap of smoldering ashes. A fire in the night had com-

286

pletely destroyed the church and all its treasures, including the wonderworking statue of Mary and her Son.

The present shrine was built to replace the burned building. The exterior is a combination of Romanesque and Gothic. Inside, the barreled ceiling with its fine paintings is pure Renaissance. The wonderworking statue has been replaced by a modern piece of statuary with far less feeling.

In the little woodland surrounding the church, the fourteen shrines for the Stations of the Cross are centered about a fine marble crucifix donated by a soldier of World War I in thanksgiving for his safe return from France. A grotto commemorating Christ's agony in the garden, and a shrine to Saint Joseph, guardian of the Holy Child, are also worthy of note. Pilgrims still throng to the shrine, and the archives are filled with the sworn testimony of the sick who have been healed of many diseases. Significant among these are several cases of tuberculosis and one case of skin cancer.

For the overnight accommodation of pilgrims a hotel has been erected one mile north of the shrine. The Sisters of the Precious Blood staff the hostel and provide meals as well as lodging for many pilgrims who come to worship here.

SAINT PAUL'S SHRINE OF
PERPETUAL ADORATION

Euclid Avenue and East 40th Street

Cleveland, Ohio

Founded 1921

ARCHBISHOP SCHREMBS OF CLEVELAND bought the Episcopal Church of Saint Paul on Euclid Avenue in 1930. The Bishop had longed to have in his Diocese a shrine of perpetual adoration in which dedicated women would pray perpetually for the welfare of the Church and of our nation. As part of this plan he had brought a group of Franciscan nuns to Cleveland from Vienna, Austria, in 1921. Mothers Mary Agnes and Mary Cyrilla were the leaders of the group.

The nuns were established in a temporary convent at University Circle, and the first cycle of perpetual adoration began that year. A second home on East Boulevard proved unsatisfactory, and when Saint Paul's was put up for sale Archbishop Schrembs bought it for a permanent adoration shrine. The interior was altered and improved, and a small fireproof monastery was built to house the nuns.

Since 1930 the foundation has been a veritable lighthouse of prayer and contemplation. Hour by hour, day and night, the faithful nuns have kept their vigil before the Sacrament. Attracted by their devotion, men, women, and children have been stimulated, sorrows have been healed, the sick of mind and body have found health, and sinners have returned to God.

The exterior of the shrine is a mélange of English Gothic influences that lack any true unity. The nave is a combination of

Tudor and medieval styles set off with fine stained-glass windows, and Romanesque pillars separate the ambulatories from the body of the nave.

The front of the church interior is, however, admirably balanced. Above a beautifully carved screen that marks off the cloistered choir of nuns shine the gilded pipes of the organ. The altar of adoration is of Carrara marble with three carved panels along the front. On the pedestals on either side six angels bend in worship.

The golden monstrance stands high on an elevated throne and the canopy over it culminates in a high Gothic peak which seems to point to a splendid crucifixion group in the intricately carved sanctuary grille. Through this openwork screen the nuns in the choir can look out upon the sanctuary, which blazes with the lights of many candles.

NATIONAL SHRINE OF
OUR LADY OF LOURDES

21320 Euclid Avenue

Providence Heights, Euclid, Ohio

Founded 1926

THE SHRINE OF OUR LADY OF LOURDES, IN suburban Euclid, Ohio, is located halfway up the hillside of Providence Heights. The property was formerly in the hands of the Sisters of the Good Shepherd and the shrine came into being after a number of the Sisters had made a journey to Lourdes.

Green lawns were laid out; trees and flowering shrubs were planted; and in the midst of these Bernadette's grotto arose—the little cave, the tall pinnacles of rock, and the niche in which the Virgin appeared. The swamp at the bottom of the hill was drained and turned into a lagoon spanned with rustic bridges and bordered with cedars.

In the pattern of Lourdes, but without the drama attending Bernadette's finding of the spring of water that brought healing and consolation to countless thousands, a spring of water was discovered near the grotto at Providence Heights. A stone from the niche in the rock at Lourdes where Our Lady's foot rested was placed in the spring, and some people have claimed that the water has healing properties. Thousands of pilgrims from many states come to pray at the grotto, and many carry away bottles of water from the spring.

Providence Heights, on which the grotto stands, is only ten miles east of Public Square in Cleveland, but its rural charm is worlds removed from bustling city life. In the distance the twinkling waters of Lake Erie are ever changing into new patterns of color and light.

SAINTE ANNE-DE-DETROIT
Saint Anne of Detroit

1000 Nineteenth Street

Detroit, Michigan

Founded 1701

THE PARISH OF SAINT ANNE OF DETROIT was established in 1701 under the leadership of the French explorer Antoine Cadillac, whose name is today memorialized in a high-priced car that is the antithesis of the hard life and weary journeys of that French aristocrat. Father François Valliant and Father Nichols de Halle, a Recollect priest, were the founders of Saint Anne, which has retained its French spelling. The first chapel was a log hut, well suited to the Fathers' hard life among the savages of the region. Father de Halle was martyred in 1704 and his church was burned by the Indians. Successive log chapels were built in 1712, 1723, and 1798.

The real importance of the parish begins about 1799 with the work of Father Gabriel Richard, a member of the Society of Saint Sulpice. He was one of the most extraordinary and most lovable priests in the pioneer history of our country. When Detroit was completely destroyed by fire in 1805, Father Richard moved his congregation first to a storehouse near the river and next to the La Salle house in the village of Springwell. Eventually a new site, a mile from the center of Detroit, was purchased, and a stone church was erected on the property in 1828. Four years later Father Richard died, and his funeral stopped all activity in Detroit.

The tribute was not astonishing, for Father Richard was undoubtedly the most influential citizen in the infant town. The driving force of the man flowed out in an amazing number of successful

291

Manning Bros., Inc.

enterprises. He founded a series of grade schools and a high school for girls, and he was one of the founders and vice president of the University of Michigan. Present-day faculty with crowded schedules will wonder how Father Richard managed to hold six of the original thirteen professorships at the University and still found time to supervise his schools and to teach the young ladies. He was also Vicar General of the area and chaplain of the first regiment of Michigan militia.

It was Father Richard who brought the first printing press, the first piano, and the first organ to Michigan Territory. Protestants admired his learning and his speaking ability, and often after a Sunday morning of labor in Saint Anne's he was invited to preach to Protestants of the community at noon.

He capped his achievements by running for territorial delegate to the Congress of the United States. Bigots opposed him vigorously and even went to the length of having him arrested for debt, but the men of good will far outnumbered the bigots and Father Richard was elected to Congress, where he served from 1823 to 1825. He is the only priest in the history of the United States to have enjoyed that distinction.

In the fire of 1805, Father Richard organized the rescue crews, and when a terrible attack of cholera ravaged the city in 1832, he went among the sick of all religions. It was during his work of consolation in the epidemic that he contracted the plague and died. Father Richard's body is buried under the altar steps of the present Sainte Anne-de-Detroit, which was built in 1886 to replace his stone church.

The architecture of this church is thirteenth-century French Gothic, while precious altars of Italian marble and Mexican onyx lend a note of Renaissance opulence. The church possesses five authentic relics of Saint Ann, with which pilgrims are blessed every Tuesday evening and during the nine days preceding the Feast of Saint Ann on July 26.

Sainte Anne-de-Detroit is fortunate in having all the records of the parish since the year 1804. These and many other historical souvenirs, including a bell rescued from the fire of 1805, attract thousands of visitors every year.

Notes of religion and patriotism are a harmonious counterpoint at the church. The splendors of the mother of Mary have a humble echo in the life of Father Richard, who tried to be "all things to all men."

SHRINE OF THE LITTLE FLOWER

Royal Oak, Michigan

Founded 1939

THE SHRINE OF THE LITTLE FLOWER, AT Royal Oak, Michigan, a suburb of Detroit, is a fine modern tribute to the "Saint of the Little Way." Set in a green frame of trees, the church looks unusual and closer examination only heightens this impression. A monolithic tower faces the four points of the compass, dramatically portraying the triumph of the Cross. Sculptured on its front is a tremendous crucifix. Other carvings at the base and top of the tower memorialize the personages and scenes of Calvary.

The church itself is octagonal in shape. This is an ancient plan of church building, beautifully adapted to the needs of the Liturgy and particularly pleasing in that it groups the congregation within easy sight of the Mass-drama.

The main altar is a huge slab of Carrara marble artfully carved with symbols of eternal life and resurrection. The candlesticks and altar crucifix are of carved ivory set in bronze to match the exquisite low tabernacle. Either side of the altar may be used for the celebration of Mass. A communion rail of Tennessee marble and bronzework surrounds the altar on all sides. The church is prodigal in its wealth of colored marble and excellent bronze.

Particularly notable is the chapel dedicated to the patroness of the shrine, Saint Therese of Lisieux. Two massive columns frame the approach to the chapel. A rectangular vestibule is ornamented with two marble statues: Saint Christopher on the right, Saint Anthony of Padua on the left. Monumental oak doors fold back from the entrance. The chapel itself is commodious enough to be used as a church in winter. Its walls are lined with soft travertine

294

I WILL SPEND MY HEAVEN
DOING GOOD ON EARTH

picked out with shining inserts of black Belgian marble. The dark blue of the ceiling is pointed with flowers in a riot of simplicity and gaiety. The altar of Saint Therese is dramatically conceived. Carved of white marble in high relief, it shows the little saint receiving her shower of roses from the hands of the Christ Child seated on Mary's lap.

The four side chapels of the church are well worth a visit. They are dedicated to Our Lady, Saint Joseph, Saint Sebastian, and Saint Perpetua. All the magnificent resources of modern art are employed in their decoration.

CHURCH OF
OUR SORROWFUL MOTHER

5121 West Jackson Boulevard

Chicago, Illinois

Founded 1874

THIRTEEN YEARS AFTER THE GREAT FIRE of 1871, two priests of the Servite Order, Fathers Austin Morini and Andrew Venturi, came to conduct a mission at Saint Patrick's Church, in Chicago. The mission proved a tremendous success, and moved Bishop Foley to suggest that the Servite Fathers establish a permanent church in Chicago. The fire that had burned the city had swept away churches, convents, and schools. Bishop Foley was making valiant efforts to rebuild, and the coming of the Servite Fathers seemed to him a heaven-sent opportunity to recruit new strength for the execution of his ambitious plans.

The parish given the Servite Fathers was out on the prairie, now Chicago's populous West Side. Within five months a two-story brick church had been built, and the Fathers had established a chain of missions to the farthest corners of their parish, which covered some ten miles of territory fairly screaming with growing pains. From their modest red-brick building, which cost $3000, has sprung a devotion to Our Sorrowful Mother that girdles the world.

By 1890 Chicago had become the nation's second largest city and Our Lady of Sorrows could no longer contain the congregation. A new church was started, superb in conception and plan. The moment the nave was finished it was hurriedly roofed in, so pressing was the need for space. Not until 1889 was the work of building resumed. The new church, much admired for its lofty towers and the Renais-

296

sance splendor of its interior, continued to serve the people of the neighborhood. Shrines of Servite piety multiplied and enriched the devotional life of Chicago citizens.

Then, after almost sixty-five years of quiet and devoted service, Our Lady of Sorrows began to attract world-wide attention. Father Keane, the pastor, decided to establish a weekly novena to Our Lady of Sorrows, intending it to be a mere parish devotion. The first novena night, January 8, 1937, a biting wind blew in from Lake Michigan, yet despite snow and wind long queues of people began to form outside the church doors and soon both the upper and lower church were jammed with people. Week after week the crowds grew. "Within a year there were thirty-eight services of the novena each Friday" for over seventy thousand people. The humble and the great, the unemployed and the rich came with their private sorrows and requests. The devotion from Our Sorrowful Mother's Shrine spread to other churches in Chicago, then to neighboring states. It went out to other nations—across the world to India and China, to Australia, Africa, and the Philippines. In slightly more than a decade five hundred million people participated in the novena to Our Sorrowful Mother. A small leaflet, "Novena Notes," told an ever widening story of requests granted. Often the letters were pathetic in their love and gratitude.

The shrine chapel has a wonderful replica of Michelangelo's *"Pietà"* executed by Ferdinand Palla, a famous Italian sculptor. The *Via Matris* commemorating Mary's sorrows, and woodcarvings from Fatima and many other devotional shrines, attract the attention of pilgrims and inspire devotion in a whole world bowed down by the cross of war and destruction.

NATIONAL SHRINE OF
THE LITTLE FLOWER

Woodlawn Avenue and 64th Street

Chicago, Illinois

Founded 1935

T HE NATIONAL SHRINE OF THE LITTLE Flower, in Chicago, was built under the supervision of the Carmelite Fathers. Every penny of the cost of the building came from members of the Society of the Little Flower, from men and women of little means or of great wealth, who had one thing in common: on them the Little Flower had conferred one of her favors, the rose leaves of good she had promised to shower upon the world.

Those who love the "Saint of the Little Way"—and their name is legion—will find the Chicago shrine one of the most interesting on the American continent. The interior of the church is built about the symbol of the rose. Even the lighting fixtures are in the form of rosebushes, and when they are lighted the statue of the Saint and her shrine altar seem to be bowered in roses of light.

Of greatest interest to pilgrims are the relics and souvenirs preserved in the shrine. A casket of crystal and gold holds a cunningly made branch of five roses, a triumph of the goldsmith's art. Each rose contains a major relic of Saint Therese. This is the most noteworthy collection of her relics outside of France.

Saint Therese had a great fondness for roses. From a tall rose tree in the monastery garden in Lisieux, France, she picked every day a fresh rose to place before the statue of the Christ Child. From this rose tree a lovely crucifix has been made. The rush-bottomed, ladder-back chair Therese used in her cell, the two plain reliquaries she hung on its walls, a lily made of locks of her hair, a toy tam-

299

bourine from her earliest childhood, a map of America drawn at the age of twelve and annotated in her own writing—all these mementos carry with them something of the artless beauty of this young saint.

Paintings of the many miracles worked through the intercession of Saint Therese hang in the shrine. One, memorialized in a past issue of *The Little Flower Bulletin,* tells the following story:

On August 27, 1909, Mrs. Dorans of the parish of Our Lady and St. Margaret's, Glasgow, was suddenly and completely cured of a cancerous tumor. The disease had so far progressed that her doctor—Dr. Colvin, a Protestant—had said on the eve of her cure that she would in all probability die on the following day. In the morning he had found the cancer gone. "If this is going to be permanent," he remarked when he had recovered from his stupefaction, "it is nothing short of a miracle. It is a good thing," he added, "for professional men like us to know that these things are in a Higher Hand. After all, I believe that there is a God."

This is one excerpt from a staggering body of testimony that grows with the years. Week after week the letters pouring in from all parts of the country show that Therese still showers her roses and that men and women of all classes and conditions still sing her praises.

300

SHRINE OF SAINT JUDE

Our Lady of Guadalupe Church

3208 East 91st Street

South Chicago, Illinois

Founded 1929

SAINT JUDE WAS ONE OF THE TWELVE Apostles and the brother of Saint James the Less. Except for his Epistle in the New Testament, one of the last letters written by an Apostle, very little is known of this saint. Tradition has it that he and his brother were martyred in Persia, where they had gone to spread the Gospel of Christ. Yet in spite of this almost unknown history, Saint Jude has a devoted following throughout the world, for he is known as the "Saint of the Impossible" because of the many seemingly impossible favors granted through his intercession.

The establishment and propagation of devotion to Saint Jude in the United States is itself a minor miracle. In 1925 the Claretian Missionary Fathers came to Chicago and assumed the care of the parish of Our Lady of Guadalupe, in South Chicago near the steel mills, whose congregation was a rich, broad sampling of the American melting pot. The Claretian Fathers infused new life into the parish and soon were in the process of building an elaborate new church. Then came 1929, when the bottom dropped out of the stock market; the steel mills cut their pay rolls to the bone; bread lines formed; and banks failed.

To Father James Tort, the pastor of Our Lady of Guadalupe, it seemed hopeless to continue the building program—there was simply no money in the parish. But the priest was devoted to Saint Jude. Night after night he begged the help of the Saint of the Impossible and promised to erect a shrine in his honor if the church could be finished.

301

302

The favor was granted. The money came in somehow—never enough to guarantee security but enough to continue the work. The church was completed during the Depression, and a modest shrine to Saint Jude was set up. To the amazement of Father Tort, the shrine drew more visitors than the church itself. People began to talk about the shrine, and their praise of the saint led Father Tort to conclude that he had been niggardly in fulfilling his promise to Saint Jude. He decided to do something about it.

One year during Passiontide, when the statues in all the churches are veiled with purple, Father Tort shifted Saint Jude's Shrine to the place of honor at the right of the sanctuary. When the veils were removed from the statues on Easter Saturday, Saint Jude was revealed in his new setting. With the approval of Cardinal Mundelein, the shrine at Our Lady of Guadalupe became a national shrine.

In the twenty-five years since this shrine was erected devotion to Saint Jude has spread widely in the United States. Saint Jude's League has been formed and approved, and streams of pilgrims in ever-growing volume come to visit his shrine. *The Voice of Saint Jude,* which has a paid subscription of 135,000, increases devotion to Saint Jude and tells abroad the wonders worked by his intercession.

BENEDICTINE SANCTUARY OF
PERPETUAL ADORATION

Our Lady of the Lake Seminary

Mundelein, Illinois, on Route 176,

north of Chicago

Founded 1928

FOR FOUR DAYS IN JUNE 1926, CHICAGO WAS the center of attraction for the Catholic world. The International Eucharistic Congress was being held, and Cardinal Mundelein was host to a distinguished assemblage. The Pope's Legate, Princes of the Church, Archbishops and Bishops, priests and nuns, and a tremendous crowd of people came to pay tribute to the Blessed Sacrament. The splendid series of ceremonies in Soldier's Field was climaxed with a magnificent procession on the grounds of the Chicago seminary, Our Lady of the Lake, in the suburb of Mundelein.

The Cardinal, ever a man of thought and faith, had in 1925 asked the Benedictine Sisters of Perpetual Adoration to establish a sanctuary on the seminary grounds which would memorialize forever the outpouring of devotion to the Eucharist expressed at the Congress. On the Feast of Corpus Christi in 1928, a temporary convent was completed. One of the large rooms was turned into a chapel of adoration, and here Cardinal Mundelein celebrated the first Mass on June 7, 1928.

The permanent chapel came into being through the efforts of many generous patrons, rich and poor. The dedication ceremonies, at which Cardinal Mundelein again pontificated, were carried out in a memorable fashion on the Feast of the Guardian Angels on October 2, 1932.

304

Since that time the Sisters have poured out their prayers before the Eucharist, which is exposed in a monstrance that is a triumph of the goldsmith's art. Many humble people sent gifts of prized jewelry that went into the making of this golden throne.

The chapel itself is in keeping with the architecture of the seminary, which is American Colonial. An atmosphere of serenity has been achieved in the pillared entrance ornamented with statues of Saints Peter and Paul, Saint John the Beloved Disciple, and Saint Thomas Aquinas, the poet of the Eucharist. The interior is a small basilica. Fine marble columns march toward the sanctuary under a rich inlaid ceiling. The sanctuary, with its wealth of marbles and pillared baldachin, is a fine setting for the lovely monstrance.

Throughout the chapel Eucharistic symbols dating from the earliest days of the Catacombs to our own time speak poetically of the Bread of Eternal Life.

305

HOLY HILL
Shrine of Mary Help of Christians

Hubertus, Wisconsin, on Route 83,

northeast of Milwaukee

Founded 1863

HUBERTUS, WISCONSIN, ATTRACTS MANY
pilgrims during the warm months of the year. The
scenery of the lake district of Dodge County is delightful; groves of
thick trees, flashing lakes, and intensely green hills provide enchanting variation. But the chief point of interest to pilgrims is Holy Hill,
which rises high above the surrounding countryside, crowned with
a noble abbey church that might have come out of the Black Forest.
The exterior of the church is German Gothic. The great rose window
in the front and the two high-pointed towers are imposing, bathed
as they are in lapping waves of greenery or the multicolored fires of
Indian summer. A solid, six-story monastery rises to the left of the
church and lends its bulk to the whole imposing mass on the hill.

Opulent Romanesque decorations were used for the interior
of the church. Carved marble contrasts beautifully with solid bronze
and delicate wrought iron. The principal shrine is that of Our Lady
Help of Christians. The votive altar is of pink-veined Kasota marble
ornamented with carved bronze and mosaic. The armories of symbolism and poetry have been ransacked to provide a setting for the
famous statue, presented to the shrine by a friend, the product of
Pustet's Munich studio. First exhibited at the World's Fair in Philadelphia in 1876, the statue was carried up Holy Hill in 1878, in
solemn procession. Eighteen young girls bore the precious burden
during the seven-mile walk up the steep hill to the church.

The present shrine is the third church built on the site. The
first building was a log chapel erected in 1863. It was replaced by a

306

more ambitious building in 1881. Diocesan priests were originally in charge of the shrine. Then, in 1906, the Discalced Carmelites took over its custody, and since that time the shrine has grown continuously in size and importance. Artfully disposed in the quiet woods that border the old road leading to the hilltop are life-size Stations of the Cross. The pilgrims seem to love them, and young and old may be seen at all hours meditating on the episodes that led to Christ's death on the Cross.

The Shrine of Mary Help of Christians seems to be afire with vigil lights. Crutches and braces have been left behind as a testimony of cures.

Long ago, Indian tradition says, Marquette planted the first cross on Holy Hill. Whether this story is true or not, the hill has been a place of pilgrimage ever since the first Irish and German families settled in Hubertus.

CHAPEL OF
OUR LADY OF GOOD HELP

Crippled Children's Home

New Franken, Wisconsin

Founded about 1861

A LITTLE GIRL NAMED ADELE BRISSE WAS walking along an Indian path in the Wisconsin woods of the Green Bay peninsula, far northward from Milwaukee. The maples arching the path dropped their flame and gold streamers. Adele was the sturdy daughter of Belgian peasant parents, but her neck was bent under the weight of a heavy sack of grain balanced on her head. Suddenly she saw a light and the sack of grain slid from her head and fell into the rustling hazel bushes.

Adele stood very still. There seemed to be a mist on the path. Near by in a clump of trees stood a lady clothed in shining white. A blue sash enclosed her waist, and the two ends of it fell almost to the hem of her gown, her hair was golden yellow and her face shone with light. How long Adele stood there she didn't know. The brightness of the vision slowly faded and finally only a light mist lingered in the air.

All the way home the girl puzzled over the sight. She was so busy thinking that she scarcely felt the weight of the grain. Adele told her mother the story. "It's probably some poor soul from Purgatory asking for prayers," Mrs. Brisse said. "You are going to Mass on Sunday. You can pray for her then."

Sunday came and Adele started for church. It was eleven miles on foot but the girl looked forward to the journey. She went off gaily with her sister Isabella and their neighbor, Mrs. Vander Nies-

sen. When they drew near the thick clump of trees Adele said impatiently, "That lady is waiting. I can see her." They all stopped. Adele's two companions watched her intent face. Finally Adele moved. "She's gone!" And the three plodded on toward the distant church talking of the "poor soul" who needed help.

When Adele went to confession that morning before Mass, she told the priest she was frightened at the vision.

"Don't be afraid, my daughter. If the vision is of God you will see it again. Then ask in God's name who she is and what she wants."

On the journey home the lady was waiting at the same spot. This time Adele knelt resolutely on the path. "In the name of God, who are you and what do you want?" Then a voice was speaking in the most musical accents Adele had ever heard. "I am the Queen of Heaven, who prays for the conversion of sinners."

A long dialogue took place between the lady and the girl. It ended with a command to Adele: "Gather the children and teach them the Catechism that they may know and love my Son."

The unlettered girl carried out the command as best she could. Her father built a little log oratory on the site of the visions, and there Adele gathered the children of the growing Belgian community and prepared them for their first communion. Eventually the grateful settlers built a small school. Pupils came, and other workers joined Adele.

The little band, under the guidance of a Belgian priest, assumed the religious habit and followed the rule of Saint Francis. They had many difficulties with priests and with the Bishop, who mistrusted the story of Adele's vision, but finally misunderstandings were cleared up and Adele continued her work until her death in 1896. She was succeeded by Sister Pauline, who had assisted Adele for many years, and the infant community was merged with the Sisters of Saint Francis of Bay Settlement.

Sister Adele's first chapel was famous in the whole district around Green Bay. She had labored mightily to teach religion to the children, and had bolstered the work of the Norbertine Fathers in bringing religious peace to the many factions in the Green Bay Diocese. In 1933 the original boarding school established by Sister Adele was turned into a home for crippled children, and a beautiful new chapel has been built in honor of Our Lady of Good Help.

The chapel has always been a place of local pilgrimage, but of late years the number of pilgrims from far places has been growing. The Church has not formally approved either the visions of Adele or the cures which are said to have taken place in her chapel.

DICKEYVILLE SHRINE

Dickeyville, Wisconsin

Founded 1918

F ATHER MATHIAS WERNERUS CAME TO
Dickeyville, in southwestern Wisconsin, in April
1918. He was assigned the pastorate of the Church of the Holy Ghost,
a red-brick building with a tall spire, set in some twenty acres of tree-
studded fields not far from the banks of the Mississippi and the Inland Waterway.

Father Wernerus combined the best gifts of two nations: the
orderliness and tenacity of the German, the imagination and lucidity
of the Frenchman. The German heart in him ached at the disorder
of the grounds about the church, particularly the old cemetery.
Weeds choked the fallen grave markers; trees, seedlings, and vines
ran riot everywhere. This condition seemed all the more sad because
living young men were returning from France leaving behind them
many World War I comrades sleeping under white crosses in a
foreign land.

"Who remembers the dead?"

Father Wernerus asked this question of his congregation.
Quietly, like a true "doer of the Word," he went out himself to
begin work on the cemetery, assisted by his sister, who kept house
for him. He cleaned and straightened the markers on the pioneers'
graves, disciplined the grass, and pruned the trees. Borders of flowers
gave a salute to the light. Passers-by, early and late, caught sight of
the stocky figure clad in faded shirt and overalls.

Already Father Wernerus had publicized his plan for a
crucifixion group in memory of the three soldiers of Holy Ghost
Parish buried in France. His congregation supported the plan and
was thrilled to see it take form. A marble cross emerged from a low

311

M. J. Robb

mound; Mary and John stood at either side; Mary Magdalen wept at its foot; and above them hung the Man of Sorrows, so soon to be turned into the Man of Joys.

The Calvary group was a spur to the great plan taking shape in Father Wernerus' mind—a shrine of love of God and love of country. He was determined to build what he saw, but there was the eternal question of funds. The treasury was empty. The priest chuckled to himself, recalling the words of the Lord: "Consider the lilies of the field how they grow; they labor not, neither do they spin." In his heart Father Mat knew the Lord would provide. Out of the money saved from his own table and the sale of chickens he

312

raised, he had a small amount of ready cash. Stone quarries were near at hand. And, thank God, he had good health and a pair of strong shoulders. He would invent a new method of building what he wanted.

The work went on and his plan came slowly to perfection. The base of all the building was reinforced concrete; walls, urns, steps, and pillars were anchored in a strong stone foundation. Set in the surface were gleanings of the past that ran back into the distant ages. Petrified wood, moss, and wasps' nests, carnelians, stalactites, old stones and colored shells, bits of white and colored glass, china cups and saucers molded on pre-Revolutionary potters' wheels, odd pieces of metal, forged bronze—the patterns swirled over the surface with the exuberance of creative genius.

A shrine to the Sacred Heart, a grotto to Our Lady, Christ the King, the Twelve Apostles, the Tree of the Holy Ghost! Visitors marveled at Father Mat's inventions and at the beauty and endless variety of the whole composition. Balancing the religious group was the patriotic plaza, with Columbus enthroned under an arch, a fountain in three tiers surmounted by a marble eagle, and superb statues of Washington and Lincoln. Huge clumps of cedars brought the glow and glitter into high relief.

Father Mat went on building until 1931, when a sick call in a February night of snow and sleet took him out on the almost impassable road. He contracted pneumonia and in three days was dead. His sorrowing congregation buried him near the crucifixion group he had created in 1918.

The Dickeyville Shrine was not raised as a monument to the humble priest. He loved his God and his adopted land and he wished to share these loves with others. Pilgrims who see his work are sure that he succeeded.

314

ASSUMPTION CHAPEL

Cold Spring, Minnesota

Founded 1877

MOST OF THE FARMERS WHO LIVED NEAR Cold Spring, Minnesota, in the 1870's were of German origin. They loved their land and their farms prospered. In the summers of 1876 and 1877, however, when the cleared farmlands were one stage beyond pioneer days, many of the farmers were worried. A plague of locusts had descended on the district and wherever the cloud landed the crops were devoured to the last blade of green.

Father Leo Winter, O.S.B., who served the two parishes of Jacob's Prairie and Saint Nicholas, was a man of the faith that moves mountains. "Have confidence in Mary," he told his people. "If this plague is removed we will bind ourselves to build a shrine to Our Lady of the Assumption and offer frequent Masses there for fifteen years." The farmers agreed. Overnight the grasshoppers disapeared.

When the crops were harvested, the farmers gathered to fulfill their promise. A piece of land was donated by John Maselter and a frame building arose among the trees, a chapel 26 feet long and 15 feet wide. Capable hands painted and decorated it. Over the altar a wooden statue was placed, carved by a local farmer named Ambroziz who had more than a little of the talent developed in his homeland by generations of devout Bavarians. Soon the chapel was bright with lights and flowers.

The farmers loved their shrine, and often when illness or sickness or the worries of making a living oppressed them whole families came to ask the intercession of Mary. Like good pilgrims they walked to the shrine, sometimes from ten miles away. Because Saturday is known in Catholic tradition as the Virgin's day, whenever work and weather permitted the farmers came on that day.

315

Then, in 1894, a terrible tornado howled through the district and the shrine was torn from its foundations. Part of it was broken to matchwood; part of it came to rest in a grove of young oak trees, bowed even to this day with the force of the blow. Only the statue of the Virgin and Child escaped the fury of the storm.

For years there was talk of rebuilding the chapel. Nothing came of it, though often enough on winter evenings the subject came up in conversation and everyone agreed that something should be done. The hard work of plowing, planting, and harvesting somehow crowded out the creative ideas of winter.

Finally, in 1951, a committee of farmers and workmen was organized. Permission to build was granted by Bishop Busch of Saint Cloud and the work started. The chapel was completed in 1952. It was built of rough pink granite. The warm greens in the trees surrounding it bring out the delicate tint of the stone and cast a muting shadow on the pointed, stainless-steel steeple topped with a large cross.

The interior of the building is lined with highly polished agate and carnelian granite. A green-black altar holds six candlesticks and a crucifix of onyx. The original statue, repainted and shining, looks down from its place of honor. Imported stained-glass windows offer a glowing tribute to many of the titles under which people pay honor to Mary.

All the material in the chapel was given free; all the work was done by farmers and local workmen. Casual pilgrims stop to offer a prayer or a bunch of simple garden flowers; farmers and workers come anew with their problems and worries. The vow was paid long ago, but faith and hope remain, and a love that has deepened into beauty.

GROTTO OF THE REDEMPTION

West Bend, Iowa

Founded 1928

T HE MONASTERY CHURCH OF THE DOMINI-
cans in Oaxaca, Mexico, fabulous even in its decay,
has an unusual ceiling. Beginning at one corner of the vast ceiling is
a vine called the Tree of Life. From a carved bust of Adam in high
relief, the Tree of Life winds in and out over the ceiling in great
sworls of green. Patriarchs, prophets, judges, kings, Apostles—the
whole Bible story is unrolled, culminating in Christ and Mary.

Something of the same conception, but immeasurably more
involved and pictorial in its appeal, is to be found in the Grotto
of the Redemption, at West Bend, in Palo Alto County, Iowa, not
far from the Minnesota border. The conception and execution of the
tremendous undertaking is the life work of Father P. M. Dobberstein, pastor of the Church of Saints Peter and Paul, West Bend. For
thirty-five years the priest has labored on his project.

Although still uncompleted, enough of the grotto has been
realized to earn the admiration of many pilgrims. The finished plan
will tell the complete story of the fall and Redemption of man. Beginning with the episode of Adam and Eve, the stones will cry out the
good tidings of God's slow-unfolding mercy.

Father Dobberstein is said to have traveled 127,000 miles in
search of material for his shrine. Rocks from mountains, deserts, and
the seashore, from all the states and famous places of the world, are
set in a concrete base. Mosaics, subtle color arrangements in the patterns employed, and the use of lovely statues of Carrara marble will
eventually make the shrine a veritable picture book of the Redemption. Beautiful trees, lawns, hedges, and shrubs already provide an
atmosphere of natural beauty which is doubly enhanced in the wide

317

mirror pool with its shimmering views of the forest of mounds, domes, and pillars.

Of the completed work, the Stations of the Cross have caused the most comment. For these Father Dobberstein has constructed a mountain background and has presented the Stations with a maximum of effective coloring. Even the most thoughtless Christian goes away from the shrine with serious ideas of the great price of our redemption. In color, form, and great tenderness of feeling, Father Dobberstein has visualized the story that never grows old.

OLD CATHEDRAL OF SAINT LOUIS

Second and Walnut Streets

St. Louis, Missouri

Founded 1770

O LD CATHEDRAL OF SAINT LOUIS, AS IT
stands today, is the fourth church to be built on the
site at Second and Walnut streets. The first building was a small,
primitive log chapel church, completed June 24, 1770. It served the
infant community of St. Louis during the first phase of its history.
In time a second and larger church was erected, but it too was replaced, this time by a commodious brick structure built in the style
of a "glorified hay barn." The cornerstone of the present building
was laid by Bishop Rosati on August 1, 1831. In the autumn of 1834
the church was completed and consecrated. When we remember the
year, the smallness of the Catholic community, and the lack of available craftsmen on the frontier, the building that emerged seems a
wonderful achievement.

The whole edifice is built in classical style. Four massive Ionic
pillars are capped with a low pediment; two false arches balance the
front of the building on each side of the portico. A series of solid
stone balustrades hides the slope of the church roof and prepares the
eye for the drama of the sturdy tower of polished stone, in two steps,
out of which a pointed steeple soars aloft holding the brightly gilded
ball and cross.

The church interior, which is a simplified basilica, contains
three aisles divided by two rows of Doric pillars of imitation marble.
The curved ceiling of the nave is beautifully paneled. The main altar
is almost a repetition of the outside portico except that its pillars are
graceful Corinthian. The side chapels are framed in columns that

319

320

repeat the pillared note in the altar screen. One chapel is dedicated to the Blessed Virgin, the other to Saint Joseph.

The museum at the back of the church is rich in fascinating relics of the past, some historical and some religious. Among these is the old church bell, cast in 1770, whose sweet tone is probably due to the two hundred silver dollars cast into the molten bronze.

Four splendid gilt reliquaries exposed on the main altar contain first-class relics of many famous saints and two relics of the crib of Our Lord. The Old Cathedral is also rich in indulgences. Bishop Rosati, who built the Cathedral, was a classmate in Rome of Pope Gregory XVI, and this Pope granted to the Cathedral in perpetuity many indulgences that may be gained from visiting the shrine. Among the most important of these are a plenary indulgence and all the indulgences attached to a pilgrimage to the Seven Churches of Rome.

The two humble log churches, a brick structure, and the Old Cathedral have looked down on a great span of history. They have seen the city of St. Louis grow and prosper under the reign of Spain, France, and the United States. Massacre, plague, poverty, magnificence—these and many famous events and much human drama have flowed about these hallowed walls. For years the business district of the city engulfed the historic shrine, but in 1939 the city of St. Louis began work on Jefferson Memorial Plaza and razed all the buildings in the area except the Old Cathedral. Some day it will be bowered in quiet trees like an old lady recounting a rosary of memories.

SHRINE OF
BLESSED PHILIPPINE ROSE DUCHESNE

Sacred Heart Academy

St. Charles, Missouri

Founded 1818

MOTHER PHILIPPINE ROSE DUCHESNE, WHO came to the United States from France in 1818, was one of that group of valiant women from homes of ease and comfort who found on the American frontier a challenge to the magnificence dormant within them. Coarse fare; the bitter cold of winter in half-heated cabins that in summer sweltered in the swampy southern heat; yellow fever; rough manners—Mother Duchesne took them all in her stride. A sense of humor buoyed her up, and a sense of hope. Beyond these virtues was a burning love of God so intense that it scoffed at wind, weather, or personal suffering endured in doing the will of God.

Bishop du Bourg received Mother Duchesne in his primitive palace at St. Louis. On his orders Mother Duchesne left for St. Charles, not far north of St. Louis, to found the Sacred Heart Academy, her school for girls, the first (1818) to be established west of the Mississippi River. The hardships of those initial years of her life on the frontier are partially revealed in her first report to Saint Madeleine Sophie Barat:

> We find all sorts of new occupations here. We dig, we water the cows, carry manure and clean the stable. It is so cold that the water freezes close by the fire, as well as the linen placed there to dry. We have had the blessing of actually being deprived of bread and water. I had always expected the first of these privations, but on the banks of the Mis-

souri, I hardly anticipated the last. Neither doors nor windows shut at all. Our firewood is too thick for use and we have nobody to chop it. Here we have to turn our hand to every sort of work, to milk cows, not in a stable, but often in mud a foot deep, in the snow and rain; one cooks, another bakes. Every moment we have to cross yards or rather quagmires which nothing can dry up. We have neither clogs nor overshoes. Such articles are unknown here and the state of the house often evinces it.

When the St. Charles venture grew but did not prosper, Mother Duchesne put all the blame on herself. She redoubled her penances and devotions. Many a night she waited for the winter dawn on her knees in the chapel. In the presence of her God time had no more meaning than suffering.

One year after its foundation, Bishop du Bourg moved the school a few miles eastward to Florissant, Mo. The time was one of terrible poverty and naked courage, but a three-story brick convent was finally erected. Twenty pupils came and the community began to flourish. Mother Duchesne then dared Providence in opening a novitiate for her society. It was soon filled with American girls who found in their superior a woman capable of passing on to them something of her own fire and simplicity. It was this ardor which made possible the foundations in Louisiana in 1821 and 1825, and in St. Louis in 1827. Mother Duchesne returned to her first failure in 1828, and this time the St. Charles school endured.

In her heart Mother Duchesne still felt the old missionary call that had first emboldened her to come to America. Long ago in France, before she had ever seen them, she had known and loved the Indians with her heart. Her work with them and for them had made her early love flower. Now a woman of seventy-two, she went with three companions to Sugar Creek, Kansas, in 1841, to found a school for Potawatamie girls. It is not astonishing that this attempt was a failure. The hardships of the place broke Mother Duchesne's health and her tired mind found it impossible to learn the difficult Indian dialect. Yet the Indians revered her. "The woman who always prays," they named her, noting her endless vigils before the Blessed Sacrament that called the light into her face.

A good general knows when to retreat, says the adage, and Mother Duchesne did not hesitate. After a year at Sugar Hill she returned to St. Louis, reproaching herself for being a worthless vessel. Her profound humility was the deep foundation of amazing love and wisdom that flashed out in her words and writings until her death in St. Charles on November 18, 1852. The daring, the insight still sparkled, but all the iron in her nature had been transmuted into gold.

Her foundation at St. Charles has grown into a brilliant and respected college. The daughters of her mind and heart have multiplied manyfold. Forty colleges and academies of the Society of the Sacred Heart in the United States, Canada, Mexico, Cuba, Puerto Rico, New Zealand, and Japan have sprung from the humble foundation made by Mother Duchesne. Her daughters have long called her blessed, and this thought has been ratified by her beatification in Rome, in May 1940. Her canonization awaits the final miracle which will not be long denied.

On the grounds of the Villa Duchesne, in St. Charles, a memorial chapel has been raised in Blessed Philippine's honor, but only the nave or body of the church has been completed. The body of the *beata* is enshrined in a tomb of rosy marble underneath the temporary marble altar. Simple draperies and abundant sunlight create an atmosphere of that hopeful prayer beloved of those who long to go on pilgrimages.

Many favors have been granted to those who invoke Blessed Philippine, but most of them have been in the realm of mind or spirit. Children especially seem to love this shrine, which is not astonishing when we recall that she spent her whole life for them.

Pilgrims going to the Shrine of Blessed Philippine will find reverently preserved the room in which she died. The deal floor, the dim old paintings, her little work table, the chair she covered with rawhide, and the brazier where she warmed her gnarled and work-worn hands are all preserved today just as they were when Mother Duchesne walked into Life.

OUR LADY OF SORROWS

Starkenburg Road

Rhineland, Missouri

Founded 1852

LIKE OUR NATION, THE SHRINE OF OUR Lady of Starkenburg began in log cabins. Rhineland, Mo., which is a little west of St. Charles and not far from Jefferson City, was still frontier when in 1852 the log chapel of Starkenburg became noted for a statue of the Virgin and Child that was admired by people of all creeds. Because of the ornamental white veil worn by the Virgin, the appealing statue was known as the White Lady.

Within twenty years the log chapel was replaced by a stone church. The old statue of the White Lady was thought to be too shabby for the new building, so it was shunted off to the attic and replaced with a more ornate figure.

One year in May the pious young sacristan, August Mitsch, found the old statue, cleaned the dust and cobwebs from it, and set it up in the church grounds under a cloud of dogwood branches. Toward the end of summer August built a little roof to protect his Lady. He continually added to this shelter until in time he had erected a small chapel which attracted many pilgrims. Among the visitors were some ladies from St. Louis, who thought the worn old statue not good enough for the shrine and offered to replace it with a statue of the Mother of Sorrows. When the pastor accepted their gift, the White Lady, like Cinderella, again returned to her attic.

Many favors were attributed to the Mother of Sorrows: good crops, the healing of mind and body, and preservation from danger. Many pilgrims found in Mary's sorrows the key to hope and strength. That God and Mary might be glorified, the numerous friends of the

326

shrine collected funds to build a beautiful stone Romanesque church, which was dedicated by Archbishop Glennon on September 15, 1910. Here the Mother of Sorrows has her own chapel at the side, and under the exquisite marble baldachin of the main altar the repainted statue of the White Lady, looking more delightfully benign than ever, is enthroned.

In the green cool of the grove that surrounds the church are Stations of the Cross and several shrines, including the simple chapel of the woods built by August Mitsch. Large pilgrimages come at all seasons of the year to gain the rich indulgences granted to the shrine. A spring, discovered in unusual circumstances, is called the Lourdes Well, and many pilgrims drink of its waters. But the real charm of the shrine is the Cinderella tale of the White Lady who preferred her Son's house to the attic.

SHRINE OF THE MIRACULOUS MEDAL

Perryville, Missouri

Founded 1830

THE SHRINE OF THE MIRACULOUS MEDAL, at Perryville, Mo., is in the Church of the Assumption. Since 1830 the church has been a beacon light not only to all the Catholics of Perryville but to those of the whole Ozark region. It has also been the chapel of the Vincentian Seminary, where young men preparing for the arduous work of Saint Vincent's Society are formed in the pattern of their Master.

In the transept of the splendid old Renaissance Church of the Assumption a humble shrine was first erected to Our Lady of the Miraculous Medal. Then, in 1930, for the hundredth anniversary of the revelation to Sister Catherine, a superb new shrine was opened for the devotion of seminarians and pilgrims. A white marble altar intricately carved and adorned holds a fine statue of the Virgin in the attitude in which she revealed herself to Catherine—hands outstretched, a gentle smile lighting up her face. Behind her is a radiant niche of gold mosaic, and this radiance is carried out in the paintings in the dome of the chapel and in the flashing marbles of the wainscoting.

The windows of the Perryville church are particularly noteworthy. They show the various apparitions of the Virgin to Saint Catherine and tell the story of the revelation with pictorial beauty.

The object of this shrine, like that of the Central Shrine of the Miraculous Medal, in Germantown, Pa. (p. 69), is the propagation of devotion to the Miraculous Medal. The medal is not supposed to be worn as an amulet or charm. Its purpose is to mark its wearer as a child of Mary, devoted to her work of assisting in the sanctification of sinners.

329

THE CHILDREN'S SHRINE

Boys Town, Nebraska

Founded 1917

"SUFFER THE LITTLE CHILDREN TO COME unto me," Christ said.

If any sentence was graven on the heart of Father Flanagan, these were the words, and the story of Boys Town is the story of his heart.

Edward Flanagan seemed to grow up bursting with the desire to serve others. His hotel for down-and-outers was his first attempt to serve. Then, in December 1917, he gathered a group of boys around him in an old two-story house in Omaha, Nebraska. All the boys were from broken homes; some were orphans, and nearly all were wayward because they had been neglected. Father Flanagan's only assets were ninety borrowed dollars and his love of God.

The group grew and grew until the walls bulged. Father Flanagan's situation was much like that of the old lady who lived in the shoe—but he *knew* what to do. He begged shamelessly from friends, strangers, and people of all creeds and colors. Money came in, and somehow mounting bills were paid.

"It's miraculous," people said, "what this priest does for bad boys." Father Flanagan answered: "There's no such thing as a bad boy." Boys needed love, love of God and love of people; boys needed activity of the mind and body; boys needed the discipline of work and governance. By multiplying himself so that he seemed to be everywhere, the Father succeeded in providing all those things. By the side of the ball diamond he taught boys sportsmanship; he led them to govern themselves and to establish just patterns of punishment for offenses. His love was like an acetylene torch burning through steel cages that young hearts had built up, cages compounded of fear, maltreatment, and misunderstanding.

330

The boys kept on coming—the haunted and unwanted, the healthy and the frail—and Father Flanagan took them in. He taught them how to work, how to play, and how to laugh. The success story of his love is today bounded in a thousand acres of farmland and playing fields. Dormitories, schools, and shops of all kinds open opportunities for the skilled minds and the skilled hands. A stadium, swimming pools, and a gymnasium help to provide sound bodies for sound minds. The boys are equally at home in the field and shops, in discussion forums and the intricacies of self-government. The Boys Town Choir is world famous, but long-hair and short-hair music also have their ardent followers.

331

The magnificent chapel, donated by a generous benefactor, is the heart of Boys Town. Here boys of diverse faiths hear the word of God and take their first steps in Divine love, which is the fountainhead of all enduring love. Respect and reverence for all religions is the cornerstone of Boys Town, for it is nonsectarian and each group is ministered to by its own pastor.

Father Flanagan died in Germany on May 16, 1948, while abroad at the invitation of the United States government, which wanted his suggestions for a plan to aid the refugee children, derelicts of war. His body was flown back to his town and buried in the chapel while the misted eyes of the boys attested how much he had meant to each of them. Today Monsignor Wegner, who was Father Flanagan's chief helper for many years, carries on the work of Boys Town in the same spirit of love and understanding.

Boys Town is a shrine of hope and of the virile love that scorns to mouth the word without the deed. "Suffer the little children to come unto me!" Like the answer of the infant Samuel, Boys Town cries, "Here I am, Lord!"

OLD COEUR D'ALENE MISSION

Cataldo, Idaho

Founded 1843

T HE STORY OF THE JESUIT FATHER DE SMET
is a saga of the Northwest that compares well with
the fabulous exploits of other missionaries who brought culture and
beauty to California and the Southwest. The influence this great
priest exercised among the Indian tribes was owing to the admiration the aborigines had for his endurance and integrity. He was a
chief among chiefs.

Other priests who helped de Smet have been nearly forgotten,
but the story of three Jesuits who labored with the Coeur d'Alene
tribe is memorialized in an unusual shrine at Cataldo, Idaho. Fathers
Ravillia and Joset left de Smet's devoted band of Jesuits in Montana
and ventured into the wilderness to found new missions. They settled
with the Coeur d'Alene Indians, were warmly received, and very
shortly, in 1843, began work on a church. A hill site was selected and
large stones were cut in the mountains. The Fathers chose their
trees from the endless forests that clothed the great slopes on every
side, and in the thick snows of winter sledges pulled the ponderous
loads to the building site. Special clay was dug and, from the tiny
patches of wheat fields, straw was gleaned to give strength to the clay
when it was formed into bricks and baked in the sun. For tools the
two Fathers had only a ripsaw, wooden hammers, knives, and axes.

Within three years the church was completed. Father Ravillia
was a genuine artist and it was he who was largely responsible for
the interior decoration. With his own clever hands he carved two of
the statues and painted several of the pictures that adorn the little
church.

333

Soon after the church was blessed the founders of the mission moved on to other fields and Father Cataldo came to replace them. He was assisted in his work by several Jesuit lay brothers. So successful was he that when lead was discovered near the mission the pioneer town that sprang up overnight was named Cataldo.

Lead mining brought money to the whites and sorrow to the Indians. Their fields and pastures became poisoned; their stock died. They complained to the United States government and were given new lands near Worley, Idaho, and some other compensation for their losses.

Today Old Coeur d'Alene Mission stands as a monument to a great pioneer past and the native genius of the men who made those years memorable. The white-pillared front of the chapel has a high scalloped gable, ornamented with a great rayed host in gold and enamel. The altars and statues inside are a colorful tribute to the talented Jesuits who built a house of God in the wilderness and brought words of faith and beauty to hearts that hungered.

INDEX

Shrines in this book are referred to in boldface type

335

337

338

340

oseph J. Caltabellotta
427 Dunlap Crossing Rd
Rivera, Calif.